Sanctifying Interpretation

Vocation, Holiness, and Scripture

SANCTIFYING INTERPRETATION

VOCATION, HOLINESS, AND SCRIPTURE

SECOND EDITION

CHRIS E.W. GREEN

CPT Press
Cleveland, Tennessee

SANCTIFYING INTERPRETATION
VOCATION, HOLINESS, AND SCRIPTURE

Second Edition

Published by CPT Press
900 Walker ST NE
Cleveland, TN 37311
email: cptpress@pentecostaltheology.org
website: www.pentecostaltheology.org

ISBN: 978-1935931-997

DEDICATION

It's still all for you, Jewels

TABLE OF CONTENTS

Preface to the First Edition   x
Preface to the Second Edition   xi
Abbreviations   xvi

Introduction   1
    Pentecostals, Scripture, and Hermeneutics   1
    A Personal Note   6

PART ONE
VOCATION

Chapter 1:
Identity and/as Vocation: Revisioning Calling in Christ
    Introduction   11
    Being and Doing   12
    Identity-in-Vocation   14
    Baptism: The Womb of Identity and Vocation   15
    Salvation, Obedience, and Theotic Participation   18
    Nature and Grace   19
    Crucified Below: The Eucharist and the Sacrificial Life   21
    Friends (of the Friend) of Sinners   24

Chapter 2:
Sanctified Bodies, Sanctifying Mediation: Sharing Christ's
Continuing Priesthood
    Introduction   29
    Christ's Body as the World's Temple   30
    The Saving Spectacle   33
    'I Have Come to Do Your Will'   34
    'A Body You Prepared for Me'   37
    'Sacrifices You Have Not Desired'   39

Chapter 3:
Saving Speech, Holy Listening: Calling, Worship, and
the Transformative Work of Interpretation
    Introduction   43
    Vocation, Language, and Meaning-Making   44
    'Speaking in Tongues': Human Meaning and Divine Pedagogy 49

The Liturgical Grammar of Priestly Vocation 55
Spiritedness, Silence, and Ex-centricity 70

PART TWO
HOLINESS

Chapter 4:
The End of Holiness
Introduction 75
Re-Righting Holiness 75
Holy as Christ is Holy 85
Godlikeness Beyond 'Goodness' 88
The Crucifixion (and Resurrection) of Conscience 90
Holding Court with God 91

Chapter 5:
The Beginning of Holiness
Introduction 97
Unwanted Beauty, Imperfect Love 97
Holiness as (In)Hospitality 98
Holiness as Transparency 105
Holiness as Endurance 107
Holiness as Transgression 109
Holiness as Strangeness 112
Holiness as Intercession 118

PART THREE
SCRIPTURE

Chapter 6:
Reading for Christ: Interpretation and (Trans)Formation
Introduction 125
Holy Scripture and Divine-Human Vocation 125
(Mis)Reading Scripture, (Mis)Apprehending God 127
Pentecostals and the Scriptures 128
Re(dis)covering Early Pentecostal Hermeneutics 130
Making Peace with the Warrior God 140
Scripture as Sacrament, Interpretation as Encounter 150

Chapter 7:
Scripture as Divine and Deifying Foolishness
Introduction 153

Sanctifying Troubledness   154
The Endurance of the Scriptures   162
Frustration as/and Redemption   164
The (Trans)Formation of Desire   166
Living and Dying by the Word   168
The Spirit, the Seed, the Soils   176

Chapter 8:
Praxis: The Ways of Sanctifying Interpretation

Introduction   181
Hearing the Whole Counsel of God   181
(Re)Reading in the Spirit   185
(Re)Reading with Community   188
(Re)Reading for Christ   193
(Re)Reading from the Heart   197
(Re)Reading toward Faithful Performance   201
The Divine Performance   206

Afterword   215

Bibliography   220
Index of Biblical References   233
Index of Authors   237

PREFACE TO FIRST EDITION

What I have to share in this book has been forged over the last several years, mostly in conversation, prayer, and study, as well as in lectures, sermons, and presentations at academic conferences. My debts, unsurprisingly, are many.

Thanks, first, to my wife Julie and to my kids – Zoë, Clive, and Emery – who sustain me, day after day after day, with endless patience and kindness. Thanks to my students and my colleagues at Pentecostal Theological Seminary, and especially to the editors of CPT Press, Chris Thomas and Lee Roy Martin, who have done so much to bring this work to publication. Thanks also to those communities (including, among others, Sanctuary Church in Tulsa, Divine Life Church in Oklahoma City, Renovatus Church in Charlotte, and New Covenant Church in Cleveland, Tennessee) who have made room for me to continue to learn with them how we are to handle the Scriptures.

Thanks to my friends who have given hours of their lives to discussing these ideas with me and to commenting on rough drafts of the chapters. They tolerated endless questions from me, and they (usually) responded graciously to my constant demands (always disguised as requests, of course) for feedback. At the risk of failing to remember everyone who should be named, I need to mention explicitly Jeff Lamp, Don Vance, Rickie Moore, Jonathan Martin, Silas Sham, and the Discluded. I trust that this book is testament to the depth of those friendships.

PREFACE TO THE SECOND EDITION

Not long after this book was published, I realized I had more that I wanted to say. And after a few of the first readers responded, I realized I had more I *needed* to say. Several people shared with me that they found my argument at crucial points too compact, too compressed; and others said that they believed they understood my 'theory' but they needed to see more extended examples of that theory put into practice. In the next couple of years, in response to those criticisms, I wrote a series of in-depth theological and spiritual interpretations of biblical texts that I found particularly troubling and difficult. Some of these were published online, and others were published in various journals and edited volumes. Just in the last few months, I sensed that the time had come for a revision, one that allowed me to say more of what I wanted to say in the first, and that also allowed me to make some of the needed corrections and clarifications. Thankfully, Chris and Lee Roy agreed that it was a good idea and that this was the right time to do it.

So, almost all of what I said in the first version I stand by, although I do want to tweak some of what I suggested about liturgy, and some of the ways I talked about the church as witness of the kingdom. More than anything, I want to be clearer and more accessible. I have eliminated much of the technical language, including Greek and Hebrew. Where the argument seemed too compressed, or where I made claims without an argument, I have tried to spell out in a bit more detail what I in fact mean. I have provided quite a few more examples, including fairly extended readings of 1 Samuel 15, Romans 9-11, Psalm 88, and 1 Cor. 11.2-16, which are passages that I find particularly difficult, although in distinct ways. When all is said and done, I hope the work I have put into this revision makes it clear that I believe God is good and that the Scriptures are good for us especially when they seem to be making trouble for us.

Those who did not read the first version will find that in this version, too, the most central claim of my argument is that God does not intend to save us from interpretation but through it. I said this more than once then, and I stand by it now. And I want to add, as

Brad East puts it, that 'there is no one right way to read the Bible'. There are bad ways, to be sure. Ways we should reject. But there are more good ways — the Spirit, after all, is infinite, and so are the possibilities of interpretation.[1] All to say, what I am arguing for in this book is not a method, per se, but first and foremost a sensibility, an attitude toward interpretation. But I am arguing for certain practices, too, not because they are the only right ones, but because I think they are helpful. And most of them I have found in what seem to me the best of ancient and medieval readings of Scripture. Eriugena summarizes the view like this: 'the fabric of divine Scripture is intricately woven and entwined with turns and obliquities ... because [the Holy Spirit] was eager to exercise our intelligence and to reward hard toil and discovery'.[2] All to say, I am convinced, now no less than before, that reading Scripture is meant to be at least sometimes difficult, soul-harrowing, purgative. We are supposed to be marked, wounded, by our efforts to make sense of these texts. Why would God burden us like this? Because the struggle to make sense of these texts works on us in ways nothing else can. Besides, these texts are *God's*. Is it really surprising that they are too much for us to take in, to manage?

In his reflections on the seventh Beatitude, Origen argues that peacemakers are blessed because of the way they handle the Scriptures (*Philocalia* 6.1-2).[3] First, peacemakers discover the peace *of* the Scriptures, which are at peace in the sense that they manifest one unified witness to Jesus Christ. Second, peacemakers know how to make peace *with* the Scriptures, reconciling the seeming contradictions within the texts — and the real contradictions between themselves and the texts[4] — as well as discerning the deeper, hidden significances of seemingly meaningless passages. That is why, peacemaking interpreters find that they are also making peace with and for their

---

[1] Brad East, *The Doctrine of Scripture: A Cascade Companion* (Eugene, OR: Cascade, forthcoming), p. 126.

[2] Joannes Scotus Eriugena, *Periphyseon: On the Divisions of Nature* IV.38 (trans. Myra L. Uhlfelder; Eugene, OR: Wipf & Stock, 1976), p. 345.

[3] For a description of Origen's view of Scripture, see Henri de Lubac, *History and Spirit: The Understanding of Scripture According to Origen* (San Francisco: Ignatius, 2007), Peter W. Martens, *Origen and Scripture: The Contours of the Exegetical Life* (Oxford: Oxford University Press, 2012); and John David Dawson, *Christian Figural Reading and the Fashioning of Identity* (Berkley, CA: University of California Press, 2001).

[4] See Stephen E. Fowl and L. Gregory Jones, *Reading in Communion: Scripture and Ethics in Christian Life* (Grand Rapids: Eerdmans, 1991), pp. 70-71.

neighbors, discovering and helping others discover the peace of God. Paraphrasing Paul, we might say that for Origen it is because there is one text that there is one body.

In the middle of this passage, Origen takes up a striking analogy. He describes Scripture as 'the music of God', and says it is a composition with strange, unexpected, and perplexingly intricate harmonies that bewilder and frustrate ill-equipped and untrained readers (*Philocalia* 6.2). This is why, Origen says, that unskilled hearers hear in the Scriptures only dissonances, as if the Old Testament conflicts with the New, or the Prophets with the Law, or the apostolic writings with the Gospels.[5] If readers hope to appreciate the divine harmonies of the Scriptures, then they have to be trained for it. The required sensibilities and skills must be seeded into them.

At this point, Origen transposes the analogy into a new image: Scripture is also the *instrument* of the Spirit. But, crucially, Origen insists that believers can only 'hear' the scriptural harmonies that they can 'play', and so they have to be made 'like another David', gifted with the abilities necessary 'to bring out the sound of the music of God'.[6] Such readers develop over time and under guidance the necessary skills for performing the divine sound; they know 'the right time to strike the chords', playing the Law, the Gospels, the Prophets, and the Apostles so as to make the 'certain sound' that is the 'one saving voice' of God's Word. In this performance, peacemakers become like David whose music 'laid to rest the evil spirit in Saul, which was choking him', 'implanting' in the spirits of their neighbors the very peace of God that all so deeply desire (*Philocalia* 6.2).

Origen's hermeneutic makes it clear that Scripture must be interpreted, made beautiful. And that depends on believers having the Spirit-given, Spirit-led skills to create good readings, readings which are good because of their effects (and not just their exegetical rigor). Good readings, as opposed to merely correct ones, actually bring the peace of God to bear in the world. Here, Pentecostals fully agree with Origen and the Patristic hermeneutical tradition: the reading of Scripture has a purpose, and that purpose is the making-present of

---

[5] Origen is insistent: Scripture is *one*. See Matthew R. Crawford, 'Scripture as "One" Book: Origen, Jerome, and Cyril of Alexandria on Isaiah 29.11', *The Journal of Theological Studies* 64.1 (April 2013), pp. 137-53.

[6] See de Lubac, *History and Spirit*, p. 193.

the works of God. And that can only be done as readers are led by the Spirit beyond the 'letter' of Scripture to discover its 'spirit'.[7]

Again, the emphasis is not so much on the right interpretations of a text, as determined by the rules of, say, the grammatical-historical method. Instead, the emphasis is on the need for good interpretations.[8] The aim is not merely exegetical: it is prophetic and priestly. Ultimately, faithful readings are known by their effects, their 'fruit': they stir up holy love for God and love for neighbor, and draw hearers on toward higher and deeper and wider faithfulness.

Origen assumes, as Pentecostals do, that Scripture is a coherent whole and that the meanings of Scripture are inexhaustible.[9] There is always more to a biblical text than has yet been or ever could be understood, but whatever is discovered in the depths of a particular text is of a piece with all other texts.[10] This is because God is infinitely generous: Scripture is his storehouse, and he is always giving gifts from it to his children.

We should, I believe, assume that biblical texts have multiple senses.[11] And these multiple senses are intimately related to the stages of spiritual maturation. Knowing this, we can see how the reading of Scripture yields different meanings at different times for different people. Hence, Gregory the Great's famous maxim:

---

[7] J. Christopher King, *Origen on the Song of Songs as the Spirit of Scripture: The Bridegroom's Perfect Marriage Song* (Oxford: Oxford University Press, 2005), p. 147.

[8] This is perhaps not far removed from what Umberto Eco, *On Literature* (Orlando: Harquart Books, 2002), pp. 222-23, describes as the difference between 'semantic' and 'aesthetic' readers.

[9] John McGuckin, 'The Exegetical Metaphysics of Origen of Alexandria', in Matthew Baker and Mark Mourachain (eds.), *What is the Bible? The Patristic Doctrine of Scripture* (Minneapolis: Fortress Press, 2016), pp. 3-20; p. 9.

[10] McGuckin ('The Exegetical Metaphysics of Origen of Alexandria', p. 11) makes it clear that does not mean, however, that all texts are the same in every sense: 'though all texts are sacred and illuminative, however, they act soteriologically in differently nuanced manners'. McGuckin discerns this loose ordering of texts in Origen's writings: John, Paul, Psalms, the other Gospels, the greater prophets, the remaining apostolic writings, and then the historical and legal books. For Pentecostals, Luke-Acts, and other biblical narratives, along with perhaps the Psalms and Revelation, seem to hold pride of place.

[11] In David Steinmetz's words ('The Superiority of Pre-Critical Exegesis', *Theology Today* 37.1 [April 1980], pp. 27-38 [38]), 'The medieval theory of levels of meaning in the biblical text, with all its undoubted defects, flourished because it is true, while the modern theory of a single meaning, with all its demonstrable virtues, is false'. See also Peter Leithart, 'The Quadriga or Something Like It: A Biblical and Pastoral Defense', in Mark Husbands and Jeffrey P. Greenman (eds.), *Ancient Faith for the Church's Future* (Downers Grove, IL: IVP, 2008), pp. 110-25 (124).

For as the word of God, by the mysteries which it contains, exercises the understanding of the wise, so usually by what presents itself on the outside, it nurses the simple-minded. It presenteth in open day that wherewith the little ones may be fed; it keepeth in secret that whereby men of a loftier range may be held in suspense of admiration. It is, as it were, a kind of river, if I may so liken it, which is both shallow [*planus*] and deep, wherein both the lamb may find a footing, and the elephant float at large.[12]

This is the sum of the matter, I think: we are called to read Scripture in its fullness just as we are being drawn along toward the fullness of God and our own fullness in God. But we have to be trained to read for fulness – mostly through Spirit-led imitation of other readers. We have to learn how to be divining readers; that is, readers who do not merely want to know what a text meant for the first hearers, or even what it means now for us, but who seek to respond wholeheartedly to the God who is speaking to us.

---

[12] Gregory the Great, *Moralia* I.IV.

ABBREVIATIONS

Early Pentecostal Periodicals

AF	*The Apostolic Faith*
COGE	*The Church of God Evangel*
PHA	*The Pentecostal Holiness Advocate*
PT	*Pentecostal Testimony*
TBM	*The Bridegroom's Messenger*
TP	*The Pentecost*
WE	*Weekly Evangel*

Other

BTC	Brazos Theological Commentary Series
CPT	Centre for Pentecostal Theology
IVP	InterVarsity Press
JBL	*Journal of Biblical Literature*
JPT	*Journal of Pentecostal Theology*
JPTSup	Journal of Pentecostal Theology Supplement
OUP	Oxford University Press
Pneuma	*Pneuma: The Journal of the Society for Pentecostal Studies*
WJKP	Westminster John Knox Press

INTRODUCTION

In the end, this is a book concerned with how we read Scripture. But I have realized that I cannot say what I want to say about reading Scripture without also talking more broadly about *vocation* – what it is that we are created to do and how everything God does for us is fitted to it – and about *sanctification* – what it means for us to be holy, and how God shares his holiness with us for our good and the good of all things. Bearing that in mind, I have arranged the book in three parts or movements. First, a series of essays on vocation, which explore what it means to take responsibility as human beings called to participate in Christ's ministry. Then, a series of essays on sanctification, which recast holiness in the light of Christ's compassionate and sacrificial intercession. Finally, a series of essays on interpretation, which attempts to celebrate the ways Scripture is designed to sanctify our hearts and minds, and so to shape us for our calling. As the book's title suggests, I hope to show not only that we need to change how we read and talk about reading Scripture, but also that if we read Scripture well, we will find that we are being changed by that reading.

Pentecostals, Scripture, and Hermeneutics

Pentecostals, by and large, hold to a high view of Scripture, almost exclusively in terms borrowed from standard Evangelical accounts. For example, the first of the Assemblies of God Fundamental Truths reads: 'The Scriptures, both the Old and New Testaments, are verbally inspired of God and are the revelation of God to man, the infallible, authoritative rule of faith and conduct'. The United Pentecostal Church International's statement on beliefs begins with this claim: 'The Bible is the infallible Word of God and the authority for salvation and Christian living'. And the Church of God in Christ's Statement of Faith begins with a similar affirmation: 'We believe the Bible to be the inspired and only infallible written Word of God'.

Familiar as these doctrines are to us and useful as they may have been at one time for some purposes, they are nonetheless insufficient. For one thing, as Billy Abraham has shown, they betray an 'overcommitment' to philosophical ideas about Scripture that in the long run subvert true understanding and faithful enactment of the gospel. If we know our histories well, we can see that these doctrines have proven themselves now to be failed attempts to solve problems raised by post-Reformation churchly controversies and post-Enlightenment critiques of Christian doctrine and theological practice.[1] And so, we should acknowledge their failures, and lay them to rest having learned a valuable lesson about how easily even the best motivations can lead us to make bad theological decisions.

It is important to remember that these Pentecostal doctrines were drafted as provisional, heat-of-the-moment apologetic measures, devised to address philosophical problems perceived as threats to believers' confidence in the integrity and authority of the Scriptures. In actuality, however, driven by fear of subjectivism and the need for a peculiar feeling or idea of certainty,[2] they bound Pentecostal doctrine to the conceptual framework of foundationalist epistemologies – to disastrous long-term, long-lasting effects.[3] In spite of the fact that they were intended to foster unity and to bolster confidence, these doctrines, and the frames of references they depended upon to be intelligible, in fact led and continue to lead to more and more fragmentation, confusion, and anxiety.

Historically and theologically speaking, what Robert Jenson says about the doctrine of inspiration in the moderately pietist Lutheranism in which he grew up is equally true of many Pentecostal churches as well:

> It tended to flatten the great and various *interests* of the Scriptures
> … [It] obscured the *way* in which the church should and classically

---

[1] William J. Abraham, *The Bible: Beyond the Impasse* (Dallas, TX: Highland Loch Press, 2012), pp. 36-46.

[2] See Kern Robert Trembath, *Evangelical Theories of Biblical Inspiration: A Review and Proposal* (Oxford: Oxford University Press, 1987).

[3] See William Oliverio, *Theological Hermeneutics in the Classical Pentecostal Tradition: A Typological Account* (Leiden: Brill, 2012).

has read Scripture ... as one great narrative of the coming of Christ and the Kingdom ... [It] flattened also the great variety of ways in which the Spirit actually *uses* Scripture in the life of the church: as liturgical readings to be heard and pondered, as the lexical and rhetorical model for worship and edifying conversation, as the text for preaching and teaching, as the occasion of mediation ...[4]

We should not scapegoat those who developed these statements, of course, or disparage their intentions, which no doubt were pure. What is more, we can and should affirm Scripture's authority, integrity, and efficacy, just as they hoped to do. But we need to disavow the philosophical foundationalism they assumed. And, even more importantly, we need to break from the bundle of ideological ambitions that led them to take on that foundationalism in the first place: the idea that Scripture's validity is dependent on its errorlessness;[5] the idea that Scripture's uniqueness is reasonably self-evident; and the idea that the meaning of Scripture is plain, at least to those who are led by the Spirit and have learned a particular method of interpretation.

All of these problems present themselves unmistakably in the Pentecostal Holiness Church's *Advanced Catechism*, which includes these exchanges:

Q. Is the Bible a perfect revelation?
A. Yes, the Bible contains all truth, and nothing can be added to make it more complete as a Divine revelation to man. All true science is in perfect harmony with the Scriptures. The apostolic writings complete the revelation. Not only is all of the Bible true; but all truth is contained in it. The better we understand it, the more this can be realized.
Q. How do we know the Bible is the Word of God?
A. Man has never been able to produce anything equal to the Bible; and its teachings cover entirely all the needs of all people,

---

[4] Robert W. Jenson, *On the Inspiration of Scripture* (Delhi, NY: American Lutheran Publicity Bureau, 2012), pp. 1-5.

[5] As I discuss in Part 2, we have imagined that the sanctified life is a sinless life, a life lived without wrongdoing. In the same way, and for the same reasons, we have imagined that Scripture is holy just insofar as it free from mistakes of any kind.

of every age. Also its perfect harmony though written by different men over a period of about 1,500 years; and its miraculous preservation.[6]

As I have already said, these ideas have proven false over time. They lead only to dead ends. Biblicisms of all kinds rightly assume that Scripture is God's Word. But they wrongly assume that that means Scripture, carefully studied, yields a single, internally coherent theological system of thought, which can then be extracted and rearticulated in our own terms without loss or remainder. In truth, however, Scripture, by virtue of its inspiration, is polyphonic and multivalent. If it is like a choir, as Chris Thomas suggests, it is like a black gospel choir – in rehearsal.[7] But we might also think of it like a great banquet buzzing with coinciding, intersecting conversations: some heated, others warm; some nasty, others sweet; some routine, others esoteric; but all lively, and all fraught with misunderstandings and missed understandings. Even in routine conversations, we always say more and less than we intend, and are rarely if ever heard to say exactly what we meant. And the same is true of these sacred texts. When all is said and done, we trust not in a concept of perfection, applied to Scripture, but in God who works perfectly in the texts' seeming imperfections – its ambiguities, secrets, complexities, contradictions, confusions, mysteries, and conundrums.

Needless to say, it would be unfair to suggest that all biblicisms, much less all biblicists, hold idolatrous conceptions of the Bible. But at least at times, they do leave the impression that the Bible shares the divine attributes. Aquinas shows a better way. He begins his *Summa Theologiae* not with Scripture, per se, but with 'sacred doctrine', emphasizing not the text itself, considered separately from God as a reality in its own right, but with the work of God through and with faithful readings of the text. In this way, Aquinas wisely assures the authority and efficacy of Scripture – without attributing divinity to it. Scripture, we might say, read in the Spirit, divines but it is not itself divine.

---

[6] Paul F. Beacham, *Advanced Catechism for the Home, Sunday School, and Bible Classes* (Franklin Springs, GA: PH Church Publishing House, 1971), pp. 9-10.

[7] John Christopher Thomas, 'The Spirit, Healing and Mission: An Overview of the Biblical Canon', *International Review of Mission* 93.370-371 (July-October 2004), pp. 421-42.

We can do that best if we shift away from what Billy Abraham calls *epistemological* to *soteriological* conceptions of Scripture. That is, we need to reject theories and practices intended to reassure us of the perfections of the text and the infallibility of our interpretations. And we need to affirm theories and practices that assure us that God is reliable and that he works even in our faulty readings of the imperfect biblical texts.

All to say, I believe we Pentecostals should turn away from biblicism, and away from the foundationalist philosophies and simplistic accounts of interpretation that accompany it. We, as well as the Evangelicals from whom we borrowed most of our conceptions and theological strategies, need a deep and broad reworking both of our doctrines of Scripture and of our interpretative practices, as well as the doctrine of God that they depend on. As in Christology, the decisive question for our doctrines of Scripture and our theories of interpretation is not How but Who?[8] That is, we should not ask, 'How can I know the Scriptures are true? How can I get the truth from Scripture and know that I have gotten the truth?' But we should ask, instead, 'Who has given us the Scriptures? Who is he making us to be?'

The Bible is not what we wish it to be. And the work of interpretation requires from us what we might not want to give. Still, once we remember *who* has given these texts – God in Christ, through the church, his Body – we can accept the Scriptures as they have come to us, in God's wisdom. And we can accept that the Scripture's uniqueness, like Christ's uniqueness, remains 'hidden', even in its manifestation. Finally, we can accept that the work of interpretation of Scripture is difficult, just as God intends it to be.

Tragically, appeals to biblical authority are far too often entirely about authority and not at all about the Bible. This comes clear as over time our authoritarianism reveals itself in our responses to the cries of the suffering. Time after time, in crisis after crisis, it becomes more and more clear that our avowals have to do primarily, if not entirely, with establishing our own authority over others, rather than God's authority over us. As Lee Roy Martin once said to me in conversation, this authoritarianism expresses itself always in the misuse of the Scriptures, and these misuses becomes obvious 'when the

---

[8] Dietrich Bonhoeffer, *Berlin: 1932–1933* (Dietrich Bonhoeffer Works 12; Minneapolis: Fortress, 2009), pp. 299–360.

interpretation (not so surprisingly) benefits the interpreter to the subjugation of weaker members of the community'. We need, then, not
only to rework our theologies of Scripture and our practices of interpretation; we first and foremost have to reject authoritarianism in all
of its forms. The Scriptures are entrusted to the church for the sake
of her ministries. If we fail to be the people of God, if we allow ourselves to be carried along by any other spirit than the Spirit of Jesus,
if we fail to act in each and every moment from humility, restraint,
and generosity, then the work we are doing is not God's – it will only
harm us as it harms others.

A Personal Note

Needless to say, everything I try to say in this book is colored and
shaped by my particular experiences in the various communities to
which I have and do belong. In fact, I wrote this book, at least in
part, because those experiences kept forcing me to work through
what I was coming to believe about the Scriptures and how we are to
read them. But let me be clear: even after having written it, I have not
arrived at some final position. As you are reading, I hope you find
that the claims or arguments I have made do not read like an effort
to have the 'last word' but instead show themselves to be nothing
less or more than an attempt to fail toward a more faithful articulation of the Scripture's use in our sanctification. I will be happy if at
least some of what I have said points to possibilities for further reflection, raises new questions (and/or old ones in new ways), and
sparks conversations as we try to discern together what it means to
be faithful hearers and doers of the holy gospel witnessed by these
sacred texts.

As many have lamented, much contemporary theology, despite its
intentions, never actually matures into genuine talk about God but
remains fixed in merely talking about talking about God. Michael
Root agrees: 'academic work in modern theology seems less the study
of God or of the Christian message about God, and more the study
of the creativity of great theologians'.[9] I hope what I have said here,
whatever its flaws and shortcomings, proves an exception to that
rule.

---

[9] Michael Root, 'The Achievement of Wolfhart Pannenberg', *First Things* 221
(March 2012), pp. 37-42 [42].

Of course, talking about talking about God is much less risky, much more manageable than talking about or to God. But I find Timothy Radcliffe's advice unshakeable: 'Get out of your depth; you should always be writing about something beyond your grasp. Don't aim to be a master: there's only one master, and that's none of us.'[10] I have tried to follow that direction.

In the first edition, I admitted I was somewhat afraid to have written this book – afraid that I had said too much or too little, afraid that what I had said would only provoke controversy or generate confusion. I meant that. But I hope in this second edition to strike a different note, a note of confidence. Theology should be hesitant, even troubled, but not anxious. It cannot afford to be anxious if it is truly concerned about others, because an anxious theology is a self-absorbed theology – a contradiction in terms. We need theologies which arise from holy compassion for others and holy familiarity with God. And that is only possible if we allow the Spirit to trouble us toward ongoing and ever-deepening repentance, praise, intercession, delight, and care. Our theology cannot be life-giving if we ourselves do not care for others as we ourselves have received care from God.

---

[10] Timothy Radcliffe, 'Preaching: Conversation in Friendship' (lecture; Preaching and New Evangelization Conference; University of Notre Dame [June 25, 2014]); available online: https://www.youtube.com/watch?v=3ePWGez_xP0; accessed: August 4, 2014.

PART ONE

VOCATION

Identity and/as Vocation: Revisioning Calling in Christ

Introduction

What does it mean to be human? What kind of creatures are we? Who are we meant to become? What are we meant to do? The Westminster Shorter Catechism famously says that our end is 'to glorify God, and to enjoy him forever'. But I am convinced that this statement turns out to be too narrowly drawn, at least if we understand the glorification and enjoyment of God as something separate from our own glorification, something separate from our own joy in ourselves and in our neighbors. Perhaps, then, we come nearer the truth in saying that we are meant for 'ever deeper communion with God and neighbor'.[1] But even that statement does not quite capture the fullness of our calling.

The NT suggests a better answer in its Christological readings of Psalm 8 and its promise of human 'dominion' over creation. The writer of Hebrews, for example, draws on the Psalm, insisting that God has subjected everything to human beings so that nothing is left outside their sovereignty (Heb. 2.5-7). But he immediately acknowledges that for now this vocation remains unfilled, this sovereignty unrealized: 'As it is, we do not yet see everything in subjection to them' (Heb. 2.8). Or, better, the writer holds that the human vocation *is* fulfilled – but for now only for Jesus, our 'pioneer', who has 'tasted death for everyone' and entered into the rest of perfection for us (Heb. 2.9-10). We have not yet seen the promise fulfilled. But we do

---

[1] Stephen E. Fowl, *Theological Interpretation of Scripture* (Eugene, OR: Cascade Book, 2009), p. 13.

not lose hope because 'we *do* see Jesus ...' (Heb. 2.8). And so we remain confident, trusting that whatever is true of him shall be true of us, because 'the one who sanctifies and those who are sanctified are all one' (Heb. 2.11).

Paul offers a similar reading. He too suggests that the promise of Psalm 8 remains unfulfilled, and he too directs attention to Christ as the one in and through whom it will be fulfilled: 'God has put all things in subjection under his feet' (1 Cor. 15.27). Christ, the 'first fruits' of the new creation, is already Lord (1 Cor. 15.30), but his rule is not yet fully established in the earth: 'he must reign until he has put all his enemies under his feet' (1 Cor. 15.25). In the meantime, believers are bound to cling to him, trusting that in his 'coming' he will finally totally destroy his enemies and ours (1 Cor. 15.24), drawing us and all creation into his share in the Father's love.

Paul's hope is wildly daring and subversive: the Son's identification with us is so radical that he shares our subjection to God: 'When all things are subjected to him, then the Son himself will also be subjected' (1 Cor. 15.28). But this subjection is not a servitude. The Son and the Father are one in their Spirit; therefore, when the Son takes our condition as his own, he alters in himself and for our sakes the nature of our relation to God. This is why Paul says the Son is subjected to God: '*so that* God may be all in all' (1 Cor. 15.28).

In his 'coming', Jesus defeats 'every ruler and authority and power' that holds us in subjection (1 Cor. 15.24), freeing us to live in his own freedom, a freedom which knows nothing of either enslavement or mastery, servility or domination. And that is why we pray 'Come quickly, Lord Jesus'. We long for God to be 'all in all', for all creation to be baptized in the Spirit,[2] because we long for fulfillment. We long to relate to ourselves and to one another the way God relates to God. And that is precisely what the gospel of Christ's 'coming' promises.

Being and Doing

These apostolic readings of Psalm 8 reveal that the human vocation is nothing less than a share in Christ's lordship, and that Christ's lordship is nothing less than a giving away of God's own life. And they

---

[2] See Frank Macchia, *Baptized in the Spirit: A Global Pentecostal Theology* (Grand Rapids: Zondervan, 2006).

also reveal that who we are is inseparable from what we are called to do.

It has been popular in some preaching and teaching to separate being from doing, insisting that the first matters more than the second. This distinction may at times prove useful, but it is more often misleading. Distinguishing being from doing obscures the truth about what it means to be human precisely because it is untrue to the ways of God with us.

The truth is, we know God only as God is at work among us. In Aquinas' words, 'God is not known to us in His nature, but is made known to us from His operations'.[3] Or, as Balthasar says it,

[Christ's] form is in the world in order to impress itself upon it and to continue to shape it: everything depends on this event; and, therefore, it is not only difficult but impossible to consider and grasp the shaping form purely in itself, before its act of shaping. We see what this form is from what it does.[4]

God is not 'a such-and-such who then, as such-and-such, does so-and-so. God *is* what he *does*. Indeed, he is the doing of it.'[5] Or, as Jesus himself says, 'even though you do not believe me, believe the works, so that you may know and understand that the Father is in me and I am in the Father' (Jn 10.38). Believe *the works* – only in this way does knowing God become possible.[6]

The way we come to know God – that is, in his works for us – reveals to us not only his character, but ours, as well. Or to say it somewhat differently, how we know God tells us how we are to be

---

[3] Aquinas, *ST* I.13.8.

[4] Hans Urs von Balthasar, *The Glory of the Lord: A Theological Aesthetics Vol. 1 – Seeing the Form* (San Francisco: Ignatius Press, 1982), p. 527.

[5] Robert W. Jenson, *A Religion Against Itself* (Richmond, VA: John Knox Press, 1966), p. 39.

[6] Barth (*CD* II.I, p. 260) makes the same affirmation: 'When we ask questions about God's being, we cannot in fact leave the sphere of His action and working as it is revealed to us in His Word. God is who He is in His works'. Barth goes on to insist that 'God's being is not reduced to God's works. Yet in Himself He is not another than He is in His works'. He of course cannot be *reduced* to his works. 'He is the same even in Himself, even before and after and over His works, and without them. They are bound to Him, but He is not bound to them.' But God is not known to us *apart* from those works, either. 'Yet in Himself He is not another than He is in His works. In the light of what He is in His works it is no longer an open question what He is in Himself.'

ourselves. Who we are comes to be known – because for us, unlike God, it comes to be at all – only in our doing of what it is that we are called to do. In Johannine language, we come to know ourselves as 'children of God' (*identity*) just as we 'walk in the light' (*vocation*), living in ever-deepening intimacy with the one who is light, and who calls us to live in the light with him, to share in his goodness (1 Jn 1.5-7). God is known to us in his works. And for that reason, we are ourselves just as we work the works of God (Jn 9.4).

Identity-in-Vocation

The story of Jesus' baptism, at least as Matthew tells it, underscores this truth about the inseparability of doing and being, vocation and identity. According to the Gospel, while Jesus is emerging from the baptismal waters, the Spirit comes to rest upon him, and just in that moment the Father speaks a blessing over him: 'This is my beloved Son, with whom I am well pleased' (Mt. 3.17). Given Christian habits of thought, we are bound to read this blessing as a statement of Jesus' identity as the eternal Son. When we hear the Father name him as 'beloved Son' we recognize an affirmation of Jesus' status as the second One of the divine Three. But the narrative of the Gospel suggests another possible and complementary reading.

Earlier (in Mt 2.15), Matthew quotes Hosea 11.1 – 'out of Egypt I have called my son' – which is clearly a reference to Israel and the Exodus-event through which God singled out Abraham's descendants as the 'chosen people' to whom and through whom the promised blessing would come to 'all the families of the earth' (Gen. 12.3). Careful readers, then, are sure to connect what God had said of Israel with what God is now saying about Jesus.

As Matthew's story continues, this connection he has drawn between Jesus and Israel deepens. For example, no sooner has Jesus been named 'Son' in that moment of his baptism in the Jordan than the Spirit leads him through the river and into the wilderness. He effectively reverses Israel's wilderness journey into the Promised Land. He moves through the baptismal waters back into that same wilderness where Israel failed to overcome her temptations. In this way, Matthew shows us that Jesus not only shares Israel's name, but he also bears Israel's burden to be the priestly people for the sake of the world.

In the wilderness, Satan tempts Jesus not so much by calling his Sonship into question as by trying to confuse him about what it means for him to bear Israel's burden and how he is to fulfill it. But Christ overcomes the temptations, entering fully into his vocation precisely by refusing to exploit the privileges of his identity as divine Son.[7] In this way, Jesus gets done in the wilderness for and as Israel what Israel could not do otherwise.

> Jesus had come through the waters of baptism, like Israel crossing the Red Sea. He now had to face, in forty days and nights, the equivalent of Israel's forty years in the desert. But, where Israel failed again and again, Jesus succeeded. Here at last is a true Israelite, Matthew is saying. He has come to do what God always wanted Israel to do – to bring light to the world.[8]

By telling Jesus' story this way, Matthew affirms Jesus' identification with Israel, and Israel's identification with Jesus. They can be called by the same name – 'beloved Son' – because they share the same vocation: to be the elect through whom all the nations are drawn gracefully into the Abrahamic family and its promised glories.[9]

Baptism: The Womb of Identity and Vocation

Bearing that connection between Jesus and Israel in mind, we can return to the words the Father speaks over Jesus at his baptism, and we can hear now that the words of that blessing are all-at-once both the affirmation of his identity and the announcement of his vocation. As we reflect carefully on the NT witness, it begins to come

---

[7] See John Nolland, *The Gospel of Matthew* (NIGTC; Grand Rapids: Eerdmans, 2005), p. 163.

[8] N.T. Wright, *Matthew for Everyone Pt. 1* (Louisville: WJKP, 2004), p. 25.

[9] Christopher J.H. Wright, *Knowing God the Father through the Old Testament* (Downers Grove, IL: IVP, 2007), p. 80, sees the description of Israel as 'son' throughout the Old Testament as

> another way of picturing the theological affirmation of Israel's election – i.e., that God had chosen Israel to be his people for the sake of bringing blessing to the nations. But [the sonship metaphor] takes it back a step further by suggesting that it was not the case that Israel was an already-existing nation whom God then subsequently decided to choose and use. Rather, Israel was brought into existence for this chosen purpose. This was what they were born for. Their creation, election and calling were 'simultaneous' realities …

astonishingly clear that the same double blessing happens to us in our baptism. Our shared fall into sin and death 'involved a fall from the royal and priestly stewardship of God's creation'.[10] But 'in the waters of baptism' we are restored to our calling, re-fashioned in Christ's priestly image for 'representing God to the world and offering the world to God in a sacrifice of love and praise'.[11] In the language of Ephesians, it is through the washing of the Word-as-water (Eph. 5.26) that we receive, just as Jesus did, an affirmation of who we are and an announcement of what it is that we are to do. The 'one baptism' births us into 'the one hope of our calling' (Eph. 4.4-5) and connects us to 'the work of the ministry' (Eph. 4.12). To be 'accepted in the Beloved' (Eph. 1.6) is to be so identified with him as to be taken up into the mission he embodies.

Too often, we Pentecostals, like many Evangelicals, think of water baptism as merely symbolic of our repentance and regeneration, our conversion and the forgiveness of our sins. But, in fact, the mystery of baptism graces us with nothing less than a share in the reality of Christ's own life and lived experience. As the Scriptures say, we have been buried with Christ and raised with him into his new reality (Rom. 6.3-5; Col. 2.12), incorporated into the one body (1 Cor. 12.13) – the 'spiritual body' of the resurrected Jesus – through which and for which God in the End rights all things. As the Spirit brings the kingdom to bear on us, we are raised together from the waters of baptism into Christ's Spirit-filled identity-and-vocation. As Rogers explains, only the Spirit makes possible this sharing in Christ's life: 'The baptism of Jesus does not make sense without the presence of the Spirit … At the baptism of Jesus, the Spirit, with her presence, indicates, marks, points out – bears witness to – the love between the Father in the Son in such a way that it can be shared'.[12]

But what does this mean? Many Pentecostals have described Spirit baptism as the gift of empowerment for mission and deep intimacy with the Father.[13] But as a rule, we have failed to recognize that water

---

[10] Frank C. Senn, *New Creation: A Liturgical Worldview* (Minneapolis: Augsburg Fortress Press, 2000), pp. 45-46.

[11] Senn, *New Creation*, p. 46.

[12] See Eugene Rogers, *After the Spirit* (Grand Rapids: Eerdmans, 2005), p. 137.

[13] See, for example, Simon Chan, 'The Language Game of Glossolalia, or Making Sense of the "Initial Evidence"', in Wonsuk Ma and Robert Menzies (eds.), *Pentecostalism in Context: Essays in Honor of William W. Menzies* (JPTSup 11; Sheffield: Sheffield Academic Press, 1997), pp. 80-95 (86).

baptism is itself already a summons to and effectual sign of the same intimacy and the same empowerment. In the sacrament of washing, the Spirit of Pentecost rests on us, so that we are set apart as co-participants in Jesus' work.[14] As Walter Brueggemann says, in baptism our bodies are 'marked in the midst of dark, bloody chaos … as carriers of God's future … marked to act differently, unafraid'.[15] As a people who have entered 'into the Yahweh narrative', we are now 'inescapably engaged in the work of mending the world' – a work that happens in and through us as we 'make our intentional, bodily investments in the narrative of God'.[16]

It may seem odd to talk about water baptism in these terms. But the mothers and fathers of the Pentecostal tradition knew what many of us have now mostly forgotten: the baptismal rite is 'the acceptance of the call to become a holy witness in the power of the Holy Spirit'.[17] Therefore, redemption cannot be separated from mission, and water baptism cannot be separated from Spirit baptism, any more than the Spirit can be divided from the Son. 'The Son and Spirit are sent, and [since] we are in the Son and the Spirit, then we are caught up into their sending. There is no union with the God of Israel that is not also a sending, no deliverance that is not also a commissioning.'[18]

---

[14] Amos Yong, *The Spirit Poured Out on All Flesh: Pentecostalism and the Possiblity of Global Theology* (Grand Rapids: Baker Academic, 2005), p. 160, writes,

> Minimally, if baptism is understood as our obedient participation in the death of Christ and our realization of new life in the power of the Spirit, then there is at least a protosacramental character to baptism as Christian initiation. Maximally, if baptism is understood not as a 'dead ritual' but as a living and transformative act of the Spirit of God on the community of faith, then baptism is not only protosacramental but fully sacramental in the sense of enacting the life and grace of God …

[15] Walter Brueggemann, *Inscribing the Text: Sermons and Prayers of Walter Brueggemann* (Minneapolis: Augsburg Fortress Press, 2004), p. 117.

[16] Walter Brueggemann, *Deep Memory, Exuberant Hope: Contested Truth in a Post-Christian World* (Minneapolis: Augsburg Fortress Press, 2000), p. 33.

[17] Steven Jack Land, *Pentecostal Spirituality: A Passion for the Kingdom* (Cleveland, TN: CPT Press, 2010), p. 110. On this point, we should be as clear as possible: in the moment of being 'filled with the Spirit', believers are experiencing what Frank Macchia (*Baptized in the Spirit*, p. 77) describes as the release of an already-indwelling presence.

[18] Peter Leithart, 'Salvation and Mission'; available online: http:// www.first things.com/blogs/leithart/2014/06/salvation-and-mission; accessed July 11, 2014.

In the waters of baptism, we receive from Christ the Spirit promised by the Father. But 'Spirit-filling must be sought daily',[19] because in this continual re-filling, we receive anew, season by season, moment by moment, the reaffirmation of our baptismal identity as beloved and so find ourselves ready to accept again our human vocation to work the works of God.

Salvation, Obedience, and Theotic Participation

I have been arguing that we are called to share in Christ's lordship for the sake of creation, which means that we cannot share in Christ's identity without also taking up his vocation. If at least the gist of what I have said is true, then we have to acknowledge our salvation does not happen apart from our being taken up into collaborative participation with God's mission to reconcile the world to himself.[20] The invitation to follow Christ is a summons to take responsibility to work his works. Or, to put it yet another way, to let his works come alive in our ours.

Scripture lays down the rubric: 'a disciple is not above the teacher, nor a slave above the master' (Mt. 10.24). Therefore, because Christ 'learned obedience through what he suffered', and only in this way was made 'perfect' as 'the source of eternal salvation' (Heb. 5.8-9), we should expect our involvement in God's work to involve just this same obedience. What Christ underwent for us, we undergo for him and for one another, so that in the undergoing we might become truly what he is, sharing in his priestly intercession for the world.

Insisting that salvation is participationist and theotic – that we commune with God so that we share in his nature – does not mean either that God does some of the work while we do the rest, or that God's work depends upon or is determined by ours in any sense.[21]

---

[19] Steven J. Land, 'A Passion for the Kingdom: Revisioning Pentecostal Spirituality', *Journal of Pentecostal Theology* 1.1 (Apr 1992), pp. 19-46 (35).

[20] As Anthony Baker, *Diagonal Advance: Perfection in Christian Theology* (Eugene, OR: Cascade Books, 2011), p. 284, says, 'God will not justify us without our mediating involvement in that work, because to do so would be a destruction of the human form'. Here, Baker is riffing on Augustine's axiom: 'He who made us without ourselves will not justify us without ourselves' (*qui ergo fecit te sine te, non te iustificat sine te*).

[21] John Webster, *Word and Church: Essays in Christian Dogmatics* (London: T&T Clark, 2001), pp. 225-20.

Too often, we talk about our cooperation with God in ways that obscure the 'sheer gratuity of the gospel', undermining the truth that salvation is by grace alone, and a reward for our obedience or devotion.[22] We are called to 'work out our own salvation' – but we can do so precisely because God is at work in us, freeing us into freedom (Phil. 2.12-13). Yes, our salvation is set before us both as – shocking, revolutionary, unpossessable – reality and also as task.'[23] Our sanctification cannot happen apart from our participation in and cooperation with God.[24] But this is not because participation and cooperation are conditions that must be met before the Father can be pleased with us. Not at all. Instead, participation and cooperation are the inevitable consequence of being conditioned by the Spirit who is the love of the Father for the Son and the love of the Son for the Father.

Nature and Grace

In one sense, vocation is given only in the call to follow Christ.[25] In other words, what the NT refers to as 'calling' does not belong to anyone by 'nature', and this calling is, as Barth says, 'certainly a new thing in contrast to his existing being in the limits set for him by God as his Creator and Lord'.[26] But we should be careful not to oppose the churchly vocation to the human one.

> We speak of baptism as a re-generation or a re-birth but we should
> not be mislead by that *re-*. Baptism is not a second birth that we
> have instead of the first; we are not discarding the first; still less

---

[22] Webster, *Word and Church*, p. 229.

[23] Webster, *Word and Church*, p. 229.

[24] See Cheryl M. Peterson, *The Holy Spirit and the Christian Life: Historical, Interdisciplinary, and Renewal Perspectives* (New York: Palgrave Macmillan, 2014), pp. 97-100.

[25] Barth's distinction between *vocation* and *profession* in this section of the *CD* is especially useful. Because of the fallenness of the world and our own frailty, our vocation simply cannot translate perfectly into any profession or work, whether 'secular' or 'sacred'. But we can and should make every effort to take up and live professions so that we can bring God's holiness to bear in our world to the fullest extent possible.

[26] Barth, *CD* III.4, p. 595. For a critique of Barth on this point, see Anthony D. Baker, 'Things Usually So Strange: Nature and Grace Reconsidered', *Syndicate* (July/August 2014); available online: http://syndicatetheology.com/anthony-d-baker/; accessed: August 4, 2014.

are we adding something on top of it – a layer of grace-life on top of the natural life we received at birth. In this second birth we are discovering the implications of our first birth.[27]

I believe, in other words, that a call to collaborate with God rests upon *all* of us just because we exist as the creatures we are. We are all of us as human beings made to mediate God's holiness to the rest of creation, to work the works of God, to do what Jesus did, to be who Jesus is. To be human is to be burdened with this vocation. And in many ways – small and large, conscious and unconscious, intentional and inadvertent – all of us are more or less faithfully and lovingly in fact fulfilling our calling, although always only in part. In Christ, the Spirit places us under that burden, strengthening us for the bearing of it. This is why the Church came to regard the sacrament of baptism as 'a kind of restoration of what it is to be truly human'.[28]

Donald Bloesch suggests the kingdom exists in three modes or realms: the kingdom of nature, the kingdom of grace, and the kingdom of glory:

> All of humanity belongs to the kingdom of *nature*, for we are all created by God and for the service of God. The kingdom of *grace* is the new order of social relationships inaugurated by Jesus Christ in his cross and resurrection victory. It is an ever-widening reality hidden in the old structures of human existence corrupted by sin and death. The kingdom of nature does not invariably lead to the kingdom of grace, because the former has been seized by the principalities and powers which defy God's reign, though God continues to reign in the midst of their defiance. The kingdom of *glory* is the final stage of the plan of salvation in which the kingdoms of the old order will be transformed into the kingdom of everlasting righteousness and peace.[29]

Using Bloesch's categories (perhaps in ways he did not intend) we can say that the kingdom of grace exists as witness to the kingdom of nature that all things are meant for the kingdom of glory. That

---

[27] Herbert McCabe, OP, *Law, Love and Language* (London: Continuum, 2003), pp. 146-47.

[28] Rowan Williams, *Being Christian: Baptism, Bible, Eucharist, Prayer* (Grand Rapids: Eerdmans, 2014), p. 3.

[29] Donald G. Bloesch, *The Church: Sacraments, Worship, Ministry, Mission* (Downers Grove, IL: IVP, 2002), p. 80.

means that the church lives only to remind the world of its true nature and its true destiny in the kingdom. And we do so by living 'differently, unafraid' by ordering our lives – or, better, by having our lives reordered – in ways that do not conform to the patterns of what the NT calls this present evil age.

What, then, of justification by faith? What of the Spirit's call to set our faith exclusively on Christ? Perhaps the difference can be described best in these terms: our broadest vocation is not so much given to us at our baptism as we are at last truly given to it. Baptized into Christ, we are awakened to and sanctioned for the vocation we always already were meant to bear. Our narrower vocation – the work we are called to do as members of Christ's body (e.g. bishop, pastor, or deacon; evangelist, intercessor, or teacher) – comes to us in our call to believe or is imparted to us in the event of ordination (1 Tim. 4.14), but always with a view to the fulfillment of the natural human call. Within such an account, those outside the church are recognized to have the same broad vocation we do. For now, however, we find ourselves called out from them, but only because we have been singled out by God to share in the work of making room *for* them. We take on the ecclesial vocation always only on behalf of others – never instead of them, much less against them. We are the called out ones whose lives are dedicated entirely to collaboration with God's work for those who have yet to hear or to submit to the call. The elect are elected always for the sake of the non-elect.[30] The church is a remnant of the world, gathered from the world to be both a temple and a kingdom of priests for the world's sake.

Crucified Below: the Eucharist and the Sacrificial Life

In one of the oddest passages in Paul's writings, the apostle claims to find joy in his sufferings because he is '… completing what is lacking in Christ's afflictions for the sake of his body, that is, the church' (Col. 1.24). What are we to make of such a claim? Scripture plainly says again and again that Christ offered himself as the atoning sacrifice 'once for all' (Rom. 6.10; Heb. 9.28; 1 Pet. 3.18). Dying, Jesus proclaimed his work 'finished' (Jn 19.30). How then does Paul dare

---

[30] See Hans Urs Von Balthasar, 'Vocation', *Communio* 37.1 (Spring 2010), pp. 111-27.

to suggest that Christ's sufferings are somehow insufficient?

To make sense of what Paul's says, John Wesley distinguishes what God did *for* us in Jesus' pre-Ascension work from what God does *in* and *through* us as the Body of the ascended Lord. He affirms that Christ's sufferings on our behalf were more than enough to effect the expiation of sin and the undoing of death. The church's sufferings add exactly *nothing* to this peculiar, once-for-all event and its accomplishments. Nonetheless, Wesley also holds that in order for Christians to be conformed to Christlikeness they must suffer and obey as he did. Suffering in imitation of and in participation with Christ, they offer what Wesley in his *Notes* calls 'testimony to [Christ's] truth', and just so find themselves drawn into sanctification, making room in their lives for others to share in the same joy.

Perhaps it would not be too much to say that Wesley believed Christ's atoning act was *inclusively substitutionary*, and that therefore Christians are called and empowered to suffer with and for Christ on the world's behalf. God's victory in Christ has made our participation in Christ's life possible. In Wesley's own words, 'God works, therefore you *can* work ... God works; therefore you *must* work'.[31] To frame it pneumatologically, we could say that because the Spirit is devoted to bringing to fullness everything the Son means to give the Father in the End, the church's sufferings are taken up by the Spirit as means of grace, provoking and enticing creation toward its eschatological redemption. Or, said differently, the Spirit makes us co-sanctified co-sanctifiers with Christ to the Father's delight.

Again, what God did for us in Christ is already accomplished. And, without doubt, Christ's sacrifice is sufficient for our at-one-ment with God. But what God means to do in and through us is not yet complete,[32] and the good news is that his sacrifice is so sufficient that it makes possible our sharing in the divine life even now, before the end in which God is 'all in all'. As we imitate Christ, offering our bodies in ways that do not merely recall the form of his sacrifice but actually partake in his new-creation life by the Spirit, we begin to take

---

[31] John Wesley, Sermon 85: 'On Working Out Our Own Salvation' III.2; see also Thomas C. Oden, *John Wesley's Scriptural Christianity: A Plain Exposition of His Teaching on Christian Doctrine* (Grand Rapids: Zondervan, 1994), pp. 244-52.

[32] So Webster (*Word and Church*, p. 224) contends that the atonement is 'an event charged with force to expand itself and establish conformity with itself, for it is an event one of whose agents is the Holy Spirit'.

on, or at least give off reflections of, God's character, enjoying the Son's intimacy with the Father in the Spirit, bearing with him his burden for the whole creation. In the words of the early Pentecostal pastor, William H. Piper:

> 'It is one of the great principles of Christianity', says Paschal, 'that everything which happened to Jesus Christ should come to pass in the soul and body of each Christian'. Jesus was hated, so will we be. Jesus was reviled, so will we be. He was forsaken by friends and relatives, so will we be. He was crucified, so must we be. He was resurrected, so shall we be. The true disciple of the Lord will pass through all the experiences of his Lord and suffering must be included.[33]

This Wesleyan vision of our participation in Christ's suffering comes clear in a Wesleyan theology of the Eucharist. Daniel Brevint's *The Christian Sacrament and Sacrifice*, which John abridged and appended to his and Charles' *Hymns on the Lord's Supper*, insists that 'as Aaron never came in before the Lord without the whole people of Israel … so Jesus Christ does nothing without his church'. The identification of Head and Body is so complete that 'sometimes they are represented as only one person'. It follows, then, that 'the church follows all the motions and sufferings of her Head'. Brevint insists that *nothing* that happened to Christ is kept from his Body in her history:

> The truth is, our Lord had neither birth, nor death, nor resurrection on earth, but such as we are to conform to; as he hath neither ascension, nor everlasting life, nor glory in heaven, but such as we may have in common with him … we shall follow him into Heaven, if we follow him here on Earth and we shall have communion with him in his glory, if we keep conformity with him here in his sufferings.[34]

These shared realities are tasted, and taken in, at the Table: 'We here thy nature shall retrieve/And all thy heavenly image bear' (*HLS* 32). At the Lord's Table, the saints invoke the Spirit with this prayer: 'Yet in this ordinance divine/We still the sacred load may bear/And

---

[33] William H. Piper, 'But Also to Suffer for His Sake', *LRE* (Jan 9, 1909), p. 7.

[34] Daniel Brevint, *The Christian Sacrament and Sacrifice* (London: Hatchard and Son, 1847), pp. 62-63.

now we in thy offering join/Thy sacramental Passion share' (*HLS* 141). Seen in this way, the Eucharist teaches – or, better, the Spirit uses the Eucharist to teach us – that we are called to share in Jesus' sacrifice, to bear the dying God's 'sacred load'. At the Table, we are reminded what his sacrifice requires of us and makes possible for us.[35] And as we embody the Eucharist, we are 'crucified below', realizing its promise in our day-to-day lives. Consumed as living sacrifices in the faithfulness of the one whose flesh and blood by faith we have consumed, we find ourselves maturing into Christ's full stature (Eph. 4.13), becoming truly his Body, 'the fullness of him who fills all in all' (Eph. 1.23).

Barth is right, then, to say that the Holy Spirit calls believers not so much into 'the enjoyment of their salvation' as into 'God's service as members of Christ's missionary people'.[36] Justification and sanctification find their meaning, their fulfillment and fullness, only in faithfully-lived vocation. If justification and sanctification together form, as Barth says, 'the external basis of vocation', then vocation, in turn, constitutes their 'internal basis or telos'.[37] In justification, God says 'I will be your God'. In sanctification, 'You shall be my people'.[38] In vocation, the church responds with God to God in an emphatic 'Yes!' – the same Yes the Son says to the Father; the same Yes the Father says to the Son – the Yes of the Spirit.

Friends of (the Friend of) Sinners

The biblical witness makes incredible claims about Jesus, which poor teaching and neglect have caused us to forget. These claims identify him as the one who bears in himself the destiny of everyone and everything. He 'tastes death for everyone' (Heb. 2.9). All die in him and are made alive in him (2 Cor. 5.14). He 'upholds all things by the word of his power' (Heb. 1.3). All things are reconciled and held

---

[35] Peter Enns, *Ecclesiastes* (The Two Horizons Old Testament Commentary; Grand Rapids: Eerdmans, 2011), p. 171.

[36] Darrell L. Guder, 'Mission', in Richard Burnett (ed.), *The Westminster Handbook to Karl Barth* (Louisville: WJKP, 2013), p. 150.

[37] George Hunsinger, *How to Read Karl Barth: The Shape of His Theology* (New York: OUP, 1991), p. 154

[38] George Hunsinger, 'Sanctification', in Richard Burnett (ed.), *The Westminster Handbook to Karl Barth* (Louisville: WJKP, 2013), pp. 192-98.

together in him (Col. 2.17, 20). Insofar, then, as the Spirit through baptism gives us a share in Christ, we are baptized into all that is his, including his vocation, which entails an absolute and unconditional solidarity with human beings at their most vulnerable, their least worthy.[39] 'The central truth of baptism, therefore, is lodged in Jesus Christ himself and all that he has done for us within the humanity he took from us and made his own, sharing to the full what we are that we may share to the full what he is.'[40]

Acknowledging this radical solidarity, we are positioned to see that these incredible claims about Christ entail astonishing implications for us, too, because, in every case, what is said of him addresses our relation to him in his relation to God. Baptism, then, effects not so much a cleansing from sin as a binding to humanity and the creation with which God in Christ has so radically identified himself.[41] In this sense, it is the sacrament of solidarity. It is, first, 'the sacrament of God's solidarity with the world in all of its sinfulness and estrangement'; second, 'the sacrament of human solidarity in Christ with each other, and especially with all those who are different, strange, and even frightening to us'; and, third, 'the sacrament of human solidarity with the whole groaning creation'.[42] Joined to him in the washing of water and by the indwelling of the Spirit, we receive Christ's priestly sensitivity to 'the need, the chaos, the darkness of the world' and his prophetic passion to enter into that darkness as 'the light of the world' (Mt. 5.14).

All to say, being baptized, being filled with the Spirit of baptism, does not 'confer on us a status that marks us off from everybody else'.[43] Baptism does not privilege us, or separate us safely from others. Indeed, it does the opposite. The truly holy life is a life lived in radical solidarity with sinners just because it is a life consumed by intimacy with the holy God. The Spirit of baptism calls us into the depths – the depths of God's joy and the depths of the world's agonies. We have been warned: 'the path of the baptized person is a dangerous one'.[44]

---

[39] Rowan Williams, 'Sacramental Living: Living Baptismally', *Australian Journal of Liturgy* 9.1 (2003), pp. 3-18 (6).

[40] T.F. Torrance, *The Trinitarian Faith* (London: T&T Clark, 1997), p. 294.

[41] Williams, 'Sacramental Living', p. 6.

[42] Daniel Migliore, *Faith Seeking Understanding* (Grand Rapids: Eerdmans, 2nd edn, 2004), pp. 293-94.

[43] Williams, *Being Christian*, p. 5.

[44] Williams, *Being Christian*, p. 5.

Comparing Jesus' baptism with Israel's baptism-like passage through the Red Sea, Bob Ekblad notes that Jesus' baptism differs from Israel's in one critical detail: unlike them, he does not pass through 'on dry ground'. Instead, he suffers *immersion* in the flood – just as Pharaoh and his armies did.[45] Ekblad infers from this coincidence that for Christ, 'descent into the waters of baptism involved a deliberate joining in solidarity with the fate of sinners'.[46] And he contends that baptism means nothing less than that for us, as well:

> Jesus' acceptance of this baptism and the entire New Testament teaching on baptism is nothing less than a call for all future followers to join in the fate of the enemies of God's kingdom, the 'them' that we may deem worthy of exclusion, punishment, or death.[47]

'Under water, God's chosen people join the damned.'[48] And at the Table, they feast in the presence of the enemies they are called to love toward reconciliation with God in Christ.

The *Apophthegmata Patrum* recounts the following story of Abba Bessarion, which captures what it means to live our baptismal identity-in-vocation: 'A brother who had sinned was dismissed from the community by the priest. Abba Bessarion stood up and walked out with him, saying: "I, too, am a sinner."'[49] This is at least part of what it means to 'go to him outside the camp and bear the abuse he endured' (Heb. 13.13).

Our share in Christ is also always necessarily a share in the lives of sinners for whom Christ gave and continues to give himself. We

---

[45] See Bob Ekblad, *A New Christian Manifesto* (Louisville: WJKP, 2008), pp. 33-38.

[46] Ekblad, *A New Christian Manifesto*, p. 36.

[47] Ekblad, *A New Christian Manifesto*, p. 34.

[48] Ekblad, *A New Christian Manifesto*, p. 37.

[49] John Chryssavgis, *In the Heart of the Desert: The Spirituality of the Desert Fathers and Mothers* (Bloomington, IN: World Wisdom Publishing, rev. edn, 2008), p. 152. Rowan Williams, *Where God Happens: Discovering Christ in One Another* (Boston: New Seeds Books, 2005), p. 22, explains that stories like these should not be taken to suggest that the saints are indifferent to sin. 'They actually believe that sin is immensely serious and that separation from God is a real possibility ... But they also take for granted that the only way in which you know the seriousness of separation from God is in your own experience of yourself'. This self-awareness floods them with mercy for their neighbor. See also William Harmless, *Desert Christians: An Introduction to the Literature of Early Monasticism* (Oxford: OUP, 2004), p. 240.

should not be surprised by such a claim. If our intimacy with God is always 'in Christ', and Christ is 'friend of sinners' (Mt. 11.19), then it is impossible to be friends of God if we are not also friends of sinners. If we hope to make sense of our calling, then we have to match Nazianzus' soteriological axiom, 'What is not assumed is not healed',[50] with a similar one: Whoever is healed desires the healing of all.

This can be seen especially clearly in the rejection of certain forms of Christian faith, which teach, explicitly or implicitly, that we need not feel any responsibility for what happens in the world, so long as we ourselves stand in right relation to God – so long as we ourselves are 'born again' and 'filled with the Spirit'. Martin Buber, in February 1942, wrote to Lina Lewy, a friend of Leonard Ragaz, explaining that in spite of the fact that he feels allied with Jesus in some respects, he cannot hail him as savior.

> I am not at all capable of believing in a Messiah who already came so many years ago, because I have too profound a sense of the world's unredeemedness to be able to come to terms with the idea of a realized redemption, be it only a redemption of the 'soul' (I do not want to live in an unredeemed world with a 'redeemed' soul).[51]

For Buber, redemption is the making right of all wrongs, the bringing to full flourishing of all creation at once and forever. And so, he cannot accept what Christians claim about what Jesus accomplished in his death. 'Redemption is a transformation of the whole of life from its very bottom, of the life of all individuals and all communities. The world is unredeemed – don't you feel that, as I do, in every drop of blood?'[52]

In a March 1917 letter to the poet and playwright, Franz Werfel, who would later write *The Song of Bernadette*, Buber says that what bothers him most about Christian theology is the suggestion that God does not need us, and that we do not need to take responsibility for what happens in the world. Citing a line from the lost *The Gospel*

---

[50] Gregory of Nazianzus, 'To Cledonius the Priest against Apollinarius', in Edward R. Hardy (ed.), *Christology of the Later Fathers* (Philadelphia: Westminster, 1954), p. 218.

[51] Martin Buber, *The Letters of Martin Buber: A Life in Dialog* (New York: Knopf Doubleday, 1991), p. 498.

[52] Buber, *The Letters of Martin Buber*, p. 223.

of the Hebrews, Buber argues that God waits on us, longing to rest upon us as he rested upon Jesus at his baptism: 'My son, in all of the prophets I waited for you … You are my rest'.

> And how could I possibly grasp what the Christians find so easy to grasp, that God does not need me! That I have been made for a plaything and not for a perfecting … No, my friend, nothing is imposed upon us by God; everything is expected of us. And you rightly say: It lies within our choice whether we want to live the true life: in order to perfect him in our uniqueness. But according to the Christian teaching, which has turned the meaning and the ground of Jesus upside down, nothing lies within our choice; rather, everything depends on whether or not we have been elected. Our teaching is: It is not a question of whether He has elected me, but that I have elected Him. For it is truly not His business to elect and to reject. Whereas the teaching that calls itself Christian hinders men, by referring them to divine grace, from making that decision which Jesus proclaimed …[53]

Buber misunderstands Christian theology. But he rightly rejects the idea that the world's unredeemedness should not concern us, as if all that matters is that our souls are saved, and that we have a personal relationship with Jesus. Or perhaps it is nearer the truth to say that Buber understands perfectly well what is wrong with the misguided Christian theology that was presented to him. After all, I would contend that a mark of a 'redeemed soul' is its awareness of its own unredeemedness, its anguish for all that is wrong in the world. And so, the Christian life can be understood as a life of deepening intimacy with the redeemer and a deepening awareness of our responsibility in the redemption he is bringing about, which inevitably makes us feel more and more the horrible weight of the world's brokenness so that we are pressed into intercession. It is perhaps not too much to say, then, that the feeling of that weight pressing down on us is in fact our calling as it is happening to us. Seeing the suffering of others, we are made to feel the weight of glory.

---

[53] Buber, *The Letters of Martin Buber*, pp. 213-14.

2

SANCTIFIED BODIES, SANCTIFYING MEDIATION: SHARING CHRIST'S CONTINUING PRIESTHOOD

Introduction

Jesus' vocation continues. 'He remains a priest forever' (Heb. 7.3) and 'lives to make intercession' for us (Heb. 7.25). This continuation is what makes the church the church, Israel Israel, and the world the world. As Chan says, 'the story of the church is the continuation of the triune economy of redemption. It is the story of the Spirit from the Father, poured out upon the church after the ascension.'[1] And what he says of the church is true not only of churchly institutions and communities, but of all faithful, loving, hopeful people. Christ's priestly ministry is for us and with us so that our work, our ministry, is included with and within his. 'We are ambassadors for Christ, since God is making his appeal through us' (2 Cor. 5.20). As Bonhoeffer insists: 'Christ's priestly work becomes the basis of our own'.[2]

Of course, it is not that the church replaces Christ or serves as a human stand-in for him in his divine, ascended absence. Instead, Christ is truly, creatively present as the church in the Spirit embodies his priestly ministry. At the heart of the church's worship, its prayers, its preaching, its sacramental celebration, is the confidence that by

---

[1] Simon Chan, *Liturgical Theology: The Church as Worshipping Community* (Downers Grove, IL: IVP, 2006), p. 60. See also Simon Chan, 'Jesus as Spirit-Baptizer: Its Significance for Pentecostal Ecclesiology', in John Christopher Thomas (ed.), *Toward a Pentecostal Ecclesiology: The Church and the Fivefold Gospel* (Cleveland, TN: CPT Press, 2010), pp. 139-56.

[2] Dietrich Bonhoeffer, *Sanctorum Communio: A Theological Study of the Sociology of the Church* (Dietrich Bonhoeffer Works, Vol. 1; Minneapolis: Fortress Press, 1998), p. 167.

the will of the Father, Jesus himself continues to act in what we are saying and doing, what we are hearing and seeing and feeling. His activity is not exhausted in our activity or our experience, of course. But he is truly, fully present in them for our good and the good of the world.[3]

We believe the church, like and with Israel, is gathered from the world for the world's sake, as the first-fruits of the world's redemption, bearing the human vocation for the sake of all human beings.[4] Israel was called out from the other nations to be a sanctified people whose way of life brought to light the truth of creation. Now, the church is also called out to be with Israel a holy people whose life together in worship brings to light the hope of the renewal of that creation.[5] In Daniela Augustine's words, 'The Church becomes the sacred space where history is faced with its own future as the demand for and inevitability of transformation'.[6] Again, this is not in superiority to or for the domination of others in the world, but only for their service. We do not seek to make all things Christian: we seek to bear witness to the ways in which in Christ all things are made whole. In this regard, Buber's rejection of Christianity shows us what our faith in fact requires of us.

Christ's Body as the World's Temple

Often, when we are talking about the church as called out from the world, we imply a contrast between the humanity of believers and the humanity of non-believers. Truth be told, Scripture itself often seems to speak this way. For example, Ephesians 2 contrasts 'the children of wrath' – those who are 'dead' in sin, 'following the course of the world', dominated by the 'passions of the flesh' (Eph. 2.1-3) – with

---

[3] Rowan Williams, *On Christian Theology* (Malden, MA: Blackwell Publishers, 2000), p. 189.

[4] Peter Althouse, 'Ascension – Pentecost – Eschaton: A Theological Framework for Pentecostal Ecclesiology', in Thomas (ed.), *Toward a Pentecostal Ecclesiology*, pp. 225-47 (47), contends that, because Pentecost brings to bear in and for us the new-creation realities of Christ's resurrection and ascension, the church is 'the sign, foretaste, and instrument of Christ's eschatological reign …'

[5] Timothy Radcliffe, 'Christ in Hebrews: Cultic Irony', *New Blackfriars* 68 (1987), pp. 494-504 (496).

[6] Daniela Augustine, *Pentecost, Hospitality, and Transfiguration: Toward a Spirit-Inspired Vision of Social Transformation* (Cleveland, TN: CPT Press, 2012), p. 19.

the 'one new humanity', which is created in Christ's body as the 'household of God' (Eph. 2.15, 19). If we are not careful, then, we leave the impression that the saints have a different humanity 'in Christ' than does the rest of the world 'in Adam'.

But such a reading misses the point. The line of thought in Ephesians 2 does not end with the contrast between the family of God and the children of disobedience.[7] Instead, Paul goes on to insist that this 'one new humanity' constituted in and as Christ's body 'is joined together and grows into a holy temple … a dwelling place for God' (Eph. 2.21-22). What is this temple if not a holy 'place' set aside for the world to meet with its God and for God to act on the world?[8] The church, participating in the renewed humanity created in Christ as a priestly people, opens a space in the midst of the world so that heaven and earth, the new creation and the old, can touch.[9] We are made by the Spirit the temple for the sake of others, so they can encounter Christ in the room he has made for them in our lives.

These images of the church as the Spirit's temple and the church as Christ's body point to our true identity and calling. Christ is the 'image of the invisible God', bearing in himself 'all the fullness' of God (Col. 1.15, 19). The church, as Christ's body, is his fullness (Eph. 1.23) and lives in being conformed to his image (2 Cor. 3.18).

---

[7] Andrew Lincoln, *New Testament Theology: The Theology of the Later Pauline Letters* (Cambridge: Cambridge University Press, 2000), pp. 100-101, appreciates the emphasis on Temple imagery, which he sees as exemplifying the Church's 'new privileged position': the church, including the Ephesian community, has replaced the Temple in Jerusalem as 'the special focus of the presence on earth of the God of heaven'. Lincoln acknowledges that the church 'form[s] the link between heaven and earth', but seems to imply that only believers enjoy the blessings of the communion. Peter T. O'Brien, *The Letter to the Ephesians* (The Pillar New Testament Commentary; Grand Rapids: Eerdmans, 1999), p. 221, comes nearer the truth, I think, in saying that Paul wants above all for the Ephesians to know the unknowable love of God 'so they might be empowered to fulfill their role in the divine purposes'. Both Lincoln and O'Brien, however, underplay what I believe is Paul's ultimate concern; that is, for the church to be for the world what Christ is for them.

[8] John 2.13-22 also draws the connection between Christ's body and the temple. See Alan Kerr, *The Temple of Jesus' Body: The Temple Theme in the Gospel of John* (London: Sheffield Academic Press, 2002), pp. 67-101.

[9] That place where God can be touched is what Paul names 'the body of Christ'. In Robert Jenson's words, 'Whatever makes a person available to and intendable by other people *is* that person's body' ('The Sacraments', in Robert W. Jenson and Carl E. Braaten [eds.], *Christian Dogmatics Vol. 2* [Minneapolis: Fortress Press, 1984], p. 359). See also Robert W. Jenson, *Systematic Theology Vol. 1: The Triune God* (New York: OUP, 1997), p. 205.

Through the church that God's manifold wisdom is made known (Eph. 3.10) – uniquely, but not exclusively – and for the church that all things are brought into their fullness (Eph. 1.22). But, again, we have to stop to say that this is always only for the sake of those 'outside'. In the church's life, God publicizes, puts on display, an image of what he has always purposed for the entire creation: 'in the fullness of time, to gather up all things in Christ' (Eph. 1.10).

Having identified the church as temple (Eph. 2.21-22), Paul immediately moves to describe his vocation in intercessory, priestly terms: 'This is the reason that I Paul am a prisoner for Christ Jesus for the sake of you Gentiles ...' (Eph. 3.1). Toward the end of the letter, he calls for the Ephesians to take their own share in the work: 'Therefore be imitators of God ... and live in love, as Christ loved us and gave himself up for us, a fragrant offering and sacrifice to God' (Eph. 5.1). Obviously, a sacrifice is not offered for its own sake. Christ gave himself for us. And in him, and as his body, we give ourselves for others. The church is not a means to an end. But neither is it an end in itself.

When Paul prays for the Ephesians to come to know 'the breadth and length and height and depth' of God's love in Christ, a love that 'surpasses knowledge', a love that fills them 'with all the fullness of God' (Eph. 3.18-19), he does so with one aim in mind: that through them God's power might accomplish 'far more than all we can ask or imagine' (Eph. 3.20) by drawing those who have been 'afar off' into the peace of Christ (Eph. 2.13-14). Drawn close to him, they are made 'fellow heirs, members of the same body, and sharers in the promise in Christ Jesus through the gospel' (Eph. 3.6).

Priestly work, then, is, from first to last, reconciliatory mediation – peacemaking. Priestly presence is, as Rowan Williams' suggests, always 'unitive, sacrificial and intercessory'. The priest is one who 'makes connections'.[10] According to Israel's Law, priests bore the responsibility to facilitate the 'two-way connection' between God and God's people.[11] And at least according to the book of Numbers, they fulfilled their responsibility by means of four primary functions: service, the protection of boundaries, mediation across boundaries, and representation.[12] They served not only 'to facilitate the regularized

---

[10] Williams, 'Sacramental Living', p. 10.
[11] David Stubbs, *Numbers* (BTC; Grand Rapids: Brazos Press, 2009), p. 47.
[12] Stubbs, *Numbers*, p. 43.

access to God centered on the tabernacle' and to guard the distinction between the sacred and the common, but also to 'mediate or extend the holy into the common and help the common move toward the holy'.[13] They did so, by and large, by 'substituting for and representing others before God'.[14]

The prophets of Israel have often been valorized by Christian interpreters, especially Protestants, and seen in opposition to the priests. But this is a false choice: priestly ministry is prophetic and prophetic ministry is priestly. And so, the church-community is not only prefigured in the temple but also, and perhaps even more forcefully, in the cities of refuge. The laws for these cities replace focus on maintaining purity with 'a stress on mercy and openness to those in trouble'. Precisely in this way, their existence and function bear witness to something essential in the call to be a priestly and prophetic people, a call shared alike by Israel and the church, although carried out in different ways.[15]

Finally, then, we need to see how the church, as Christ's priestly and prophetic people, bears the same responsibility he bore and fulfills it in the same basic ways that he did. The work of connecting God to the people and God's people to one another, as well as to the world that God has entrusted to their care, requires us, as it did Israel, and as it did Jesus, to rely on the priestly functions of service and protection and mediation and representation, as well as the prophetic functions of challenge and threat and summons to see the world otherwise. The only question is whether we are enacting these functions faithfully; that is, in ways formed by love through faith and hope in what God has done, is doing, and has promised still to do in Christ.

The Saving Spectacle

Paul, as we have seen, envisions the church as an embodied word, a corporate, ongoingly enacted announcement to the world of the creation's true identity and purpose.[16] God's wisdom, which is made known to all creation through the church's corporate worship and

---

[13] Stubbs, *Numbers*, p. 46.

[14] Stubbs, *Numbers*, p. 47.

[15] Stubbs, *Numbers*, p. 241.

[16] According to the *Book of Order* for the Presbyterian Church (USA), the church is 'a provisional demonstration of what God intends for all of humanity'. Quoted in Allen Verhey and Joseph S. Harvard, *Ephesians* (Louisville: WJKP, 2011), p. 105.

shared witness, must be made known in ways appropriate to God's character as revealed in Christ, who is in person the wisdom of God (1 Cor. 1.24) – a wisdom that seems like foolishness to the world. Therefore, the church's proclamation of Christ must play on this foolishness. What Paul says of himself and the apostles, is true of the apostolic community wherever it finds itself: 'God has exhibited us … last of all, like criminals sentenced to death, so that we have become a spectacle to the world …' (1 Cor. 4.9). The church, in its life of prayer, teaching, and simple service, lives as a spectacle that remains from the world's perspective strange and strangely subversive.

Bearing Paul's vision of the church in mind, we can say that the people of God are like a play staged within the play that is creation's history: God puts us on display so that through our 'performance', which, always is a failed performance, in one way or another, others may find themselves unexpectedly, gracefully unsettled and intrigued – and just in this way drawn toward the possibility of repentance, self-emptying, and transfiguration. To take up language from Jesus' Sermon on the Mount, it is just as we are following the ascended Nazarene's command to 'practice our piety' hiddenly that God puts his own character on display so that our good works – in spite of our best efforts to keep them secret – are seen in such a way that the Father's goodness is celebrated and all are drawn to him who is the desire of all nations.[17]

'I Have Come To Do Your Will'

As we have seen, Paul and the writer of Hebrews are clear that any account of our vocation necessarily begins with Christ and his calling. In an astonishing passage, Hebrews allows us to overhear the Son praying about his vocation (Heb. 10.5-7):

> [5]Consequently, when Christ came into the world, he said,
> 'Sacrifices and offerings you have not desired,
>   but a body you have prepared for me;
> [6]in burnt offerings and sin offerings
>   you have taken no pleasure.
> [7]Then I said, 'See, God, I have come to do your will, O God'
>   (in the scroll of the book it is written of me)'.

---

[17] Cf. Mt. 5.16 and 6.1-6.

What we might call Jesus' vocational prayer shows that he understood his incarnational mission, his 'coming into the world', as the outworking, the enacting, of his eternally-decided calling. He comes into the world just to do the Father's will – to offer his body, received as gift, back to the Father through the Spirit as sacrifice – *the* sacrifice. But what, exactly, is it that God desires for him to do? The writer of Hebrews, anticipating the question, provides the answer: 'it is by God's will that we have been sanctified through the offering of the body of Jesus Christ once for all' (Heb. 10.10). Jesus' vocation was nothing either more or less than this: to mediate God's holiness to us, drawing us into the sanctifying communion he enjoys, reveals, and creates.

And that is our vocation, too. Or, better, that continues to be Christ's vocation, which we now share as he lives his sacrificial ministry in us. Through the Spirit, our vocation is Christ's vocation, just as surely as his identity is ours. Through the Spirit, we are so at-one-ed with Christ that our experience and his are intertwined. What is true of him is true of us, now and/or in the End. As we 'look to Jesus' (Heb. 12.2), we recognize that we are created in him to bring the beauty of God's holiness to bear on everyone and everything. Needless to say, we do not always look like Jesus. We are all such poor mediators and intercessors, never fully faithful – although we do desire to be, or at least desire to desire to be. But what matters first and foremost is that we always look to him, knowing we do not yet look like him. In that way, even in our failings, we bear a weak but indispensable witness to the promise that in the glory of God's Kingdom all things are brought into their peculiar glories, and in mediation we ourselves are brought into our own glory (1 Cor. 2.7).

Of course, God often uses our neighbors, strangers, and enemies – including unbelievers and people of other faith traditions – to draw us into new or renewed awareness of our calling. Think, for example, of Melchizedek, Rahab, Abigail – 'outsiders' who in one way or another save 'insiders' from themselves. Even after proclaiming that the Spirit was promised to 'all flesh' at Pentecost (Acts 2.17), Peter still doubts that God in fact means to include the Gentiles in the kingdom. So, in a graceful twist, God gives him Cornelius (Acts 10), and we learn, as he did, that we need those whom we are called to serve with the gospel at least as much as they need us.

Something on the same order happens in the story of Ruth. She, a Moabite, belongs to a neighboring people typically portrayed as dangerous for Israel, a threat to Israel's holiness. But, as the story continues, we see that in spite of the fact that Israel has been unfaithful to her vocation, God is saving her future through the faithfulness of this gentile. And, astoundingly, when Boaz praises her, he speaks of her as a new Abraham: 'you left your father and mother and your native land and came to a people that you did not before' (Ruth 2.11; cf. Gen. 12.1).[18]

In his masterful *Andrei Rublev* (1966), Andrei Tarkovsky portrays the now-famous painter undergoing an acute spiritual crisis. Rublev has been asked to paint an icon of the Trinity, but he resists, drowning in his own sense of unworthiness.

> He believes his crisis of faith, his struggle to reconcile the love of God with the evil and brutality which he has observed in the world and in his heart, disqualifies himself to paint icons, to open heaven through paint. And so Rublev fasts. He fasts from speaking. He fasts from community. And he fasts from his vocation.[19]

In time, Rublev, wandering through the countryside, happens upon a boy, Boriska, whose father, a well-respected bell-maker, has recently died, leaving the boy with the task of casting the bell the Grand Prince has commissioned for the village church. Afraid of losing the job, Boriska claims to know his father's mysterious secret for bell-casting. But he in fact never learned it. So, under the threat of death, he forges ahead into the seemingly impossible task, brashly insisting at every turn that he *does* know the secret, trusting himself to his instincts and hoping against hope that the casting somehow will work. Unbelievably, it does work, and as the bell rings, with the Prince and the priests and the villagers gathered around the bell in celebration, Boriska collapses in exhausted relief and disbelief at his own success.

---

[18] See Robert Alter, *The Art of Biblical Narrative* (New York: Basic Books, 2011), p. 71. See also Alain Marchadour and David Neuhaus, *The Land, the Bible, and History* (Bronx, NY: Fordham University Press, 2007), p. 36.

[19] Daniel A. Siedell, 'You Will Make Bells and I Will Paint Icons', *Cultivare* (March 12, 2012); available online: http://www.patheos.com/blogs/cultivare/2013/03/you-will-make-bells-i-will-paint-icons/; accessed: September 26, 2014.

Rublev, having seen it all from a distance like Peter at Christ's trial and crucifixion, rushes to the boy when he collapses, gathers him up in his arms, and breaks his long-held vow of silence with a promise: 'You will cast bells. I will paint icons'. In that moment, Rublev, the believing, doubting monk, is freed anew for his vocation:

> Rublev's breakthrough occurs when he discovers his neighbor – not God – in his vocation. Through Boriska – observing and comforting him and promising to care for him as a father – by being Christ to his neighbor, as Luther once said – Rublev receives his vocation anew. He receives it liberated of the burden to justify himself through paint before the face of God. Sitting in the mud with a broken, grieving orphan, Rublev is truly free. He is free to paint icons.[20]

Perhaps, in the end, we, like Rublev (and Abraham, David, Boaz/Israel, and Peter, among others), can truly bear our vocation only as we receive unanticipated, unwarranted grace from others, especially those others we understand as most in need of our care. Only our openness to the gifts they bear for us, whether they intend them as gifts for us or not, can instill in our bodies the wisdom needed to speak the gospel gracefully to them. As the story of Abraham tells us, God's friends are always those who are most hospitable to strangers.

'A Body You Have Prepared for Me'

In his vocational prayer, the Lord rejoices that he has been given a body to do God's will (Heb. 10.5). This points to the fact that fulfilling our vocation has everything to do with how we use our bodies.[21] Ephraim Radner puts it directly: 'reconciliation is about bodies and what you do with them'.[22] To understand what this means, we

---

[20] Siedell, 'You Will Make Bells and I Will Paint Icons', n.p.

[21] Pentecostals are often more comfortable talking about the work of the Spirit within the individual believer's interiority. But if Christ dwells in our hearts through faith (Eph. 3.17), it is only because the Spirit rests on our bodies, just as she did on Christ's body.

[22] Ephraim Radner, 'The Church's Witness of Reconciliation in the Twenty-First Century'; 2009 Palmer Lecture Chapel (Seattle Pacific University). Audio

need to connect the call to collaborate with God's 'ministry of rec-onciliation' (2 Cor. 5.19) with Jesus' Beatitudes (Mt. 5.3-10), which are concerned with 'where Jesus has placed his body so that the world might be saved'.[23] The Beatitudes embody, so to speak, Jesus' politics, a politics that calls for the shrewd use of our bodies for good. 'The Beatitudes show us how our bodies are to be used by showing us how Jesus used his body, the one given him by the Father for the sake of his vocation.'[24] This is hard to learn for those of us shaped by Christian teaching that talks only about the heart, about intentions, about feelings.

Before we can hear what the Beatitudes expect from us, however, we have to see how Jesus embodies them for us. Completely in the fullness of his person, he simply is true meekness, poverty of spirit, hunger and thirst for righteousness. But, as our savior, he embodies this fullness for us in way that makes it possible for us to share in his character. Therefore, because of our baptismal identification with Christ, the Beatitudes not only describe the use Jesus made of his pre-Ascension, earthly body, but they also describe a way of life for us as his ecclesial body, formed together with him as 'one flesh' in the Spirit.

We misunderstand Radner if we think he is describing an individ-ualistic, moralistic call. The Sermon on the Mount gives not a 'list of requirements', but 'a description of the life of a people gathered by and around Jesus':

> To be saved is to be so gathered ... No one is asked to go out and try to be poor in spirit or to mourn to be meek. Rather, Jesus is indicating that given the reality of the kingdom we should not be surprised to find among those who follow him those who are poor in spirit, those who mourn, those who are meek. Moreover, Jesus does not suggest that everyone who follows him will possess all the Beatitudes, but we can be sure that some will be poor, some will mourn, and some will be meek.[25]

---

available online:https://itunes.apple.com/itunes-u/palmer-lectures-in-wesleyan/I d389 794952? mt =10. Accessed July 2, 2014.

[23] Radner, 'The Church's Witness of Reconciliation in the Twenty-First Cen-tury', n.p.

[24] Radner, 'The Church's Witness of Reconciliation in the Twenty-First Cen-tury', n.p.

[25] Stanley Hauerwas, *Matthew* (BTC; Grand Rapids: Brazos Press, 2007), p. 61.

Jesus embodies the virtues the Beatitudes and the Spirit rested, and continues to rest, on him in his mission. The Spirit continues to rest on him and so on us. Through the Ascension/Pentecost event, the Spirit who came to rest on Jesus at his baptism (Mt. 3.13-17) has come to rest on us, so that we can continue to body forth his ministry, his presence. 'The Spirit gave the Word a body so that those with bodies might receive the Spirit.'[26] In other words, because Christ is the site of the Spirit's work, his life is the life described in the Beatitudes. And because the Father has placed us in Christ, we too live at the site, and so our lives are being worked to fit that description. This is not a matter of law and condemnation for our failures, but a matter of grace and a summons toward fulness.

'Sacrifices You Have Not Desired'

Although it might not seem obvious to us at first, in making such a claim on our bodies, the Beatitudes show themselves to be concerned with power. Following Radner's line of thought, then, we can say that true power – the power of the Spirit of holiness (Rom. 1.4) – is first and foremost the power of unanxious and reconciling presence, a power brought to bear on behalf of those who suffer in isolation, those forgotten or ignored by the powers-that-be, whose only hope is 'another body that comes and stands beside and in the midst ... and will not move'.[27] As our lives are made in even the smallest ways to be like Christ's, we become noticeably less anxious, less needy, less defensive, and increasingly determined for others to be treated with the dignity that is theirs as God's delight.

To this end, the church must be 'a body of people who have learned the skills of presence', skills that are developed only in a community 'pledged not to fear the stranger', where the practice of being present with those in suffering 'has become the marrow of their habits'.[28] The work of the Spirit of Pentecost is to overcome our fear,

---

[26] Rogers, *After the Spirit*, p. 126.

[27] Radner, 'The Church's Witness of Reconciliation in the Twenty-First Century', n.p.

[28] Stanley Hauerwas, 'Salvation and Health: Why Medicine Needs the Church', in Stephen E. Lammers and Allen Verhey (eds.), *On Moral Medicine: Theological Perspectives in Medical Ethics* (Grand Rapids: Eerdmans, 2nd edn, 1998), pp. 72-83.

preparing us to be there graciously and without pretension or ambi-
tion for those in need. Sometimes, the Spirit limns our actions so that
they body forth the power of Christ's compassion and wisdom in
ways that we and others can sense. But whether we or they can sense
it or not, our confidence in God leads us to say that he is always
everywhere at work doing good. So, by being there, by showing up
and staying put, we 'present our bodies as a living sacrifice' (Rom.
12.1-2), which, when all is said and done, is probably the only way
that truly overcomes evil with good (Rom. 12.21). Thus, that is the
sacrifice with which God is pleased.

We often wrongly imagine sacrifice not as gift but as forfeiture,
not as self-giving but as self-destruction. Christ, however, reveals that
God hates whatever destroys us, just as surely as he hates whatever
we might do that destroys others. And, as the last sacrifice, his priestly
ministry is the apocalyptic bringing-to-bear of the Great Commandment, which is why his sacrifice is the end of all sacrifice. Christ
makes of himself a sacrifice, and so all sacrifices, if they are true to
themselves, must be what his was: a free and freeing gift of reconciliation and healing and blessing.

When asked 'What is the greatest commandment in Torah', Jesus
replied: 'Love God, your Lord, with everything in you. That is the
greatest commandment. But another commandment goes with it:
You must love your neighbor just as you would love yourself' (Mt.
22.36-40). Having said this, Jesus also insisted that everything in
Scripture ('the Law and the Prophets') depends on these two commandments. We assume we know this commandment, and obviously
in some sense we are familiar with it. But in our circles, it is easy to
confuse the call to love God with the call to have a 'personal relationship' with God. It is easy to imagine that so long as we have devout feelings for God, loving our neighbor will happen 'naturally'.
But that is a dangerous misunderstanding. Loving God is inseparable
from loving neighbor. In fact, loving our neighbor just *is* the way we
love God. The apostle Paul insists that the whole Law and all of its
commands can be 'summed up' in *one* command: 'Love your neighbor as yourself' (Rom. 13.9; Gal. 5.14). And he directs the Galatians:
'Bear one another's burdens, and in this way you will fulfill the law
of Christ' (Gal. 6.2). The apostle John makes the same claim: 'this is
the message you have heard from the beginning, that we should love
one another' (1 Jn 3.11). We have confidence before God only if we

are loving one another – laying down our lives for one another, as Christ laid his down for us, caring for one another 'not in word or speech, but in truth and action' (1 Jn 3.14, 18-19).

Reading these passages, we are perhaps pressed to ask if the apostles are not contradicting Jesus. But it only seems like a contradiction if we wrongly imagine that loving God is something other and more important than loving neighbor. The point bears repeating: loving our neighbors is loving God. Loving God always takes the shape of loving our neighbor as Christ loved us on the cross. 'If you love me', Jesus says, 'you will keep my commandments … And my commandment is that you love one another just as I have loved you' (Jn 14.15; 15.12). In this way, we live in God and the love of God lives in us. Loving one another, we are abiding in God (Jn 15.9-10).

It is perhaps easy to miss the point, because we have been taught to make God a priority, as if God were one more person in our lives – the most important person, to be sure, the one whose jealousy requires our attention and demands our devotion. But in truth God is not just one more person in our lives: he *is* our life (Col. 3.4). 'In him we live, and move, and have our being' (Acts 17.28). And so, loving our neighbor is not a proof that we love God. It is the form loving God takes. As Rahner says, the God we desire to love is 'reached' only in the neighbor.[29] What we do to 'the least of these', we truly do to him (Mt. 25.40).

Jesus directed the accusing Pharisees to 'go and learn what this means: "I will have mercy and not sacrifice"' (Mt. 9.13). What did he expect them to find? What is meant by 'mercy' and how is it better than 'sacrifice'? Jesus intended for them to learn that God is not concerned about our devout feelings for God but with how we care for our neighbor. This is why he instructs us to leave our gift at the altar and seek reconciliation (Mt. 5.24), and why Paul says that mountain-moving faith and charismatic powers mean nothing if they are not offered in service of those who need to be borne along by longsuffering patience and kindness (1 Cor. 13.1-7).

In an astounding passage, Nikitas Stithatos, a disciple of St Symeon the New Theologian, directed his monks to this very

---

[29] Karl Rahner, 'Reflections on the Unity of the Love of Neighbour and the Love of God', in *Theological Investigations* 6 (London: Darton, Longman and Todd, 1969), pp. 231-49 (235).

wisdom:

> If while you are singing a song of prayer to God, one of your brethren knocks at the door of your cell, do not opt for the work of prayer rather than that of love and ignore your brother, for so to act would be alien to God. God desires mercy, not the sacrifice of prayer. Rather, put aside the gift of prayer and speak with healing love to your brother. Then with tears and a contrite heart once more offer your gift of prayer to the Father of the spiritual powers, and a righteous spirit will be renewed within you.[30]

This is the wisdom we must learn if we hope to move toward fulfilling our vocation, to partake truly in Christ's ongoing priestly ministry. Living lives of mercy rather than lives of sacrifice, we will in fact become a kingdom of priests who are, like our High Priest, both offerors and offerings, 'living sacrifices' (Rom. 12.2), the 'aroma of Christ' (2 Cor. 2.15), and a 'fragrant offering ... pleasing to God' (Phil. 4.18). As the prophet Samuel said to the king Saul, God takes no pleasure in sacrifices: he desires obedience (1 Sam. 15.22). Jesus reveals that the obedience that pleases God is always the doing of mercy.

---

[30] Nikitas Stithatos, 'On the Inner Nature of Things', 76 in *The Philokalia Vol. 4* (London: Faber and Faber, 1995), pp. 121-22.

3

SAVING SPEECH, HOLY LISTENING: CALLING, WORSHIP, AND THE TRANSFORMATIVE WORK OF INTERPRETATION

Introduction

Shockingly, God has from the beginning put his word and his name at risk in human hearing and speaking, in our shared 'interpretive, institutional, lyrical, testimonial activity'.[1] Why would God take such a risk? And why would he put us in such an impossible position? I am convinced the way we answer that question lays bare the heart of our understanding of what it means to be human. And I am convinced that the answer is as profound as it is simple: God so risks because God has made us for mediation, because only as mediators can we truly understand who he is to us and so reveal to the rest of creation who he is in us. Therefore, God remains determined at all costs (to himself and to us) not to save us from, but by, interpretation. And in this way, to learn and teach the meaning of his name. We are made for mediation, and mediation is inextricably bound up with the work of meaning-making, the work of interpretation. And needless to say, in this fallen world, that work is fraught with all kinds of difficulties. Still, this seems to me the bottom line: how God saves us must be inseparable from what God saves us for. Therefore, if it is in fact true that we receive the glory for which God made us only in participation with Christ in his priestly vocation, and if in fact we are created to mediate God's holiness to the rest of creation, then God's work of redeeming and glorifying us must involve us in interpreting what we experience. God is bound in his freedom to save us

---

[1] Walter Brueggemann, *Theology of the Old Testament: Testimony, Dispute, Advocacy* (Minneapolis: Fortress Press, 1997), p. 702.

in ways that make us truer interpreters. How else could we fulfill our vocation as mediators of God's divine-human holiness?

Vocation, Language, and Meaning-Making

The human is 'the linguistic animal'.[2] As Jenson says, 'we exist as human only in the tradition of speech'.[3] Being the 'articulate animals that we are, our bodies speak to one another, and through word and gesture we share in friendship the universe we inhabit'.[4] In fact, everything we do is in some sense language – in ways we intend and do not intend; in ways we understand and in ways we do not understand. All of our behavior 'says' something about us, about the world, about God.[5] Fulfilling our vocation as mediators of God's holiness, therefore, depends on what we say, even in our silence, and how we say it (via gesture, posture, writing, speaking, etc.).

It is an obvious truth, but one we often forget – perhaps because it is so obvious: we know Jesus because of what others have 'said' to us. This is uniquely true of the Scriptures, of course.[6] But we know the Scriptures, and know their uniqueness, only because of what we have learned from others. If we can grasp this truth, then we can see how our salvation is inextricably bound up with language, with 'meaning(s)' made and unmade, given and received. 'God has pulled human language into the center of his purposes.'[7]

> The Christian faith makes a daring declaration, and it is that God has so to speak got his hands on human language, appropriated human words for his purposes in order to reconcile us to himself.

---

[2] McCabe, *Law, Love and Language*, p. 68.

[3] Robert W. Jenson, *The Knowledge of Things Hoped For: The Sense of Theological Discourse* (New York: OUP, 1969), pp. 178, 180.

[4] Denys Turner, *Thomas Aquinas: A Portrait* (New Haven, CT: Yale University Press, 2013), p. 269.

[5] McCabe, *Law, Love and Language*, pp. 91-92.

[6] John Behr, *Formation of Christian Theology Vol. 1: The Way to Nicea* (Crestwood, NY: St Vladimir's Seminary Press, 2001), pp. 11-16. Behr contends that our relationship to God is, 'in a broad sense, literary' (p. 15).

[7] Jeremy Begbie, 'Language: Can We Speak About God Without Words?', n.p. (2010 New College Lectures; September 14-16, 2010; University of New South Wales [Sydney, Australia]). Excerpt available online: http://youtu.be/4fyNg8cupls. Accessed: 1 June, 2014.

He has used human language as intrinsically, integrally part of that process.[8]

But even if we can be convinced to see language as a creational gift, we are reluctant to regard the work of interpretation as anything other than a curse. In his *Fall of Interpretation,* James K.A. Smith explains how a certain Augustinian description of the Fall has come to hold our imagination captive, forcing on us the conviction that hermeneutics belongs to the disorder of the corrupted world. On this reading, our experience of language 'signal[s] a rift opened between *signa* (signs) and *res* (what is signified)'.[9] Prior to the Fall, so the theory goes, *signum* and *res* were perfectly matched to one another. Tragically, however, the entrance of sin ruptured the immediacy we were meant to enjoy.[10] Understood in this way, hermeneutics and the necessity of interpretation are experienced as a punishment 'from which we look for redemption in a paradise where interpretation is absent and immediacy is restored'.[11]

Smith finds this account irredeemably problematic, and he proposes a counter-vision, which he names a 'creational hermeneutic'. Interpretation, he insists, is not a necessary evil forced on us by the Fall. Nor is it overcome now or in the Eschaton. Instead, interpretation belongs to human be-ing as such, and so is perfected, not superseded, in Christ. Hermeneutics, he concludes,

> … is an inescapable aspect of human existence; it is a state of affairs that is affected by the Fall but not completely corrupted by fallenness nor the product of the Fall; and it is an aspect of human be-ing that is primordially good and remains such in a postlapsarian world, and therefore it is not to be construed as necessarily violent nor understood as a state of affairs to be 'overcome'.[12]

This is the crucial point: the work of interpretation is not a curse we must bear. We are created to interpret. And we discover our creatureliness, as well as our own creativity – and, above all, the limits of our creativity, limits which are not hindrance for God, in the work of

---

[8] Begbie, 'Language: Can We Speak About God Without Words?', n.p.

[9] James K.A. Smith, *The Fall of Interpretation* (Grand Rapids: Baker Academic, 2nd edn, 2012), p. 147.

[10] Smith, *The Fall of Interpretation*, p. 147.

[11] Smith, *The Fall of Interpretation*, p. 153.

[12] Smith, *The Fall of Interpretation*, p. 156.

interpretation. We are, both by nature and by grace, mediating interpreters (or, what is the same thing, interpreting mediators). And language is not merely rebellious and broken. It remains, even under the
conditions of our fallen existence, God's gift to us, fastening us to
our created purpose. So, to return to a claim already made, God is
not going to save us from interpretation but by it and for it.

All that said, we should not gloss over the troubles that daunt all
our efforts to make sense of the world, threatening every attempt,
however well-intentioned, to communicate with God or neighbor.
Our situation is not hopeless, to be sure, but it *is* tragic. Due to the
nature of things 'in Adam', language works against us even as we try
to make it work for us. The poet knows best what we all experience
in manifold ways: 'words are nervous when we need them/most
and shutter, stop, or dully slide away/so everything they mean to
summon up/is always just too far, just out of reach'.[13] The fact that
we can communicate at all is a wonder that should drive us to our
knees. And our communication is glorious in ways we are still only
beginning to see. Still, there is so much that we find we cannot
share. In part, because the world as we know it 'does not form a
single linguistic community'. Thus, 'full communication' is always
unachieved, even unachievable. And that inevitably frustrates our
loving. 'Because I cannot express myself to all men I cannot fully
give myself to any.'[14]

As I said at the beginning of this chapter, God puts his message,
and so his reputation, his name, at risk in our representation, so that
'where [our] speech and act are distorted, Yahweh is distorted'.[15]
And where our speech about God is too distorted, not merely af-
fected by our limitations but effectively effaced, our priestly ministry fails, largely if not entirely. If we cannot make faithful meaning
of our lives, speaking to God and of God truthfully, then we cannot
bring God's holiness to bear on creation. It follows, then, that
God's saving us for and with others depends upon God saving our
language, our capacity for communication, and just so saving us by
enabling us to 'speak' and to 'hear' in ways that are truly loving and
life-giving.

---

[13] Andrew Motion, 'The Voices Live'; available online: http://www.theguard-
ian.com/books/2001/nov/30/andrewmotion; accessed: 22 September 2014.

[14] McCabe, *Law, Love and Language*, p. 99.

[15] Brueggemann, *Theology of the Old Testament*, p. 702.

How does God work this salvation? He does so primarily and ultimately, in and through Jesus, the Word. 'The coming of the Word in flesh establishes, we might say, the nature of fleshly being as word, as sign.'[16] But because Jesus refuses to be known apart from his people, including many who remain anonymous to us, God also saves our language in and through the words of Scripture,[17] in and through the *viva vox* of the worshipping and witnessing Church — indeed in and through all attempts to bring the truth to speech, in whatever form, whether that happens in ways we recognize as Christian or not.

Whatever else we might want to say, when we confess that Scripture is 'inspired' we mean that the *language* of Scripture (in our various translations) is taken up mysteriously into God's purposes for us. We mean that somehow God has brought about and continues to take up these words in these texts, in whatever language we are reading them, making them apt for our good, using them for the 'training in righteousness' necessary for us to live as faithful witnesses of his salvation. That is why we should reject any account of biblical inspiration that suggests the difficulties of making meaning are somehow suspended in the writing and/or reading of the sacred texts. Instead, we should embrace the fact that those difficulties are revealed, and shown to be necessary for our sanctification.

The biblical texts are made 'Scripture', we believe, because they participate, somehow, in the life Christ shares with God and with us. That means the human *words* of Scripture are in some sense 'icons' of the divine-human *Word*. Jenson formulates it with his distinctive art: 'this personal Word comes to someone who is so opened to him by the Spirit that the Word can speak not only *to* the prophet but [also] *from* him'.[18]

Jesus' word is true for all without reserve or distinction: 'the communication he offers is unmixed with domination or exclusiveness'.[19]

---

[16] Rowan Williams, 'Language, Reality and Desire in Augustine's *De Doctrina*', *Journal of Literature & Theology* 3.2 (July 1989), p. 142.

[17] Telford Work, *Living and Active: Scripture in the Economy of Salvation* (Sacra Doctrina; Grand Rapids: Eerdmans, 2002), p. 58, contends: 'God offers these verbal signs as divinely ordered means of grace, to do God's saving work in a cosmos of confused and manipulated signs. The world's darkness does not overcome their light'.

[18] Jenson, *On the Inspiration of Scripture*, p. 29.

[19] McCabe, *Law, Love and Language*, p. 129.

The coming of Jesus, then, a coming we anticipate every Advent and celebrate every Christmas, is the in-breaking of that new language that makes possible the communication necessary for us to be truly human, and for all creation to see the beauty of God's holiness.[20] That in-breaking has already happened once-for-all. And yet it also continues to happen just as the Church, gathered and scattered by the Spirit, strives to hear and to speak this 'new language',[21] embodying the Word.

Of course, we continuously fail in these efforts. We cannot in this life speak this new language fluently, or hear it fully. No matter how knowledgeable, skilled, or mature we are, we never fail to send mixed messages. But through the Spirit, our words, however mixed with untruths, bear witness to Christ as the truth. Our witness, even at its best, is only ever adequate. But thankfully it *is* adequate, because God is happy with it. And this is why Paul can boast, in spite of everything: 'What does it matter? Just this, that Christ is proclaimed in every way, whether out of false motives or true' (Phil. 1.18).

In the moments before he went to the mountain garden where he usually prayed, Jesus asked his disciples a seemingly innocent question: 'When I sent you out without a purse, bag, or sandals, did you lack anything?' They answered that they had not lacked a thing. He then gave a strange saying (Lk 22.35-37):

> But now, the one who has a purse must take it, and likewise a bag. And the one who has no sword must sell his cloak and buy one. For I tell you, this scripture must be fulfilled in me, 'And he was counted among the lawless'; and indeed what is written about me is being fulfilled'.

The disciples share that they have two swords between them, and Jesus replies, 'It is enough' (Lk. 22.38).

Obviously, this is a mystifying exchange, made all the more mystifying by the fact that earlier he had forbidden his disciples to carry swords (Lk. 10.3-4), and by the fact that in the garden, only hours later, Peter would use one of these swords against Jesus' enemies — and would be rebuked for it: 'No more of that!' (Lk. 22.51). Why would Jesus instruct the disciples to carry swords they are not

---

[20] McCabe, *Law, Love and Language*, p. 129.
[21] McCabe, *Law, Love and Language*, p. 142, says, the church exists to 'articulate' the cosmic difference Christ's resurrection has made, 'to show the world to itself'.

supposed to use? Why allow them to carry swords he knows they will use to harm?

Unsurprisingly, scholars do not agree on what this story means. But it strikes me as instructive: we are the 'lawless ones' among whom Jesus means to be counted, not the ones called to protect him from evil; and our words are 'enough' – not to defend him against his enemies, but to show them he does not want or need to be defended, and to assure us that he can heal everyone we wound in our reckless zeal to secure the will of God.

'Speaking in Tongues': Human Meaning and Divine Pedagogy

I have already tried to say how God saves our language, but now I have to answer a related question: How and why does God use our language to save us, to co-sanctify us and make us co-sanctifiers? 'God has imbued our language at its fullest with the ability to make us perfect.'[22] And this sanctification happens as we are 'making the unmakeable name of the beyond-perfect God'.[23] But, again, what does this *mean*? It means that God uses our agonizing and never-quite-successful efforts to speak faithfully to God and for God as grace for us and for others. Our effort to bring God's self-revealing Word faithfully to bear in our own words actually somehow sanctify us, both as speakers and as hearers.

For this reason, we should be especially wary of glib, too-easy speech about God. If we are called to 'make' God's 'unmakeable' name, then our God-talk is worthy – that is, worthwhile – only if it shown to be 'under pressure' to do what cannot be done. Only so does something of the 'infinite, unconditioned mystery' of God 'soak through' our words.[24]

Truthful speech, then, is always unfinished, and its very unfinishedness witness to what St Paul says of his own life is true of our theology as well: we 'strain toward' a reality that is too much for us (Phil. 3.12), a peace that passes all understanding (Phil. 4.7).

---

[22] Baker, *Diagonal Advance*, p. 300.
[23] Baker, *Diagonal Advance*, p. 300.
[24] Williams, *Edge of Words*, p. 3.

Speaking and Hearing Differently

We see the difficulty of making God's unmakeable name known in Acts' account of the apostolic church, beginning with the story of Pentecost. Whether Pentecostals usually read it this way or not, Luke's story is a story about language and mediation – and so, about the human identity-in-vocation. He tells us that the Spirit broke like a storm into the disciples' gathering, with the sound of a 'rushing mighty wind' filling their ears and 'tongues of fire' dancing over their heads. We are told that they were heard speaking the native languages of '*every nation* under heaven' (Acts 2.5), a wonder that not only signals the reversal of 'Babel' – an overcoming of the confusion and fear and conflict that poisons our attempts to live together in shalom – but also points to the reconstitution of the people of God as a 'nation' of priests for the world.

Luke Timothy Johnson observes that Luke's account of Pentecost parallels his genealogy of Jesus (Lk. 3.23-38):

> Immediately after the gift of the Spirit in Jesus' baptism (Lk. 3.21-22), the generations of Jews are traced all the way back to Abraham, and even further, to Adam. Now, after this 'baptism in the Spirit' of the apostles and their company, Luke lists all the lands from which Jews have gathered. The parallelism fits the pattern of Luke's story: Jesus is the prophet who sums up all the promises and hopes of the people before him; in his apostolic successors, that promise and hope (now sealed by the Spirit) will be carried to all the nations of the earth.[25]

This is why the coming of the Spirit is witnessed by 'speaking in tongues' – as a sign to speakers and hearers alike (including us, as readers) that Christ, according to prophecy, has been exalted as Lord, which means that the church, as Abraham's sons and daughters, can in fact begin to open the promises and hopes of Israel to 'every nation, tribe, and tongue'. Then and there, in the Temple courts, 'Abraham' (the church) speaks not in his own 'tongue' but in the tongue of 'Adam' (the nations).

But in calling the church to open Israel's promises to every nation, tribe, and tongue, the Spirit impels us into the incredibly difficult

---

[25] Luke Timothy Johnson, *The Acts of the Apostles* (Sacra Pagina; Collegeville, MN: Liturgical Press, 1992), p. 47.

work of interpretative mediation. On the day of Pentecost, the Spirit performs a wondrous sign (in the speaking and/or in the hearing)[26] that establishes – in anticipation of the Eschaton – what McCabe calls 'full communication'. The Spirit, just for that moment, heals the brokenness of language so that all of the nations (represented by those gathered to the city for the feast) hear the gospel's praise of God in their own 'tongue' and so see, however fleetingly, a 'preview' of the eschatological banquet. But the stories that follow in Acts tell us that the miracle was not repeated. Yes, of course, 'tongues' continue to break forth in the church's prayers, but always as a re-affirming sign of the inaugural event. The Spirit never again miraculously translates the witnesses' message to their hearers.[27] Instead, it is as if on Pentecost the Spirit gave the primitive church-community a miraculous glimpse of what the End will be when God is all in all, and then repeatedly called them back to that vision as a way of drawing them toward the 'future' it promises. Post-Pentecost experiences of 'speaking in tongues', therefore, were signs of that inaugural sign – hearkening back to the events of Pentecost and just so 'forward' to the final realization of the Spirit's mission.[28]

Pentecost does not eliminate diversity, but creates a community devoted to learning how to live together patiently, peacefully, in a world of 'impatient violence'.[29] That means that the miracles of Pentecost are a summons to hear and to speak differently.

---

[26] See Max Turner, *Power from on High: The Spirit in Israel's Restoration and Witness in Luke-Acts* (JPTSup 9; Sheffield: Sheffield Academic Press, 2000), pp. 270-74.

[27] There are, of course, exceptional examples to be drawn from the church's history, including, perhaps most notably, testimonies from the early Pentecostal movements. But these exceptions prove the rule, I believe. For in-depth exploration of tongues-speech in Luke-Acts, the NT, and Christian traditions, see Gerald Hovenden, *Speaking in Tongues: The New Testament Evidence in Context* (JPTSup 22; Sheffield: Sheffield Academic Press, 2002), and Mark J. Cartledge (ed.), *Speaking in Tongues: Multi-Disciplinary Perspectives* (Milton Keynes: Paternoster, 2006).

[28] We might say that the inaugural tongue-speaking event was a burst of uncreated light from the eschatological kingdom, while the subsequent events of tongue-speaking were bursts of 'darkness' that kept alive in the church's memory the promise of that eschatological light. Thanks to David Han for suggesting this line of reflection to me.

[29] Stanley Hauerwas, *War and the American Difference: Theological Reflections on Violence and National Identity* (Grand Rapids: Baker Academic, 2011), p. 132.

To be human is to be able to speak, to say 'Yes' or 'No'; to be able to *respond* to places, times, and people, and, perhaps, to God … To be human is to be able to speak. But to be able to speak is to be 'answerable', 'response-able' to and for each other, and to the mystery of God.[30]

If being human is being able to hear and to speak responsibly, then to be 'Pentecostal' is to be divinely empowered for that essentially human task. Sometimes, at our worst, we Pentecostals have talked as if the sanctified, Spirit-filled life is a life lived beyond the limits of the 'normal' day-to-day existence to which others are subject. But in truth the Spirit intensifies human existence, creating forms of life that delight in the good God has made and defy to the death every power that seeks to spoil that goodness. And so, as on the Day of Pentecost, the Spirit comes and dwells among us to renew our vocation, to reignite our longing to bring God's goodness to bear in the world for our neighbors' good.

The Spirit, (Im)Mediacy, and Human Responsibility

Because it bears us into the work of interpretation, 'the gift of Pentecost entails slow, hard work'. In point of fact,

> … the gift of Pentecost is but the beginning of hard and painful lessons in failure. Yet even failure turns out to be a gift if through failure the church is reminded that others are included in God's promise. At its best, the church learns to receive the stories of different linguistic communities and in the process discovers that our own speech requires constant revision.[31]

The truth is that we *must* struggle, both in our attempts to understand and in our attempts to make ourselves understood. The difficulty itself is graced. And it must be, because if our words come too easily – as they did for Job's friends, for example, and for so many of Jesus' friends and enemies – it is a sure sign that we are keeping God and the awareness of God at bay, suppressing the Spirit's efforts to transform us through our speaking and listening. Scripture warns us: 'God is in heaven and you upon earth; therefore let your words be

---

[30] Nicholas Lash, *Holiness, Speech, and Silence: Reflections on the Question of God* (Burlington, VT: Ashgate Publishing, 2004), pp. 63, 65.

[31] Hauerwas, *War and the American Difference*, pp. 132-33.

few' (Eccl. 5.2). But not only few: our words must also be *care-full*, born of fear and trembling. True, at times we must speak, and sometimes we should do so boldly. But authentic boldness is possible only where there is deep, abiding humility born of 'the-fear-of-the-Lord' and sensitivity to the deepest needs of our weakest neighbors.[32] We cannot speak boldly in any godly sense if we do not know how to listen fearlessly.

Again, the problem is that some of us sometimes talk as if the Spirit saves us from the trouble of interpretative mediation, taking over our mouths or our ears so that we are freed from the difficulties of judgment, meaning-making, and communication – as if by the Spirit we are taken up beyond human, worldly limits. This is perhaps especially true of the way we describe speaking in tongues and prophecy:

> … in contemporary pentecostal practice and understanding, one often encounters a sense that tongues (and prophecy) are immediate deliveries from the divine, without mediation or translation. In other words, in the popular imagination, glossolalia is often thought to be a quintessentially unmediated, divinely given, ecstatic discourse that bypasses the conditions of interpretation – a kind of pure conduit from God, without the static or supposed distortion of semiotic mediation.[33]

Certain diseased forms of our spirituality tempt us to confuse the dynamics of the human spirit with the work of the divine Spirit. Take, for example, how often we imply that God is most powerfully present and active in those events that are least easily explained and so seem the most 'supernatural'. For example, one early Pentecostal pastor says of the disciples' speaking in tongues on the Day of Pentecost: 'the human spirit was in this case set aside, and the work was of God'.[34] But God is no less present in what seem to us to be 'natural' events than in those that seem 'supernatural'. And God gives us no unmediated, otherworldly, more-than-human mode of speech. Again, it is obvious once we think of it: how else would humans know? Still, the crucial point is that truthfulness, as opposed to mere

---

[32] Eugene Peterson, *Christ Plays in Ten Thousand Places: A Conversation in Spiritual Theology* (Grand Rapids: Eerdmans, 2005), p. 42.

[33] James K.A. Smith, *Thinking in Tongues: Pentecostal Contributions to Christian Philosophy* (Grand Rapids: Baker Academic, 2010), p. 138.

[34] *Confidence* 1.2 (Jan 1909), pp. 8-9.

self-expression or naked honesty, is the aim of Christian speech. And truthfulness requires at every turn the work of mediational interpretation – for everyone, including Spirit-led believers.[35] Therefore, glossolalia, like prophecy,[36] is nothing more or less than a particular Spirited outworking of our struggle to speak and to hear the Word of God intelligibly. We can be sure that the Spirit will not save us from the work of interpretation, but pressure us further and further into it, burdening us with it by gifting us for it. Why? Because this is what we are made for and this is what the world needs, including, first, our neighbors who are most in need. When all is said and done, then, we have to come to terms with the fact that God's gifts are not meant to carry us out of this world or beyond our humanness, but are purposed to ground us more firmly in the world that has been entrusted to our care.

Pentecost Sunday is not the end of the liturgical year. And the coming of the Spirit is not the end of the Christian life. It is true that Pentecost leads into what is called 'ordinary time', which we might take as a reminder that the Spirit is with us even when everything seems to have returned to normal. No doubt, our day-to-day communication, whether with God or with one another, is sure to seem dreadfully unexceptional most of the time, in spite of the fact that it is always far more exceptional than we can imagine. Indeed, this is the wisdom of so many Spirit-filled saints: grace is always at work in us, even, or perhaps even especially, when we are not aware of it. This is true in our sleep of course, but also in our waking. And it is true whether we are involved in church work or simply going about the living of our lives together. We can trust that whether everything seems ordinary or not, the Spirit is with and within us, alongside us, upon us. What 'follows' Pentecost, liturgically and spiritually, is

---

[35] Smith, *Thinking in Tongues*, p. 138.

[36] Many Pentecostals and charismatics think of prophecy, like a message in 'tongues', as direct communication from God, as opposed to something born from human knowledge, understanding, or wisdom. For example, Julie C. Ma and Wonsuk Ma, *Mission in the Spirit: Towards a Pentecostal/Charismatic Theology* (Oxford: Regnum Publishers, 2010), p. 161, describe the gift of prophecy as finding its place when 'in a real life setting, [where] there are many situations that require decisions which have nothing to do with ethical or Christian principals. In these instances, "direct revelation" is sought ...' For an exploration of what constitutes 'prophecy' in the Pentecostal/charismatic communities, see Margaret Poloma, *Main Street Mystics: The Toronto Blessing and Reviving Pentecostalism* (Walnut Creek, CA: AltaMira Press, 2003), pp. 115-36.

simply the ongoing ministry of Christ, exalted in his resurrection and ascension as the ruling source and guide and goal of the whole creation made entirely new. Pentecost is not the end, but the beginning. To receive the Spirit is not to 'arrive' at the fullness of spirituality, but to be pressed toward fullness. And people of the Spirit live into this beginning in every dimension of their lives, including the mundane and the routine and the seemingly unimportant.

God's transfiguring work in and through us happens just as we are in the throes of working to understand and be understood. Because we were created for God, our rational, meaning-making 'nature', as it is being restored and transfigured by grace, finds its perfection in our doing what we were made to do: mediating God's divine-human holiness sanctifyingly to the rest of creation, and, in the process, receiving our own transfiguration in the image of the one from whom, in whom, and for whom we live. Yielded to the Spirit, walking in the Spirit, living a Spirit-filled life, we become more and more *responsible* and *response-able*, pressed deeper into our creatureliness, drawn nearer the heart of the world. Ellul is exactly right: the Spirit makes us 'fully responsible'.[37]

The Liturgical Grammar of Priestly Vocation

'We were made to fashion divinity in the world.'[38] That is, as we have already said, we are made to make God's unmakeable name. But if we are to 'fashion' God rightly – speaking to God and of God faithfully and transformatively – then we must remain always in apprenticeship to the Spirit in the church, learning to hear and to speak faithfully, hopefully, lovingly.

Reflecting on God's praise for Job, Rickie Moore argues that prayer is 'both the end and the beginning of all God-talk', so that all talk *about* God fits within the experience of talking *to* him. Hence, prayer is not rendered 'subsequent and secondary' to theology, but is seen to be primary, definitive. Theology, in order to be itself, must arise from and return to worship.[39] Moved by God, we break our

---

[37] Jacques Ellul, *The Subversion of Christianity* (Grand Rapids: Eerdmans, 1986), p. 13.

[38] Baker, *Diagonal Advance*, p. 188.

[39] Rickie D. Moore, 'Raw Prayer and Refined Theology: "You Have Not Spoken Straight to Me as My Servant Job Has"', in Terry L. Cross and Emerson B. Powery

silence to speak of the Word. And we speak until we find ourselves brought to silence by that same Word. As Rahner says, faithful speakers are sooner than later 'reduced to stammering'. And all their explanations do nothing to expose the mystery of God. 'Theology is not the unmasking of the mysterious in the self-evident but rather a gaze into the bright darkness of divine mysteries. Total clarity would be a sure sign that the spurious self-evidence of human rationalism had been mistaken for the truth of God.'[40]

No one knows naturally how to do these things rightly. Faithful co-participants in Christ's continuing priestly work are made, not born, and they are fashioned over time by the Spirit in the fires of the church's shared life of adoration, service, and witness to the Father. So, if we are going to interpret the Scriptures and our experiences in the world faithfully – that is, if we are going to make the kind of sense that remains true to the New Creation established in Christ – then we must be *taught* to speak and to hear in ways that bear witness to the Word spoken and heard in Christ's life, death, and resurrection. If we hope to find Jesus in the Scripture or in our neighbor; if we desire to be made apt for God and the beautifying transfiguration that comes through being in Christ; if we aspire to embody the divine politics in and for the good of the world; then we must remain subject to the required training, which takes the whole of our lives.

In the church, God gives us ordained (and lay) ministers, women and men, who nurture us toward maturity in Christ, providing spiritual direction and pastoral care, holding us up in prayer, instructing us in the faith, offering wise counsel, standing with us in times of crisis. But the divine pedagogy also gives us certain ecclesial practices that, faithfully enacted, form us in faithfulness, training us in what it means for us to be a priestly, sacrificial people.[41]

This is particularly and principally true of liturgical worship, which, necessarily, all Christian worship is. By 'liturgy' I mean agreed-upon pre-scribed and prescriptive forms that order and direct our worship, including, among other things, readings from the Scriptures,

---

(eds.), *The Spirit and the Mind: Essays in Informed Pentecostalism* (New York: University Press of America, 2000), pp. 35-48 (47).

[40] Karl Rahner, 'Listening to Scripture', in *Theological Investigations: Vol. 16, Experience of the Spirit* (Darton, Longman and Todd, 1961), pp. 173-74.

[41] See Stanley Hauerwas, *Unleashing the Scripture: Freeing the Bible from Captivity to America* (Nashville: Abingdon Press, 1993), p. 56.

sermons, songs, and prayers. And by 'liturgical worship' I mean the communion with God that takes place as we gather in Christ's name at set-aside times in set-aside places to 'follow' the liturgy – or, sometimes, break from it – as it helps us find our way into apprehending that communion.

Why is liturgical worship necessary? Because worship, for Christians, is an act of communal witness, not an act of self-expression. And as such, it depends upon shared language, shared gestures, shared places and times. And if it is truly communal, then it develops over time, as wisdom is gained and proved through experience. And if that community is truly ecclesial, if it is truly led by the Spirit, then we should take that wisdom with utmost seriousness. Scripture directs us not to forsake the assembly because we simply cannot be a people formed in the Spirit by the whole counsel of God without the regular, common experience of approaching the Triune God together in the same way that all of God's people before us have done and in the same way that all of God's people after us will do: in shared prayer, the communal hearing and speaking of the Word of this God, the call to responsive prayer in the altar and to the celebration at the Lord's table.[42]

Each Sunday, and perhaps also on other days, the Spirit gathers us again as one people into the 'worshipping and obeying community … at the center of everything God has done, is doing, and will do' in the world.[43] Precisely so, we are positioned to hear and to tell the story of the Triune God revealed in Israel's Christ and his church as one story – a story that reveals, however strangely, the truth not only about us but also about everyone and everything – and therefore as a story large enough to include everyone and everything in its freedom.[44] As we worship, we see and hear ourselves narrated into that story as actors in the ongoing drama.

In worship, then, however formal or informal, we are joined not only with the other persons in the room but also with the entire

---

[42] See Chris E.W. Green, 'The Altar and the Table: A Proposal for Wesleyan and Pentecostal Eucharistic Theologies,' *Wesleyan Theological Journal* 53.2 (2018), pp. 54-61.

[43] Eugene Peterson, *Eat this Book: A Conversation in the Art of Spiritual Reading* (Grand Rapids: Eerdmans, 2006), p. 76.

[44] See Robert W. Jenson, 'Can We Have a Story?' *First Things* 101 (Mar 2000), pp. 16-17 (17).

saintly communion – including strangers and neighbors, both living and dead.[45] And together with them, we intentionally turn our attention to God, and allow ourselves to realize, if only fleetingly, that he is always attending to us even from long before we were born. And the liturgy itself bears witness to the fact that this way of life is not one we found on our own, or are making for ourselves. It is a way of life that we received from others, who taught us what it means to love God, and to live with God and for others.

The (Im)Possibility of Liturgical Pentecostalism

But can Pentecostals go along with claims like these about the liturgy? That may seem unlikely, at first, but Pentecostal worship is already liturgical.[46] Besides, Pentecostals are not so much anti-liturgical as anti-*ritualistic*.[47] The question, then, is not if Pentecostal worship should be liturgical, but only how.

Obviously, for liturgical worship to be recognizably Pentecostal it must be spirited. But this should not be confused with emotionalism. Spirited liturgical worship is lively worship, lively not because it is always cheerful or enjoyable, even less because it is always energetic, but because it intentionally embraces the whole of the human experience – its highs and lows, its light and shadows, its foregrounds and backgrounds – and in that way leaves room for everyone – truly, everyone – to lift up their hearts to the Lord.

But worship is not only a matter of spiritedness. Liturgical worship may be either dead or alive. But it may also be either true or false, and that should concern us every bit as much. Either the liturgy narrates worshippers into the full sweep of the story of God, the long, winding, often dark, always surprising story of Israel's crucified and resurrected Christ – or it does not. Either it identifies this

---

[45] Robert W. Jenson, 'What if It Were True?', *Center for Theological Inquiry Reflections* 4 (2002), pp. 2-20 (3) is I think exactly right: 'of course it is a mind-bending exercise to consider in what ontological mode dead believers make one living company with living ones, but do they or don't they?'

[46] Walter Hollenweger, 'The Social and Ecumenical Significance of Pentecostal Liturgy', *Studia Liturgica* 8 (1971-1972), pp. 207-15, holds that Pentecostal liturgy entails most if not all of the elements/movements of traditional Christian liturgies. See also Daniel E. Albrecht, *Rites in the Spirit: A Ritual Approach to Pentecostal/Charismatic Spirituality* (JPTSup 17; Sheffield: Sheffield University Press, 1999).

[47] Telford Work, 'Pentecostal and Charismatic Worship', in Geoffrey Wainwright and Karen B. Westerfield Tucker (eds.), *The Oxford History of Christian Worship* (Oxford: OUP, 2006), pp. 574-85 (576).

crucified and resurrected Christ as 'very God of very God', worthy of worship with the Father and the Spirit – or it does not. Either it characterizes this God as utterly reliable and trustworthy; infinitely generous, attentive, and caring; inviolable and mysterious – or it does not.

All to say, Pentecostals, like all Christians, aspire to truthful, lively worship. And truthful, livable liturgies are necessary to that end. So, we should ask ourselves if the liturgies currently in use in our services are in fact truthful and livable. *Truthful*, in that they rightly identify and characterize God, and faithfully narrate the full sweep of his story. *Livable*, in that they bear witness to the full complexity of human experience: life as well as death; sorrows as well as joys; healing as well as sickness; miseries as well as consolation; gains as well as losses; ignorance as well as knowledge; wisdom as well as foolishness; bitterness as well as sweetness; strength as well as weakness; faithlessness as well as faithfulness; light as well as darkness; fear of death as well as fear of the Lord.[48]

If our liturgies fall short of this truthfulness and livability, they need to be revised. But how? What liturgical forms are fitting for Pentecostal worship? Given that Pentecostalism emerged from the fusion of Black and Wesleyan-Holiness spiritualities,[49] I would argue Pentecostals should return to the Anglican liturgy, which is articulated in the Book of Common Prayer. Historically, this liturgy shaped the traditions that made Pentecostalism possible. And so, as they return to it, Pentecostals will find that the liturgy affirms their deeply held intuitions about what Christian worship is meant to be and to do. And they will find that the liturgy does not stifle the Spirit, but teaches us how to yield to the Spirit's Lordship.

Needless to say, no liturgy is perfect. But liturgies are more or less faithful. And Anglican liturgy, like all faithful liturgies, is God-centered, deeply communal, steeped in the Scriptures, and rooted in the

---

[48] While it is true that 'the medium is the message', and that liturgical form and content are inseparable, even if distinguishable, I believe it remains possible to perform the liturgy in different 'styles'. Think, for example, of the different stage and film adaptations of Shakespeare's 'Romeo and Juliet' or Hugo's *Les Misérables*.

[49] See Chris E.W. Green, 'Fulfilling the Full Gospel: The Promise of the Theology of the Cleveland School', in David Bundy, Geordan Hammond, and David Han (eds.), *Holiness and Pentecostal Movements: Intertwined Pasts, Presents, and Futures* (Penn State University Press, forthcoming).

beliefs and practices of the apostolic church.[50] And it is structured to bear worship that is both sacramental and charismatic, doxological and missional,[51] and calls for the participation of all the gathered people of God.[52] It follows the Christian calendar, leading worshippers from Advent through Epiphany and Lent to Good Friday and Easter, and from Easter through Pentecost to Ordinary Time. In this way, worshippers are required to attend to the full sweep of God's story, and to the entire range of their own experiences. And in much the same way, the lectionary readings require the congregation, and the preacher, to attend to the 'whole counsel of God'. At its heart, Anglican liturgy insists on the integration of Word and Sacrament, so that preaching, while remaining central, is never an end in itself, but always leads toward the call to meet God in the altar at the table. In all of these ways, and others not named, the Anglican liturgical tradition promises to serve Pentecostals well.

To be clear, the Anglican liturgical tradition should not be taken as 'an inflexible standard of correctness'. Nor should any other tradition, liturgical or theological. But Pentecostals can benefit from submitting to it, allowing it to instruct our worship, because in that way we can acknowledge the truth that we are living in the wake of God's work with others in the Body of Christ, who have responded to that work in ways we should imitate. In short, 'we are not our own authors', and our liturgy should reflect our awareness of that dependency on others' knowledge of God.[53]

The Anglican order of service involves two movements: the Service of the Word and the Service of the Sacrament. A Pentecostal elaboration of this tradition might articulate these as the Service of the Spirit-Word and the Service of the Altar and Table. The first movement, the Service of the Spirit-Word, would begin with a call to worship, the reading of a passage from the Psalms, and an invocation of Christ to pour out his Spirit on the gathered community. It would then move into a time of singing, in which adoration, praise,

---

[50] Winfield Bevins, 'Why Do Anglicans Have a Liturgy?' *Seedbed* (20 Oct 2016), n.p.; available online: https://www.seedbed.com/untitled-45/; accessed: 30 Mar 2020).

[51] See Land, *Pentecostal Spirituality*, p. 31.

[52] See Cheryl Bridges Johns, *Pentecostal Formation: A Pedagogy among the Oppressed* (JPTSup 2; Sheffield: JSOT Press, 1993), p. 89.

[53] See Williams, *Why Study the Past*, pp. 110-11.

thanksgiving, petition, and lament are given voice. Following that, there would at least sometimes be time for testimonies, and then readings from the Scripture, intentionally chosen from both the Old Testament and the New, and shaped by the Christian seasons. The sermon would be drawn from these readings, and would open out in invitation to the Service of the Altar and Table.

The Service of the Altar and Table would begin as response to the word of the Lord given in the sermon, opening an extended time for corporate and personal prayers – scripted and spontaneous, directed and undirected. Often, if not always, it would also include the laying on of hands and anointing with oil for healing, as those in need gather around the eucharistic table. The service would then culminate in the celebration of Communion, and sometimes in both foot-washing and Communion, and conclude with a final invocation of Jesus to pour out the Spirit on his friends as they return to the world renewed for mission.[54]

Work of the People, Work of God

We are often reminded that liturgy is the 'work of the people'. But this has to be qualified on (at least) two fronts. In the first place, liturgy – and, more importantly, the worship that it serves – is always already God's work before it is ours. Worship is not our gift to God until it is God's gift to us. And, because God is Trinity, even our gift to God is made possible just by God giving God to God through us. In the second place, the liturgy is the church's work before it is ours. The liturgy in its various expressions belongs to the 'one, holy, catholic and apostolic Church' and not to my/your 'tribe' or tradition. Faithful liturgies, therefore, emerge and are developed over time from 'the accrued wisdom of the body of Christ, led by the Spirit'. That means the liturgical heritage of the church belongs to all Christians.[55] 'These rituals are the gifts of God, for the people of God.'[56]

I have argued that in liturgical worship, as the church gathers to hear and to tell the story of God, we are uniquely positioned for the

---

[54] For a similar model and a rationale for it, see James K.A. Smith, *Desiring the Kingdom: Worship, Worldview, and Cultural Formation* (Grand Rapids, MI: Baker Academic, 2009), pp. 155-214.

[55] James K.A. Smith, '"Lift Up Your Hearts": John Calvin's Catholic Faith', Meeter Center Lecture (Oct 2012), p. 15. Available online: http://www.scribd.com/doc/109817080/Lift-Up-Your-Hearts-John-Calvin-s-Catholic-Faith; accessed: 24 August 2014.

[56] Smith, 'Lift Up Your Hearts', p. 15.

sanctifying work of the Spirit. Thanks to the Spirit's presence, as we liturgically enact and reenact the story, we are shaped by it. Entering into the play and work of liturgical worship, taking its words and gestures as our own, aligning ourselves to it shape, we make ourselves available to be altar-ed. But to state the obvious, the liturgy in and of itself does not sanctify any more than culture in and of itself civilizes. So, it is worth asking: how does this sanctifying work of the Spirit take place? In what ways does the Spirit use the liturgy to form us?

As the people of Israel are entering their 'Promised Land', they are warned against worshipping as the locals do, according to their own desires (Deut. 12.2-8):

> You must demolish completely all the places where the nations whom you are about to dispossess served their gods ... Break down their altars ... You shall not worship the LORD your God in such ways. But you shall seek the place that the LORD your God will choose out of all your tribes as his habitation to put his name there. You shall go there ... And you shall eat there in the presence of the LORD your God ... You shall not act as we are acting here today, all of us according to our own desires ...

God's people are called to 'seek the place' where God has 'put his name'. They are told that they must go 'there', that true worship can take place only 'there', in that chosen-for-them place. The same holds true for us now, I believe.

Christ is the 'there' where God has placed his name. And so, worship is faithful only as it gathers in, through, and for him. The purpose of liturgy, then, is to bind us to ways of worshipping that bind us to Christ and so to God and to one another.

Pentecostals often, and for good reason, talk about freedom in worship. But worship is first concerned with obedience. It is that obedience which frees us, teaching us that we are in fact unfree, and how to live in the freedom God is and makes possible for us. Worship, then, is concerned primarily not with self-expression, but with self-control and self-denial.

In some respects, what Iris Murdoch says about the work of learning to speak and to read Russian applies at least in some ways also to the askesis of liturgical worship:

> ... I am confronted by an authoritative structure which commands my respect. The task is difficult and the goal is distant and

perhaps never entirely attainable. My work is a progressive revelation of something which exists independently of me … something which my consciousness cannot take over, swallow up, deny or make unreal.[57]

Confronting the alienness of the liturgy in its 'authoritative structure' – a structure that cannot be 'taken over' or 'swallowed up' – humbles us, and in this way unites us with Christ, who humbles himself for us and reveals God's humility.

Handing On, Handed Over

'In the liturgical act agency is handed over to the tradition in a kind of asceticism.'[58] As an askesis, a christmorphing discipline, the liturgy not only burns with the light of the New Creation, but also casts the shadow of the Cross. Bonhoeffer presses the point home: 'Either I determine the place in which I will find God, or I allow God to determine the place where He will be found'.[59] What does this mean? Simply that a 'God' who meets us always where our desires demand is not in fact the God of Jesus Christ.

If it is I who say where God will be, I will always find there a God who in some way corresponds to me, is agreeable to me, fits in with my nature. But if it is God who says where he will be, then that will truly be a place which at first is not agreeable to me at all, which does not fit so well with me. That place is the cross of Christ.[60]

We might say that what we *hand on* in the traditioning of the faith is, at its heart, the awareness that we must again and again be *handed over* to the faith and the example of the faithful.[61] In faithful liturgical worship, then, we are handed over to prescribed words, gestures, and postures to which we must submit our bodies and thus our hearts and minds. 'The body has a place within the divine worship of the Word made flesh, and it is expressed liturgically in a certain discipline

---

[57] Iris Murdoch, *The Sovereignty of Good* (London: Routledge, 2001), p. 87.

[58] Gavin Flood, *The Importance of Religion: Meaning and Action in Our Strange World* (Malden, MA: Wiley-Blackwell Publishers, 2012), p. 110.

[59] Dietrich Bonhoeffer, *Meditating on the Word* (Nashville: Cowley Publications, 1986), p. 44.

[60] Bonhoeffer, *Meditating on the Word*, pp. 44-45.

[61] See Richard B. Hays, *First Corinthians* (Interpretation; Louisville: WJKP, 2011), p. 198.

of the body, in gestures that have developed out of the liturgy's inner demands and that make the essence of the liturgy, as it were, bodily visible.'[62]

While our bodies are 'going through the motions', whether we sense it or not at the time, our affections are enflamed and our desires, re-ordered. We are in this way 'primed' for godly witness to the kingdom through 'a set of habits or dispositions that are formed in us through affective, bodily means'. Ritual, routine devotional and liturgical practices, over time 'grab hold of our hearts through our imagination' and draw us toward the God whose nearness transforms us.[63]

It is the role of liturgy to bind us to faithful witness, ordering our bodies and minds and hearts into a shared, corporate posture of openness to God in our neighbor and our neighbor in God, 'inscribing watchfulness in the rhythm of the human body'.[64] Liturgy, in this sense, is like a yoke: bearing it rightly, we find ourselves gracefully restricted and redemptively directed. Or, to change the image, the liturgy is like a trellis: dead and rigid, but just so capable of supporting our growth toward God(likeness).[65] Or, to change the image yet again, the liturgy is like a 'bundling sack'[66] that binds us in the presence of our all-desirable one, frustrating our passions and just so arousing in us divine and deifying longing for our beloved's 'appearing'.

In liturgical worship, we practice speaking a strange language that is always new to us. And the Lord's Supper is the heart, the center of that practice. Without the scandal of the Eucharist, the liturgy has no gravity. As G.F. Taylor, early Pentecostal editor of the *Pentecostal Holiness Advocate* put it, 'The real purpose of the Supper is to humiliate us, to teach us the spirit of Jesus, and to unite us as a church in the

---

[62] Joseph Ratzinger, *The Spirit of the Liturgy* (San Francisco: Ignatius Press, 2000), pp. 176-77.

[63] Smith, *Desiring the Kingdom*, p. 63.

[64] Rowan Williams, 'The Theological World of the *Philokalia*', in Brock Bingman and Bradley Nassif (eds.), *The Philokalia: A Classic Text of Orthodox Spirituality* (Oxford: OUP, 2012), p. 111.

[65] Thanks to Bishop Ed Gungor for suggesting this image to me.

[66] For an explanation of this practice, see Bruce C. Daniels, *New England Nation: The Country the Puritans Built* (New York: Palgrave Macmillan, 2012), pp. 161-63. Thanks to Justin Spears for suggesting this image to me.

spirit of fellowship'.[67] And these last cannot happen without the first.[68]

And so, to sum up briefly, we need a truthful and livable liturgy, because in enacting a truthful liturgy, we practice living the truth, living truthfully. The shape of the liturgy is the shape of Christ, and as we follow it, we are bent out of our own shape and into his. This does not, of course, 'work' magically or mechanically. The liturgy does not transform us: God does. And, needless to say, he does not need the liturgy – or anything – to do his work. But we do need it, and so do our neighbors.

We need it especially in relation to our work of interpreting the Scriptures. The truth is, Scripture is Scripture – and not merely as 'the Bible'[69] – as it is received in the church's worship, and given in the church's mission. Both the giving and the receiving are embodied in the liturgy, but the receiving is primary. The story of Mary, which is the story of all the prophets, the story of Israel, and the story of the church, reveals that faithfulness, at its heart, is receptivity: 'Here am I! Let it be with me according to your Word' (Lk. 1.38). Precisely for that reason, Scripture is heard in public before it is read in private.[70] And private – we might say 'monastic' or 'prophetic' – readings are valid just insofar as they exist in service of public – 'ecclesial' – readings.

> Devotional reading of Scripture is a kind of extension of liturgical reading: a chapel branching off from the nave of the great hermeneutical cathedral. On its own, it is nothing. It relies upon and contributes to the central thing. It takes its cues from the weekly rhythm of the prophets and Psalms, the apostles and evangelists; it is a local practice contingent upon the global … In both cases,

---

[67] *PHA* 3.11 (July 10, 1919), p. 2.

[68] Hence, Herbert McCabe, 'Eucharistic Change', *Priests and People* 8.6 (June 1994), pp. 217-21 (219), warns, 'Anything which seems to take the scandal or mystery out of the Eucharist must be wrong'.

[69] See Joel Green, *Seized by Truth: Reading the Bible as Scripture* (Nashville: Abingdon Press, 2007), pp. 1-6.

[70] Rowan Williams, 'The Bible Today: Reading and Hearing' (The Larkin-Stuart Lecture; April 2007), n.p.; available online: http://aoc2013.brix.fatbeehive.com/articles.php/2112/the-bible-today-reading-hearing-the-larkin-stuart-lecture; accessed: 31 March 2020).

the aim is the same, whatever the particular end of the individual reader: to hear God speak through the embassy of his servants.[71]

We will misunderstand this if we think, flatly, that the 'liturgical' is more important than the 'devotional' or that the communal is more important than the personal or the priestly more important than the prophetic. We need, instead, to realize that in Christ the liturgical and communal and priestly are to be inseparably bound up with the devotional and the personal and the prophetic. What Paul says about 'prophecy' in 1 Corinthians 14 applies equally to all interpretation of Scripture: we should strive to excel not for our own benefit but for the building up of others. Our interpretations are worthwhile only if they are loving: if they grace the lives of those who hear us.

Christians have always been people of the Scripture. But they have not always been people of the Scripture *as a book for everyone*.[72] This truth is so obvious that it is easily overlooked. In other words, Christians have from the first read and heard and studied the sacred texts – long before it become possible for everyone to have her or his own Bible, written in her or his own native language. Again, I would not be the first to point out that this shift, which the printing press and the rise of the modern national consciousness made possible, radically altered the way Christians interpreted Scripture – and not entirely for the good. But this is not the place to retell that history or to lament those changes. What needs to be remembered is that there are various ways in which the church can be people of these texts. And in some ways, our devotionalistic bookishness is working against us. So, it is important to re-place our readings in the context of the worship gathering, assuring that that reading – the one the church gives and receives as a gathered community – takes precedence over our 'private' readings.

I sometimes ask my students to compare a famous painting, *Saint Paul Writing His Epistles*, painted either by Valentin de Boulogne or André Tournier in the early 1600s, with an icon of St Paul and an icon of the prophet Jeremiah. In the painting, the apostle is pictured at a desk, head down, pen in hand, absorbed in writing; an open Bible sits on the desk to his right, along with a smaller, closed book. A

---

[71] East, *The Doctrine of Scripture*, p. 137.

[72] Karl Rahner, 'Holy Scripture as a Book', in *Theological Investigations: Vol. 22, Humane Society and the Church of Tomorrow* (Darton, Longman and Todd, 1991), p. 223

sword, representing his imminent martyrdom, rests against the wall behind him. In the icon, St Paul looks directly at the worshipper, intently and authoritatively; a closed, bejeweled Bible held against his chest by his left hand. His right hand makes the traditional sign of blessing. In the other icon, the prophet Jeremiah is turned to his right, looking up, captivated by God. He holds an open scroll in his left hand, which assures us that God is a God who is near, and not far off. It too is turned toward God.

On the one hand, the painting images a bookish spirituality, one in which the individual reader is enveloped in his own world, communing with texts. The icons, on the other hand, image a relational spirituality, one in which worshippers are taken into another's world, as they together hear the apostle's blessing spoken over them, and overhear the blessing of God spoken to the prophet. Instructively, the apostle's Bible is closed, and the prophet's text is open to us, but the apostle himself offers us his attention, and the prophet himself directs our attention to God.

These ways of living are not incompatible, of course. But the relational-ecclesial takes precedence over the monastic bookishness, just as the iconic takes precedence over the artistic. And it does so because receptivity takes precedence over creativity. Paul instructed Timothy to give attention to exhortation and to teaching, but only after he instructed him to give attention to the public reading of the Scriptures (1 Tim. 4.13). And Luke praises Jews in Berea for searching the Scriptures 'to see whether these things were so', but only after he celebrates the fact that they were 'more receptive ... [and] welcomed the message very eagerly' (Acts 17.11).

And this is why the authoritative interpretation of Scripture happens in the context of the church's eucharistic celebrations.

> To read Scripture in the context of the Eucharist – which has been from the beginning of the Church the primary place for it – is to say that the Word of God that acts in the Bible is a Word directed towards those changes that bring about the Eucharistic community. The summons to the reader/hearer is to involvement in the Body of Christ ... and that Body is what is constituted and maintained by the breaking of bread ... For Paul ... what is shown in the Eucharist is a community of interdependence and penitent self-awareness, discovering the dangers of partisan self-assertion or uncritical reproduction of the relations of power and status

that prevail in the society around. So if Scripture is to be heard as summons or invitation before all else, this is what it is a summons to. And the reading and understanding of the text must be pursued in this light.[73]

This, then, is how we know true readings from false: they arise from the community's mutual response to the Word, and seek only to 'edify' that community in the Spirit, that is, to open it up to renewal and blessing.

At first glance, this understanding of the Scripture's authority may seem at odds with Pentecostal sensibilities and concerns. But I would argue that it is not, at least not necessarily. Pentecostals have always encouraged one another to search the Scriptures for themselves, and in spite of the fact that their rhetoric often betrays deep-seated biblicist notions, notions sometimes entangled with anti-Catholic and anti-intellectual sentiments, and almost always dependent on historical and theological misunderstandings – including, especially, the deeply troubling idea of a 'right' to read Scripture privately, and the even more problematic idea that the Bible, and in particular, the NT is the only 'rule of faith' – they have also always insisted that 'no Scripture is of any private interpretation', resisting those who claim to have no need of the church's teachings, as well as those whose readings prove divisive.[74] 'The Spirit will teach us if we are humble enough, but it will agree with the Word, for no scripture is of any private interpretation.'[75] 'Let us take the Bible as the Word of God,

---

[73] Williams, 'The Bible Today', n.p.

[74] Typically, Pentecostals have proposed that the best way to counter 'private interpretations' is by 'comparing Scripture with Scripture'. So, for example, Arthur Townsend, *PHA* 34.10 (6 July 1950), p. 4:

> When we interpret the Word of God, we must never permit individual theories and private interpretations to influence us. We should accept the Word the way it has been written, or given of God, comparing Scripture with Scripture, to arrive at a clearcut (sic) interpretation. There are many portions which seem contradictory, but in reality are not. Should we discard, however, the tried and proven rule, to compare and balance Scripture with Scripture, we shall go to extremes, one way or the other'.

For examples of anti-Catholic sentiment, see the cover of *PE* 2268 (27 Oct 1957), which celebrates Reformation Sunday and G.H. Montgomery's article, 'Ockenga Exposes Catholic Efforts to Change American Culture', in *PHA* 29.3 (17 May 1945), pp. 3, 10-11.

[75] *LRE* 3.2 (Nov 1910), pp. 2-7 (6).

and as a thing that can not be entirely circumscribed to our own manner of thinking.'[76]

In spite of the fact that their rhetoric is almost always biblicist, perhaps because most Pentecostals are familiar only with folk Evangelical theologies, Pentecostals *in practice* are *not* biblicist, at least not consistently. In truth, Pentecostal spirituality is a form of mysticism,[77] and so the reading and hearing of Scripture happens as an event of divine-human encounter.

This is evident in C.H. Mason's Azusa St Spirit baptism testimony:

> The second night of prayer I saw a vision. I saw myself standing alone and had a dry roll of paper in my mouth trying to swallow it. Looking up towards the heavens, there appeared a man at my side. I turned my eyes at once, then I awoke and the interpretation came. God had me swallowing the whole book and if I did not turn my eyes to anyone but God and Him only, He would baptize me. I said yes to Him, and at once in the morning when I arose, I could hear a voice in me saying, 'I see ...'[78]

'God had me swallowing the whole book ...'

Pentecostals leave room for mystical encounters like these to happen in the 'prayer closet', of course. But normally it is expected to happen in the worship gathering, as it did for Bishop Mason. He was driven to prayer by the desire awakened through William Seymour's 'sweet' sermon. And he says that as he was praying,

> The Spirit came upon the saints and upon me ... Then I gave up for the Lord to have His way within me. So there came a wave of Glory into me and all of my being was filled with the Glory of the Lord. So when He had gotten me straight on my feet, there came a light which enveloped my entire being above the brightness of the sun. When I opened my mouth to say Glory, a flame touched my tongue which ran down me. My language changed and no word could I speak in my own tongue. Oh! I was filled with the Glory of the Lord.

---

[76] *PHA* 13.41 (13 February 1930), pp. 1, 8 (8).

[77] See Daniel Castelo, *Pentecostalism as a Christian Mystical Tradition* (Grand Rapids: Eerdmans, 2017).

[78] Quoted in Elsie W. Mason, 'Bishop C.H. Mason, Church of God in Christ', in Milton C. Sernett (eds.), *African American Religious History: A Documentary Witness* (Durham: Duke University Press, 1999), pp. 314-24 (321).

'The Spirit came upon the saints and upon me ...'

Pentecostal spirituality, at least in practice, is usually neither biblicist nor individualistic, but finds its center in the worship service, and especially in the Word given not only in preaching, testimony, and prophecy, but also in the loaf and cup of Communion.[79]

Spiritedness, Silence, and Ex-centricity

I have tried to make the case that if we hope to hear the Word of God, and to live the will of God, then we need new – that is, more traditional – liturgical forms, forms that better tell the truth, identifying and characterizing God, unspooling the lines of his story, and creating room for us to recognize something of the scale of the enormous mystery that is our life together with God. And I have tried to make the case that our performance of that liturgy must be spirited. As Jenson reminds us, 'the question of our liturgy as liturgy of the Spirit is not so much a question about any particular things we do, as about the *spiritedness* of the whole performance'.[80] A lifeless performance of the liturgy is a betrayal of our calling.

That being said, it also has to be acknowledged again that a spirited liturgical performance is not the end-all, be-all experience either. In a sense, the truth about the faithfulness or unfaithfulness of our liturgy and liturgical performance comes to light only 'outside' the worship-event, that is, after the service ends. The question is: do we 'walk worthy' (Eph. 4.1) of the gospel we are enacting and recalling liturgically? Are our hands, lifted in praise, in fact covered with the blood of our neighbors (Isa. 1.15)? As we all already know, it does no

---

[79] Often, early Pentecostals spoke of 'appropriating their inheritance', the 'benefits' of Christ's work, sometimes stringing together texts like the command for John to eat the 'little book' (Rev. 10.8-9), the words of Jeremiah, 'Thy words were found, and I did eat them' (Jer. 15.16), a line from Psalm 1, 'Whose delight is in the law of the Lord', a line from Ps. 34.8, 'O taste and see that the Lord is good', the command to 'take, eat' the bread of Communion (Mt. 26.26), and Jesus' promises that those who eat his flesh and drink his blood have his life in them (Jn 6.56). See for example Aimee McPherson Hutton, 'Appropriate the Blessings of the Lord and "Take", "Eat" of the Sacraments of the Holy Communion Rite', *Foursquare Crusader* 6.15 (27 Jan 1932), p. 3. See also A.L. Sisler, '1 Kings 17th Chapter', *PHA* 3.9 (26 June 1919), p. 5; Lilian B. Yeomans, 'Eat the Book', *PE* 1178 (5 Dec 1936), pp. 2-3; Paul F. Beacham's response to readers' questions in *PHA* 19.27 (31 Oct 1935), p. 2; *PHA* 21.51 (28 Apr 1938), p. 8; *PHA* (2 May 1940), p. 8.

[80] Robert W. Jenson, 'Liturgy of the Spirit', *The Lutheran Quarterly* 26.2 (May 1974), pp. 189-203 (189).

good to *claim* love for God if we in fact neglect caring for those in need (1 Jn. 3.17). So, Bonhoeffer is unquestionably right: 'only where hands are not too good for deeds of love and mercy in everyday helpfulness can the mouth joyfully and convincingly proclaim the message of God's love and mercy'.[81]

If, then, we hope to reform and perform our liturgies faithfully, both ex-centricity and apophasis are required. That is, we must be led outside ourselves, led beyond what we know and think we know. Again and again, at the end of our attempts to 'make the name' and 'fashion divinity in the world', whether in prayer or song or sermon or theological essay, we have to let ourselves be reduced to awed, grateful silence in delighted fear and trembling before the 'unmakeability' of the divine name. We have to come to silence.

This coming to silence is vital. The silence that matters, the silence that shows God has acted, is 'achieved' (although of course not earned). It has a history behind it – and a history ahead of it.[82] Faithful speech about God, personal and corporate, spontaneous or liturgical, moves in and out of silence as it finds it cannot not speak of the God who gives the name above every other name.

In silence – no, in coming to silence – we learn why it is that liturgical worship must not be reduced to its usefulness. Sadly, for so many the decisive question put to liturgical worship is, 'What did I get out of it?'[83] But that is a bad question.[84] The encounter with God of course affects us. But the work of the God beyond all naming is itself not so easily named. Therefore, asking what one gets from liturgical worship is a bad question not only because it reduces the true and the beautiful to the 'valuable', but also because it assumes God's work is always identifiable and describable. In truth, God's work happens in the depths of our hearts, depths he alone can reach. Only rarely does that work show itself on the surface, and even then, always in surprising ways. And in the same way, worship, led by the liturgy, not only does good for us, but simply is good because it celebrates the God whose goodness holds us in being.

---

[81] Dietrich Bonhoeffer, *Life Together* (San Francisco: HarperOne, 2009), p. 100.
[82] Williams, *The Edge of Words*, p. 178.
[83] Nicholas Wolterstorff, *Until Justice and Peace Embrace* (Grand Rapids: Eerdmans, 1983), p. 148.
[84] Wolterstorff, *Until Justice and Peace Embrace*, p. 151.

We are silenced because we have heard. And we are silent so that we can listen. And we can listen, because we are people filled with the listening Spirit: 'When the Spirit of truth comes, he will guide you into all truth, for he will not speak on his own, but will speak whatever he hears ...' (Jn 16.13). As God listens in us, we find we can listen to him and through him to others, even to ourselves. And so cannot help but live ex-centrically, kenotically, and epicletically: like God in the going out of ourselves, the pouring out of our gifts without reserve, and the coming alongside others in their joy and in their sorrows, opened to their world in all of its otherness so we might open for them room to be with God. Just so, we 'fashion divinity' in the world, bringing divine-human holiness to bear, making the unmakeable name.

PART TWO

HOLINESS

4

THE END OF HOLINESS

Introduction

If, as I have argued, to be human is to be called to live a priestly life, a life that brings God's holiness to bear in the world, then to be baptized is to be claimed by that calling, joined to Christ, identified with him in his intimacy with the Father and partnered with him in his mission with the Spirit. Living that life, we both sanctify and are sanctified.

But how can this be? What does it mean to say we cooperate with God, either in our sanctification or in the sanctifying of others? And what is the character of the holiness we are called to mediate? These are not new questions, of course. But we need to ask them again, because so much depends on how we answer them, and so much of what we have imagined is off, out of tune.

Re-Righting Holiness

Pentecostals have a long history of talking about holiness. But if we are honest, we have to admit that that history is a 'mixed blessing'.[1] For sure, there is much to be grateful for, but all of that good notwithstanding, the history of the holiness movements has been at too many places a painful, tragic history, a history of manipulation,

---

[1] Macchia, *Baptized in the Spirit*, p. 28. For exploration of the relationship of early Pentecostal movements to the Wesleyan-Holiness traditions, see Donald W. Dayton, *The Theological Roots of Pentecostalism* (Grand Rapids: Baker Academic, 1987); Dale Coulter, 'Recovering the Wesleyan Vision of Pentecostalism: 5 Theses', *Pneuma* 40 (2018), pp. 457-88; Vinson Synan, *The Holiness-Pentecostal Tradition: Charismatic Movements in the Twentieth Century* (Grand Rapids: Eerdmans, 1997).

incomprehensible teaching, and false promises.[2] So, it is past time for revisioning. If holiness theology and spirituality is to have a future, we, as heirs of the movement, must have 'the courage to recall and repair the way holiness has been depicted in their past'.[3] Our concern should not be so much to save the holiness movement, but to remember that we are called to live lives that resemble God's, lives of intercession and compassion, lives of sacrifice and hospitality – and that we therefore depend at every turn on the transformative work of the Spirit.

Beyond Sinlessness
The holiness traditions were right to take sin seriously. Unfortunately, they left us, by and large, with a drastically reductionist and hyper-individualist accounts of sin.[4] They were right to call us to personal responsibility, but unfortunately left us with an oversimplified, overly-optimistic account of human be-ing, and an inability to account for the deep complexity of life the world.[5] Perhaps most troublingly, however, these traditions taught us to think of sanctification in terms of overcoming sin rather than in terms of being conformed to Christ. Against that teaching, then, we should shift our attention away from the darkness of sin to the light of the glory revealed in the radiating face of Jesus Christ (2 Cor. 4.6), whose blessing is the light that is our life (Num. 6.24-26; Jn 1.4).[6] We should, like Paul, desire

---

[2] It is 'tragic' just because of the promise. See Donald W. Dayton, 'The Holiness Churches: A Significant Ethical Tradition', *The Christian Century* 92 (26 February 1975), pp. 197-201.

[3] Daniel Castelo, 'A Holy Reception Can Lead to a Holy Future', in Lee Roy Martin (ed.), *A Future for Holiness: Pentecostal Explorations* (Cleveland, TN: CPT Press, 2013), pp. 225-34 [234].

[4] See J. Ayodeji Adewuya, *Holiness and Community in 2 Cor. 6.17-7.1: Paul's View of Communal Holiness in the Corinthian Correspondence* (New York: Peter Lang, 2001) and Baker, *Diagonal Advance*, pp. 276-82.

[5] See Mark H. Mann, *Perfecting Grace: Holiness, Human Being, and the Sciences* (London: T&T Clark, 2006), pp. 1-2.

[6] It is perhaps instructive to compare what I am proposing here with A.B. Simpson's description of sanctification, which Bernie Van de Walle, '"How High of a Christian Life?": A.B. Simpson and the Classic Doctrine of Theosis', *Wesleyan Theological Journal* 43.2 (Fall 2008), pp. 136-53 (144-45), summarizes in this way:

> For Simpson, the change that occurs within humanity in salvation … is neither the enhancement of the human constitution nor the amplification of an inherent, yet dormant human capacity or potentiality. 'It is not the old life improved.' 'It is not the improvement of our natural character, not even the cleansing of

more than living 'above sin'. After all, even apart from Christ Paul was capable of blamelessly keeping the Law (Phil. 3.6). Instead, we should, as he did, desire to be made like Christ, regarding blamelessness as 'rubbish' by comparison (Phil. 3.8-11). 'I count it all as nothing', he says:

> in order that I may gain Christ [9]and be found in him, not having a righteousness of my own that comes from the law, but one that comes through faith in Christ, the righteousness from God based on faith. [10]I want to know Christ and the power of his resurrection and the sharing of his sufferings by becoming like him in his death, [11]if somehow I may attain the resurrection from the dead.

We should not aspire merely to live sinlessly, because that aspiration is born not of the Spirit but of a desire to overcome our need of God and neighbor. A life so lived cannot in fact bear witness to the beauty of holiness. We should, instead, aspire to receive the end the gospel promises us: sanctifying participation with Christ and his Spirit in their intercessory, priestly mission, which draws us into intimacy with the Father and empowers us to take responsibility for what happens in his world.

Of course, that participation wreaks havoc with the sin at work in and around us. 'Those who have been born of God do not sin, because God's seed abides in them; they cannot sin, because they have been born of God' (1 Jn 3.9). And, of course, it is not for no reason that we are warned by the Scriptures against persisting in willful sin (Heb. 10.26), and are directed to 'put to death' everything in us that remains at odds with the New Creation, including 'fornication, impurity, passion, evil desire, and greed (which is idolatry)', as well as 'anger, malice, slander, and abusive language' (Col. 3.5, 8). But all that we are called to do depends on our being united to Christ. In baptism, which is our circumcision, we once-for-all 'put off the body of the flesh' (Col. 2.10-12) and are thereby freed to live Christ's life with him. Bluntly put, there is a sinlessness that is achievable apart from

---

our own spirit.' [It] is far more than a return to or renovation of some Edenic, pre-fall innocence. This work of God offers 'something infinitely higher than mere human perfection.' It is, rather, a change that results in a new estate, a new nature, and so thorough going [sic] as to truly result in a 'new life' ... God is not involved in a work of renovation but of reconstruction. This new life is something beyond merely human nature super-charged by divine impulse. It is a new structure altogether.

Christ, and Christ means more for us than simply not sinning: he means for us to be one with the Father as he is. He means for us to be overflowing with the Spirit.

Beyond Separation and Purity

Focused on sin and sinlessness, our accounts of holiness have been dominated by the intertwined metaphors of separation and purity. Framed in these terms, we can hardly help but hear the call to be holy 'as God is holy' (1 Pet. 1.16) as a call to distance ourselves from our neighbors, keeping ourselves from the impurities that threaten to spoil our sanctity. God has sanctified *us* – so we have to 'come out from among *them* and be separate', maintaining at all costs the purity we have been given (or achieved).

But this account of holiness is confusing and at least somewhat misleading, if not out-and-out unfaithful. The truth is, we know God's otherness only because God has already overcome and trans-figured the distance, disclosing Godself to us truly and gracefully, drawing us into divine intimacy. Coming to us in Jesus Christ and his Spirit, God has given to us the paradigm of the sanctified life: sepa-ration *from* the world is but the first sweep of a movement that has as its goal saving identification *with* the world. Our having-been-set-apart in Christ belongs to our having-been-given-over by the Spirit to those whom God loves through us. In God's economy, otherness, set-apartness, is always only for the sake of the other, the 'non-elect'. The Spirit, resting on us in Christ, draws us deeper and deeper into God's devotion to our neighbors, generating in us a passion for their good.

Without question, Scripture *does* call us to purity and a life of moral set-apart-ness. James insists that 'pure religion' entails keeping one-self 'unstained by the world' (Jas 1.27), and Peter instructs the 'exiles' to strive for lives of 'holiness and godliness' that are 'without spot or blemish' (1 Pet. 1.1; 2 Pet. 3.11, 14). The Apostle John warns his community against loving the world or the things of the world (1 Jn 2.15), encouraging them to purify themselves in imitation of Christ (1 Jn 3.3). Paul prays for the Philippians to be 'pure and blameless on the day of Christ' (Phil. 1.10), and he instructs Timothy to keep him-self pure by refusing to participate in the sins of others (1 Tim. 5.22).

Surely, in the light of these texts, and others like them, we have to say that holiness has *something* to do with separation and purity? Yes and no. The difference between the yes and the no comes clear in Paul's instructions to the Corinthians in 2 Cor. 6.14-7.1:

> Do not be mismatched with unbelievers. For what partnership is there between righteousness and lawlessness? Or what fellowship is there between light and darkness? What agreement does Christ have with Beliar? Or what does a believer share with an unbeliever? What agreement has the temple of God with idols? For we are the temple of the living God; as God said, 'I will live in them and walk among them, and I will be their God, and they shall be my people. Therefore come out from them, and be separate from them, says the Lord, and touch nothing unclean; then I will welcome you, and I will be your father, and you shall be my sons and daughters, says the Lord Almighty'. Since we have these promises, beloved, let us cleanse ourselves from every defilement of body and of spirit, making holiness perfect in the fear of God.

This text is easy to misread. Isolated from the context of the letter and filtered through unfaithful accounts of the gospel, Paul's words seem to call for a strict separation from unbelievers. In fact, on this misreading, God's welcome – indeed, the covenant itself – seems to rest on the strength of our initiative and our efforts in keeping ourselves from defilement by relationship with unbelievers and their wickedness. If we hope to remain the people of God, then we have to break away from the world, maintaining our innocence and purity at all costs. By this logic, we save ourselves by hating our neighbors.

But this reading is in fact a misreading, as should be apparent to any careful reader of Scripture. Hans Dieter Betz contends that 'the theology of 2 Cor. 6.14-7.1 is not only non-Pauline but *anti*-Pauline'.[7] He is wrong, I believe, but even if we disagree with his account of why and how the unit came to be inserted into the text of 2 Corinthians, we nonetheless have to agree that Paul's writings and his lived life embody exactly what the theology expressed in 2 Cor. 6.14-7.1 seems to warn against.[8] The theology of the letter to the Galatians, in particular, seems to show that the apostle is diametrically opposed to

---

[7] Hans Dieter Betz, '2 Cor. 6.14-7.1: An Anti-Pauline Fragment?', *JBL* 92.1 (Mar 1973), pp. 88-108 [108].

[8] Betz, '2 Cor. 6.14-7.1', p. 108.

a theology of purity-through-separation, laying bare his determination to disprove such thinking as accursed.[9]

What, then, are we to do with this passage? How are we to read it faithfully? We cannot simply dismiss it as an anti-Pauline interpolation.[10] And yet we also cannot ignore the ways it fits so awkwardly with what Paul says elsewhere. What we have to do, I am convinced, is press toward a closer, more nuanced reading. And that closer reading begins with the recognition that in the immediate context, Paul is begging the Corinthians to remember him as their father and themselves as his children.[11] In fact, the instructions in 6.14-7.1 are nested between the cry of 6.13 – 'I speak as to children … open wide your hearts' – and 7.2: 'Make room in your hearts for us'. If, then, we take the text in its given form, we have to hear Paul's call for the Corinthians to 'come out from the midst of them and be separate' as – somehow – a movement toward reconciliation.[12] He is asking them to break ranks with those who have divided the community by their claims to superior holiness and spiritual power.

Paul assumes they know already that light has no fellowship with darkness, righteousness no partnership with lawlessness, Christ no agreement with demons, the temple no alliance with idols, the believer no part with an unbeliever; and so he anticipates a forceful 'Nothing!' in response to each of these questions.[13] But we should

---

[9] Betz, '2 Cor. 6.14-7.1', p. 108.

[10] See Adewuya, *Holiness and Community in 2 Cor. 6.17-7.1*, pp. 2-4, 15-29.

[11] William Webb (*Returning Home: New Covenant and Second Exodus as the Context for 2 Corinthians 6.14-71* [JSNTSup 85; Sheffield: Sheffield Academic Press, 1993], p. 178) argues that in his attempt to bring about reconciliation with the Corinthians, Paul is calling for them to experience a 'new exodus'. They have abandoned him (and gone after the 'super-apostles') because they, like Israel in Egypt, have forgotten who they are. And like Israel they need an 'exodus' that truly re-fashions their corporate identity so they can recognize him as their Moses-like father in the Lord.

[12] For examples of holiness readings of 2 Cor. 6.14-7.1, see Adewuya, *Holiness and Community in 2 Cor. 6.17-7.1*, pp. 5, 34-43. He finds three basic problems with the way readers in the holiness traditions have interpreted the passage: first, they impose their own soteriological terms on the passage rather than attending to the nuance of Paul's statements; second, they focus exclusively on the personal aspects of sanctification, ignoring the corporate and communal aspects (which Adewuya believes are predominate); and third, they fail to grapple with the text as a whole, narrowly focusing on 7.1 instead.

[13] Why is Paul asking these questions at all? N.T. Wright, *Paul for Everyone: 2 Corinthians* (Louisville: WJKP, 2004), p. 74, argues that Paul wants the Corinthians

not rush past these questions unthinkingly, at least not if we hope to find a gospel-fitting reading of this text. On deeper reflection, we are reminded that the believer relates to the unbeliever in at least two senses. The believer differs from the unbeliever only in the sense that the believer lives by faith in Christ and in hope of his coming justice, which will renew all things and bring them into their fullness. In that sense, then, and only in that sense, the believer has no agreement or partnership with the unbeliever. They trust in and long for altogether different orders of reality. But in another sense, the believer lives only *for* the unbeliever, because the order to which the believer belongs in Christ – the order of new creation, the order of the kingdom – exists precisely for the sake of those enslaved to the old, evil age – the order that is passing away. By grace, the believer has been rescued from this darkness and saved from its lawlessness precisely so that she, as Christ's friend and partner, can by that same grace participate with the Spirit and all the saints in delivering others into the future the Father promises his creation. Again, the point is that separation is for the sake of later unification. The elect are elected for the sake of the non-elect.

Reading 2 Cor. 6.14-7.1 in this alternative way, we hear what sounded before as a call for a dramatic and final move away from the world as in fact a call to re-settle in the heart of the world's darkness. What seemed to be a turning *from* unbelievers – or wavering, unfaithful believers – is in fact a kind of turning *to* them.

So, it is that our 'turning away' is never like that of the Levite or the Pharisee, but is always like that of the Samaritan, who turns away from what he had in mind to do and gives himself wholly to the wounded, dying man at his feet (Lk. 10.25-37). We 'keep ourselves in the love of God' only as we 'have mercy on those who are wavering' and 'save others by snatching them out of the fire' (Jude 21-23). In this way, we come to be like Christ, who was 'separate from sinners' (Heb. 7.26) just because he was 'numbered with the transgressors' (Isa. 53.12).

The holiness to which we are called, the holiness without which we cannot see the Lord (Heb. 12.14), is a holiness we are called to make possible for others. 'See to it', we are told, 'that no one fails to obtain

---

to 'look around at the pagan world', see it for what it is, and 'take action appropriately'. In other words, 'he doesn't want them to enter into close partnerships with those who are still living by the old way of life, which is in fact the way of death'.

the grace of God' (Heb. 12.15). We intercede, then, so that others may be drawn into the same beauty that we have come to desire.

> As Christ bore with us and accepted us as sinners, so we in his community may bear with sinners and accept them into the community of Jesus Christ through the forgiveness of sins. We may suffer the sins of one another; we do not need to judge. That is grace for Christians ... Because each individual's sin burdens the whole community and indicts it, the community of faith rejoices amid all the pain inflicted on it by the sin of the other and, in spite of the burden placed on it, rejoices in being deemed worthy of bearing with and forgiving sin.[14]

We live truly in the light not by keeping our distance from the darkness, but by penetrating into the heart of that darkness for the sake of those enslaved there. We are called to 'lay aside the works of darkness and [to] put on the armor of light' (Rom. 13.12) just because we are meant to serve as 'a guide to the blind, a light to those who are in darkness' (Rom. 2.19). We can live such a life as 'children of the light' (Eph. 5.8) because the same God who in the beginning called light into being from nothing 'has shone into our hearts to enlighten them with the knowledge of God's glory, the glory on the face of Christ' (2 Cor. 4.6) – the very glory we reflect to others in the darkness. After all, even darkness is light to the God who dwells in unapproachable light. And only if we are willing to enter the 'thick darkness' of his presence – a presence always overshadowing the lost, the forgotten, the forsaken – can we draw near to God. Only in *that* light can we see light.[15]

Beyond Otherness

These two fundamental mistakes – (1) framing sanctification in terms of overcoming sin rather than participation in Christ and his ministry and (2) describing holiness as separation from sin rather than radical, intercessory identification with (the friend of) sinners – are often justified by a certain explanation of God's holiness. Christian theologians commonly use 'holiness' to name whatever it is that makes God different from all that is not-God. Jean-Luc Marion, for example, says that 'God is distinguished from the world and from other gods

---

[14] Bonhoeffer, *Life Together*, p. 102.
[15] See Ps. 139.12; 1 Tim. 6.16; Exod. 20.21; Ps. 36.9.

insofar as he is "majestic in holiness, terrible in glorious deeds" (Exod. 15:11)'. God reveals himself to creation in such a way that no one can enter 'the vicinity of his holiness, which separates him from any other as the Wholly Other'.[16] Orthodox theologian Dumitru Staniloae offers a similarly typical account:

> Holiness can be said to reveal to us all the divine qualities in a concentrated way. It is the luminous and active mystery of the divine presence. In it there is concentrated all that distinguishes God from the world.[17]

Such descriptions are true so far as they go. But they are finally insufficient. John Webster is right: God is what God does; therefore, 'God's holiness is to be defined out of God's works'.[18] Hence, given that Jesus is the full embodiment of all God's works, we have to look to Jesus and his storied witness of God if we want to know what holiness means.[19] Jesus just is, in himself, 'the event of the coming of that holiness which crosses the great divide …'[20] 'What he does and what is done to him – his whole life history – is … the manifestation of holiness.'[21]

What do we find when we look to Jesus to see God's holiness? We find that holiness is 'a mode of relation'.[22] It is, in fact, *the* mode of relation that God enjoys as Father, Son, and Spirit – the very mode of relation God opens to us as creatures. God's holiness is the freedom made possible because Father, Son, and Spirit exist for, in, and with each other. Or, to put it the other way around, because God is holy and in goodness shares that holiness with all things, God is the God God is, and we are the creatures we are, in our life together with God and before God in the world.

---

[16] Jean-Luc Marion, 'The Invisibility of the Saint', *Critical Inquiry* 35.3 (Spring 2009), pp. 703-10 (708).

[17] Dumitru Staniloae, *The Experience of God Vol. 1: Revelation and Knowledge of the Triune God* (Brookline, MA: Holy Cross Orthodox Press, 1994), pp. 222-23.

[18] John Webster, *Holiness* (London: SCM Press, 2003), p. 39.

[19] Michael J. Gorman, *Inhabiting the Cruciform God: Kenosis, Justification and Theosis in Paul's* (Grand Rapids: Eerdmans, 2009), p. 113.

[20] Craig Keen, *After Crucifixion: The Promise of Theology* (Eugene, OR: Cascade Books, 2013), p. 94.

[21] Keen, *After Crucifixion*, p. 94.

[22] Webster, *Holiness*, p. 5.

In other words, holiness is simply love given and received in over-flowing, unending, ever-increasing fullness. Therefore, to be holy is to live as God lives – in a fulness that does not violence, but gives fulness to others as deep calls out to deep.

This share in God's life is made possible through the 'communication of attributes' in Christ and then in the outpouring of his Spirit in our hearts. God's holiness, which we might call his natural relationality, holds the divine and human natures together in Christ without confusion, division, change, or mixture so that the human is healed, perfected, and transfigured by the divine. And it not only preserves the integrity of the two natures in the person of Jesus, but also effects the deification of the human nature through its communion with the divine in Christ through the Spirit. 'When the Logos of God took on human nature, he bestowed on it the fullness of his grace and delivered it from the bonds of corruption and death. They consequence of this hypostatic union of the two natures in Christ was the deification of the human nature.'[23] And when we receive his Spirit, so that we are at-one-ed with him, our nature is also sanctified, made to share in the divine nature. 'Our human nature is purified and taken up, through our participation in Christ's humanity (made possible by his participation in ours), into the divine life and fulfilled in its humanity, through that participation.'[24]

All that to say, God is holy in that God relates both immanently, with himself as Trinity, and economically, with us as his creatures, in ways that are simultaneously free and freeing, lively and life-giving, just and justifying. Because God is holy, we can experience goodness, truth, and beauty in relationship with God in ways that make us good and true and beautiful. To narrow it to a single statement: God's holiness is the way God has of relating to us so that we can not only know God, but in knowing, become like God. Because God is holy, God can be with us, the 'holy one in our midst', not unmaking our humanness but perfecting it, drawing us into humanizing deifica-

---

[23] Veli-Matti Kärkkäinen, *One with God: Salvation as Deification and Justification* (Collegeville, MN: Unitas, 2004), p. 28.
[24] Douglas Harink, *1 & 2 Peter* (BTC; Grand Rapids: Brazos, 2009), p. 144.

tion.[25] As Keen says, 'God's holiness is a freedom for what is far gone from holiness'.[26]

Holy as Christ is Holy

So far in this chapter, I have tried to make the case that because God is holy, we can and must be holy. And I have insisted that our sanctification is nothing less than transfiguring participation in the incarnate Lord's life and ongoing priestly ministry.[27] All that reflection has unearthed a deeper stratum of questions. *How* do we participate in Christ's life and work? And what does that participation mean for us?

We participate in Christ's life-work primarily through our share in the sacramental and charismatic, diaconal and kerygmatic ministry of the Church. But we share in his intercession for the world also through the mundane work of 'keeping' one another (Gen. 4.9) in the course of day-to-day life – madcap playing with our children; gaping at the sun-ravished horizon; sharing embarrassing stories with long-time friends over a good meal; sitting in long prayer with the sick and dying; struggling to find the right words in a conversation; refusing to take offense when others wrong us; listening with compassion to the broken-hearted, refusing to burden them with cheap advice.

Over time, we find – actually, I should say others find for us – that this participation is altering our character and our disposition toward God and the world, ourselves and others. Through the Spirit's wisdom, we are clothed with Christ's virtues. We become 'faithful and true' (Rev. 19.11) in him. Not that we are merely imitating his example. We are in fact living life as he lives it. Or, better, he is living his life in us, even as we fail to make adequate room for him. His own virtues – his faith, his hope, his love, his tenacity, his meekness, his prudence – become ours, worked into us like artful shape is worked into the clay by the potter. Awash in the Spirit, we receive God's own love 'shed abroad in our hearts' (Rom. 5.5) so that as we

---

[25] See Webster, *Holiness*, pp. 5, 9, 43, 45.

[26] Craig Keen, 'A Quick "Definition" of Holiness' in Kevin W. Mannoia and Don Thorsen (eds.), *The Holiness Manifesto* (Grand Rapids: Eerdmans, 2008), p. 238.

[27] Jordan Cooper (*Christification: A Lutheran Approach to Theosis* [Eugene, OR: Wipf & Stock, 2014]) argues for a distinction in the accounts of theosis put forward by the early Patristics and those who followed Dionysius the Areopagite's lead. But Baker (*Diagonal Advance*, pp. 197-230) contends that the definitive break comes later (in the 14th century), with the rise of Franciscan spirituality.

yield and resist and yield again, we undergo a constant re-energizing and re-ordering of our loves. In this way, we learn again and again, over and over, not only to love what is good but also to love what is good in lovely ways. The Spirit frees us from loving the wrong things; then, more deeply, trains us to love the right things the right way. Finally, the final resurrection alters our being so that we become utterly at-one-ed with God's love.

Of course, sanctification does not happen all at once. And it does not happen in some neat progression from less to more or from weakness to strength. As I have already said, to be sanctified is not to be sinless, or even to be progressively less sinful. That way of imagining the holy life misses the point entirely. To be sanctified is instead to be perfectly loved by God. Or, to say that the same thing another way, to be sanctified is to be joined to Christ so completely that we become one with him in intimacy, partners with him in his work, and heirs with him of all that the Father desires for him. To be called saints is to be reminded that what can be said of Christ in fact can also be said of us in promise.

But if what I have said is true, then not only our character, but also our very nature must be changed in the end.[28] Theosis is the fulfillment, and not negation, of what it means to be human.[29] Stithatos speaks of a triadic perfection that comes in the Paraclete's 'threefold gift of peace'.[30] The Spirit first gives us peace from 'hostile passions', that is, from the unnatural. Then, the Spirit gives us peace that frees us to live according to our 'true nature'. Finally, the Spirit gives us a share in God's own peace, so that we are 'perfected into what is beyond nature'.[31] In the words of his master, St Symeon, all who are

---

[28] As Craig Keen asserts (*The Transgression of the Integrity of God: Essays and Addresses* [Eugene, OR: Cascade, 2012], p. 224), 'The theosis that the Spirit works, then, is a movement that transgresses the integrity of the creature precisely as the creature participates in the Trinity, that is, in the Spirit, through the Son, to the Father, an unfathomable abyss'. See also Robert W. Jenson, 'Theosis', *Dialog* 32.2 (1993), pp. 108-112.

[29] See Andrew Louth, 'The Place of *Theosis* in Orthodox Theology', in Michael J. Christensen and Jeffery A. Wittung (eds.), *Partakers of the Divine Nature: The History and Development of Deification in the Christian Traditions* (Grand Rapids: Baker Academic, 2008), p. 39.

[30] Nikitas Stithatos, 'On the Inner Nature of Things and On the Purification of the Intellect: One Hundred Texts', *The Philokalia, Vol. 4* (London: Faber and Faber, 1995), p. 121.

[31] Stithatos, 'On the Inner Nature of Things', p. 121.

counted worthy to partake of the divine nature become, in the End, 'altogether superior to the good things that God has prepared for them'.[32]

> The union to which we are called is neither hypostatic – as in the case of the human nature of Christ – nor substantial, as in that of the three divine Persons: it is union with God in His energies, or union by grace making us participate in the divine nature, without our essence becoming thereby the essence of God. In deification we are by grace (that is to say, in the divine energies) all that God is by nature, save only identity of nature …'[33]

In other words, we are meant not only for everlasting life in the new creation, but for being with God in ways that conform our nature to his, so that we know as we are known, alive with his very life.

We need to remind ourselves again that the hope of resurrection we confess is more than the endless prolongation of our lives.[34] To be resurrected into God in the End is not simply to be kept from dying, but to be united to God fully, truly at-one-ed with God's knowing of God and God's knowing us and all things. As Scripture says, seeing Christ in his fullness alters us, so that we are like him (1 Jn 3.2). And that face-to-face encounter, which comes as the fulfillment, but not in any sense the result or outcome, of our strivings toward Christ, transforms us so that we are fitted to eternal, infinite communion with and within the delights of the Father, Son, and Holy Spirit.[35] Our hope is more than simply that death will not have the final word, but that we shall live in God and God in us so that we experience life in ever-increasing fullness.

---

[32] Symeon the New Theologian, 'Discourse Ten', C.J. de Cantanzaro (trans.), *The Discourses* (New York: The Missionary Society of St Paul, 1980), p. 162.

[33] Vladimir Lossky, *The Mystical Theology of the Eastern Church* (Crestwood, NY: St Vladimir's Seminary Press, 1976), p. 87.

[34] Christian Wiman, *My Bright Abyss: Meditation of a Modern Believer* (New York: Farrar, Straus and Giroux, 2013), p. 165.

[35] Daniel B. Clendenin (*Eastern Orthodox Christianity: A Western Perspective* [2nd ed; Grand Rapids: Baker Academic, 2003], p. 184) insists that theosis does not effect 'the transformation of our essence'; instead, it is 'natural, ethical, and in accordance with grace'. He is right, I believe, to say that deification names 'the union of the whole person with God as unrestricted happiness in the divine kingdom', but he is wrong when he says that human nature is, in the end, 'remade into its original beauty'. In the End, unlike the beginning, human beings share in the divine nature. Inevitably, then, the beauty of human beings in the End infinitely outshines the 'original' beauty, but does not violate it.

Godlikeness Beyond 'Goodness'

Salvation, then, is deification. And deification means we come to share God's character and God's nature so that we flourish in fullness as God is all in all. That is, we do not become merely good in some abstract sense: we become Christlike; that is, we become good with his goodness.

We often, always at terrible cost to ourselves and to others, confuse the sanctified life for a moral life. But the truth is, holiness is beyond morality and immorality. And theotic participation in God's holiness inevitably forces us into conflict with the moral standards of our various worlds and their regnant worldviews. Holiness is, as Milbank insists, 'a thing so strange, that it must be declared immoral or amoral according to all other human norms and codes of morality'.[36]

Tellingly, Jesus, the holy one, is again and again throughout his ministry charged with immorality, and at last he is betrayed and tortured and murdered because his life does not fit into the story the powers of Rome want to tell or the story many of Israel's leaders want to tell. His life calls into question the moral standards of both the Empire and the Temple-system. As Paul says, Christ crucified is 'a stumbling block to Jews and foolishness to Gentiles' (1 Cor. 1.23).

As with him, so with us: the holy life is never a consistently moral life because it never fits neatly and consistently into worldly 'value systems' – including religious systems. Not to put the point too sharply, but authentic sanctification begins to take root in us just as we let the Spirit rend apart and break open the moral frames of reference formed in us 'naturally' by the disordered powers that give shape and energy to the way things happen our world. Self-righteousness and despair assert themselves whenever good people (by the standards of their 'worldview') settle into *that* goodness, refusing the Spirit the right to re-order their being-in-the-world after the image of Christ and *his* goodness.

The truth of this conflict between the kingdom of God and the morality of the world is dramatized for us in Matthew's account of Peter's confession. Peter, Matthew tells us, receives a revelation from God – 'Blessed are you, Simon, son of Jonah! For flesh and blood has not revealed this to you, but my Father' (Mt. 16.17) – and he

---

[36] John Milbank, *The Word Made Strange: Theology, Language, Culture* (Malden, MA: Blackwell Publishing, 1997), p. 219.

makes a true confession: Jesus *is*, in truth, 'the Christ, the son of the living God' (Mt. 16.16). But Peter, who had been called 'the rock' in the receiving of that revelation and the giving of that confession, is nonetheless a 'stumbling-stone' for Christ because what he bears in his heart and his mind in receiving that revelation and making that confession is *false*. Satanically false, in fact. Peter, like all of us, un-knowingly appropriates divine revelation to his frame of reference, reshaping it to make sense in the terms of his worldview and offering his confession on those terms.

On the Day of Pentecost, Peter stands and proclaims that the Spirit, as prophesied by Joel, is now being poured out on 'all flesh' (Acts 2.17). At one level, this too is a true confession. But of course what he meant by 'all flesh' was in fact 'all *circumcised* flesh', which subverts the truth of his confession with a lie. We know this because of what he later admits to Cornelius: '*Now* I know that God is no respecter of persons' (Acts 10.34-45).

Even after this second eye-opening encounter, Peter still does not quite understand. Pressured by some in the Jerusalem churches, he withdraws from table fellowship with Gentile converts and so betrays the gospel (Gal. 2.11-14). It is not that Peter lacked moral integrity. If anything, his reluctance to join himself to Gentiles was a mark of his integrity. But his integrity was a self-integration on the terms of the worldview he had received. It was not an integrity founded on the terms of the gospel's kingdom.

Like Peter, we learn the 'languages of moral and spiritual discern-ment' only in 'ongoing conversation with those who bring us up'.[37] And giving ourselves to those 'languages', we learn to be 'good'. In the same way, we learn the language of holiness only in ongoing con-versation with the people whose lives are graced to happen at an an-gle to the world. In the process of giving our lives unstintingly to the gospel, we are required to *un*learn our accustomed way of making sense of ourselves in the world. We learn holiness only by *un*learning 'goodness'. The call to holiness is a call to break free from morality, which, at its heart, is always about power and control.

Brueggemann provides a model for thinking about this conflict. He suggests that we see ourselves as 'scripted' by the manifold

---

[37] Charles Taylor, *Sources of the Self* (Cambridge: Cambridge University Press, 1989), p. 35.

processes of cultural formation that are imprinted on us through the 'liturgies' of ideological propaganda. To be sanctified, then, is to be de-scripted, saved from the illusions of the worldly script through the church's 'steady, patient, intentional articulation of an alternative script'.[38] The church's witness – especially as it is embodied in the lives of the saints – confronts us with the saving strangeness of God, bewildering and subverting our scripted expectations, awakening in us a desire for the ways of God, which are always too good for us to have believed.

The Crucifixion (and Resurrection) of Conscience

This saving bewilderment takes place primarily in the realm of *conscience*, where the foundations of our sense of right and wrong, good and bad, the fitting and the unsuitable are crushed under the weight of the gospel's otherness. Christ alone tells the whole truth about us, and not until the Last Judgment is the truth truly set out plainly for one and all. Knowing this, we have to keep the claims of conscience 'under authority' – ready to submit to them insofar as they conform to the gospel, and ready to defy them when they do not. Conscience, whatever service it might offer, cannot claim the ultimacy that belongs to Christ alone. As Radner insists, the NT expects believers to surrender their rights, laying down their right to judgment 'for the sake of another's conscience and for the goals of "peace"'.[39] Conscience is not so much tamed as crucified.

Such a claim makes a sense only if the voice of conscience is considered a manifestation of sin, an expression of our attempts to be a law unto ourselves. And that is precisely Bonhoeffer's argument. When Christ, the 'Lord of conscience', becomes in faith 'the point of unity of my existence', then my autonomy is mercifully undone. Jesus alone is the *nomos* who orders my existence before God in the world. He names me, and so gives me myself. So, Bonhoeffer puts it directly, and with force: 'Jesus Christ has become my conscience'.[40] As Lord, he 'sets the conscience free for the service of God and of our

---

[38] Brueggemann, 'Counterscript', p. 23.

[39] Ephraim Radner, *A Brutal Unity: The Spiritual Politics of the Christian Church* (Waco: Baylor University Press, 2012), p. 378.

[40] Dietrich Bonhoeffer, *Ethics* (Dietrich Bonhoeffer Works Vol. 6; Minneapolis: Augsburg Fortress Press, 2005), p. 278.

neighbor'.[41] In that freedom, we come into being, into the promised abundant life.

Bonhoeffer is right, I think, in saying that conscience must die, because the 'script' uses its voice to exert binding claims on us. After all, the call to deny ourselves in bearing his cross (Mk 8.34-35) would mean little or nothing if it did not require dying to our moral sense. But Bonhoeffer seems to forget that if conscience is crucified with Christ, then it is also *resurrected* with him. Grace not only destroys the *un*natural in us (that is, whatever it is that turns our conscience against us, God and neighbor). Grace also perfects the natural.[42] And conscience is natural.

Still, before the End, conscience is saved only in hope – and 'hope that is seen is not hope' (Rom. 8.24). Short of the Last Judgment, therefore, self-knowledge and self-judgment, like all knowledge and all judgments, remain strictly provisional. Radner has it exactly right: Christian conscience must be 'unceasingly relearned'.[43] If it is not, then we cannot live the life for which the Spirit gathers us. But if we allow the Spirit ceaselessly to unrest and reorder our sense of judgment, then we can begin to learn how to live together toward and into the oneness purposed for us. Belonging to Christ, we belong also to one another (Rom. 12.5); therefore, any understanding of conscience that assumes we need only a 'personal relationship' with God and do not need to listen to the wisdom of our neighbors, including the wisdom of our brothers and sisters in Christ, must be wrong.[44]

Holding Court with God

Human beings are created to share in God's judgments. We might even say that God saves us just *for* judgment. When Paul says 'the saints judge the world' (1 Cor. 6.2) he has in mind, I think, both Psalm 8, which, as I have already argued, points to our God-given

---

[41] Bonhoeffer, *Ethics*, p. 240.

[42] In Baker's (*Diagonal Advance*, p. 230) words: 'a rational being receives the grace of revelation as the constant completion of her own natural orders of loving and knowing'.

[43] Radner, *A Brutal Unity*, p. 380.

[44] See Chris E.W. Green, '"Not I, but Christ": Holiness, Conscience, and the (Im)Possiblity of Community', in Lee Roy Martin (ed.), *A Future for Holiness: Pentecostal Explorations* (Cleveland, TN: CPT Press, 2013), pp. 127-44.

responsibility to mediate the divine beauty to all creation, and Psalm 82, which describes our vocation as a share in God's royal court: 'God has taken his place in the divine council; in the midst of the gods he holds judgment' (Ps. 82.1).[45]

Coming to Judgment

I have, I hope, already made the case that God does not save us from interpretation, but for it and through it. 'To be human is to interpret; to experience the world is to interpret the world.'[46] The only question, then, is whether or not we interpret those experiences rightly. And that, in turn, depends entirely on our having good judgment and making good judgments.

In conversation with Oliver O'Donovan, who focuses on judgment as a political act,[47] Oliver Davies suggests that judgment is best understood as 'the way in which we self-position in life'.[48] He agrees with O'Donovan that judgment is a form of moral discernment, concerned with getting to the truth and 'dividing right from wrong … to resolve moral ambiguity and to make right and wrong in a given historical situation clear to our eyes'.[49] But Davies wants to argue that judgment is more than action: it is 'the form of our orientation to others in the world', undergirding 'the structure of our social relationships'.[50] 'Judgment', in this sense, names the spiritual/moral vision through which we interpret life in all of its complexity, drawing it into a meaningful – and if possible coherent (but never totalizing) – narrative. 'A meaningful human life is one that is shaped by judgment, making what we believe about the world and how we act in the world consistent and convergent.'[51]

1 Corinthians makes clear that Paul expected believers to make judgments. He tells them they are bound to judge one another – and bound *not* to judge outsiders (1 Cor. 5.9-13). In laying out his orders

---

[45] See 'Divine Council', in Walter Brueggemann, *Reverberations of Faith: A Theological Handbook of Old Testament Themes* (Louisville: WJKP, 2002), pp. 55-56.

[46] Smith, *Thinking in Tongues*, p. 137.

[47] See Oliver O'Donovan, *The Ways of Judgment* (Grand Rapids: Eerdmans, 2005), pp. 3-12.

[48] Oliver Davies, *Theology of Transformation: Faith, Freedom, and the Christian Act* (Oxford: OUP, 2013), pp. 177-78.

[49] O'Donovan, *The Ways of Judgment*, p. 7.

[50] Davies, *Theology of Transformation*, p. 178.

[51] Davies, *Theology of Transformation*, p. 178.

for worship and instructions for living faithfully in the 'everyday' world, he writes that he expects them to judge for themselves the truth of what he is saying (1 Cor. 10.15; 11.13). He even suggests that if the Corinthians had judged themselves rightly, discerning the Eucharistic/ecclesial body in faith, they would not have continued to fall under the corrective judgment of God (1 Cor. 11.31-32).

But these calls for the Corinthians to make judgments come only after Paul has told them how little he cares if or how they judge him (1 Cor. 4.3-5):

> [3]But with me it is a very small thing that I should be judged by you or by any human court. I do not even judge myself. [4]I am not aware of anything against myself, but I am not thereby acquitted. It is the Lord who judges me. [5]Therefore do not pronounce judgment before the time, before the Lord comes, who will bring to light the things now hidden in darkness and will disclose the purposes of the heart. Then each one will receive commendation from God.

We see, then, that Paul holds a distinction between the kind of judgments we can and must make here-and-now and the kind of judgment the Lord gives in the End. Our interpretations and judgments are penultimate and so provisional. God's judgment in Christ's final appearing is ultimate and final.

What are we to learn from Paul's distinction? First, it means that we can and must in this life develop good judgment, learning to interpret our experiences as faithfully as we can. After all, Jesus commands us to 'judge with good judgment' (Jn 7.24). And he would not command it if it were simply impossible.

Second, it means that until the Final Transformation, the believer's judgment remains itself under judgment, always incompletely renewed and imperfectly conformed to Christ's character. And that means we have to make provisional and penultimate judgments, holding our interpretations of Scripture, as well as our experiences of God and one another lightly, making room within our judgments for the judgments of our neighbors and enemies, as well as the judgment of God.[52] In other words, our judgments and interpretations are

---

[52] See, for example, Paul's instructions to the Roman Christians about eating meat that had been offered to idols (Romans 14-15).

trustworthy only if they remain tentative, open to critique, allowing for reasonable and charitable differences and inviting collaborative and corrective responses. Totalizing judgments, because they refuse to leave room for God, are necessarily false judgments, even when they are technically true.

Third, it suggests that we come into maturity in this life only by risking our penultimate and provisional judgments, which we offer in meekness and humility – and always for the sake and in the hope of the righting of all things in Christ so that God may be all in all. If we trust wrongly in our own judgments, we shall be only self-righteous. But if we refuse to make any judgments at all, out of fear of self-righteousness, then we will never participate with Christ in bringing about justice in his Father's world.

Perfecting Judgment

Iris Murdoch, in her terrific if sometimes puzzling *The Sovereignty of Good*, contends that the good life is more than choosing well or doing right. In fact, she holds that our character is shaped mostly by what happens between the choices.

> The moral life, on this view, is something that goes on continually, not something that is switched off in between the occurrence of explicit moral choices. What happens in between such choices is indeed what is crucial.[53]

Murdoch borrows from Simone Weil the notion of 'attention', and argues for the primacy of moral vision. She insists that we can only choose within the constructs of the 'world' we envision. How we see one another, ourselves, the world – that is what makes us who we are. Everyone is always, continuously, knowingly or not, attending to the world, constructing the 'structures of value' that order a way of being-in-the-world. 'The task of attention goes on all the time', so that even at 'apparently empty and everyday moments we are "looking", making those little peering efforts of imagination which have such important cumulative results'.[54] We are always 'looking', Murdoch insists, even if we are not 'attending'. The only question is whether or not we have the moral imagination to see what in fact is

---

[53] Murdoch, *The Sovereignty of Good*, p. 36.
[54] Murdoch, *The Sovereignty of Good*, p. 42.

there to be seen. 'The only thing which is of real importance is the ability to see [reality] clearly and respond to it justly ...'[55]

Murdoch, I believe, shows us how to re-imagine what it means to judge rightly. If we are to reign with Christ, then we must judge as he judges by seeing as he sees. But, we have to ask, how do we learn to see rightly so we can live justly? Murdoch is convinced that this kind of learning happens only with forceful, focused effort over long stretches of time. We influence our desires, and thereby our will, only through 'sustained attention to reality'. We are shaped for living justly only through long-term, intense moral struggle. 'Attention' – and *only* attention – 'is rewarded with knowledge of reality'.[56] We have to give everyone and everything, as well as every situation, our 'patient, loving regard' if we want to live a truly sanctified and not merely 'moral' life. Because God's holiness is graciously at work in us, we find we can painstakingly, longsufferingly, look to him at all times and look after our neighbors with graced attention that is as good for us as it is for them. Reality shows itself only to 'the patient eye of love'.[57]

This judgment has to show itself both in how we read Scripture for ourselves and how we read it for others. And so, Mary's Song (Lk 2.46-55) provides a necessary framework: We can rejoice rightly in God and in God's judgments only as we enter more and more completely into the lowliness of Mary and her Son. And our readings of Scripture can be true only if they help to bring about what it is that God truly desires for us – exalting the humble and satisfying the needy, while at the same time scattering the high-minded in confusion, exposing the pretensions and dissembling of the powerful, and leaving the rich with the emptiness of their gains and achievements.

And if there is anything that proves we lack this judgment it is the history of racism in the American Christian tradition – including the Pentecostal tradition.[58] For generations, we have handled the Scriptures and all of our churchly ministries so that the powerful are established and the wealthy enriched, while those already oppressed and abused are subjected to further humiliation and neglect. Now is the time to acknowledge that history, to own the corruptions at the

---

[55] Murdoch, *The Sovereignty of Good*, p. 85.
[56] Murdoch, *The Sovereignty of Good*, p. 87.
[57] Murdoch, *The Sovereignty of Good*, p. 39.
[58] Chris E.W. Green 'The Spirit That Makes Us (Number) One: Racism, Tongues, and the Evidences of Spirit Baptism', *Pneuma* 41.1 (2019), pp. 1-24.

heart of our ministries, and to open ourselves up to the judgment of God. That, and only that, can save us from the self-deception that makes what we imagine to be God's work into nothing more than vainglory and the cruelest violence.

5

THE BEGINNING OF HOLINESS

Introduction

As I have been arguing, we need to tell a different story about holiness and sanctification, a stranger and more beautiful story that moves us to live more faithfully and does justice to the complexities of human be-ing and the mystery of God. More than anything, we need to think of holiness not in relation to sin, primarily, but in relation to Christ. And that means we must reimagine the sanctified life not as a sinless life, but as a life lived for those harmed by sin. To be a saint is to be loved by God so deeply that we are caught up in spite of ourselves in his ways of caring for our neighbors. Only so can we honor the work of the Spirit in our history and the work of the father and mothers of our tradition.[1] What follows, then, in this chapter is an initial attempt at that kind of reimagining.

Unwanted Beauty, Imperfect Love

Scripture calls for us to worship God 'in the beauty of holiness' (1 Chron. 16.29; Ps. 29.2). But what does that mean? And how do we make sense of it? Given that for us 'Jesus is the first saint',[2] we begin by asking in what sense *Christ* is beautiful. And as soon as we start to think along these lines, we crash into the words of the prophet: '*he has no beauty* that we should desire him' (Isa. 53.2). What sense does

---

[1] See Castelo, 'A Holy Reception', pp. 231-34.

[2] Herbert McCabe (*God, Christ, and Us* [London: Continuum Books, 2003], p. 48). As McCabe explains, Jesus is obviously not the first saint in history, but is 'the first in the sense that all other saints have their godliness from him'.

it make to talk about the beauty of the one who has no beauty?

Of course, Christians do find Christ beautiful. As the mystics say, he is the all-beautiful one (Song 5.16), 'the one my soul loves' (Song 3.3-4), the 'desire of the nations' (Hag. 2.7), whose love 'satisfies the desires of every living thing' (Ps. 145.16). And our best theologians remind us that only there, in the disfigured body of the tortured Nazarene, can we begin to see beauty and goodness as it truly is, rather than as we merely imagine it.[3] Living as he lived and dying as he died, Jesus exposed our ugliness, and showed us how in so many ways we have confused evil for good and good for evil. But he did more than expose what is wrong. He also revealed the divine goodness that precedes and supersedes all evil, and the divine justice that will stop at nothing to put right all that has gone wrong in and around us. Seeing his beauty that shines out even through his disfigurement, we come aware of our own disfigurement and our own beauty, which is a gift of this God who desires us and is in no way put off by our ugliness.[4]

But our hearts are so deeply marked by the wrongs we have done and the wrongs that have been done to us that we often cannot see his loveliness in ourselves or in others, and we often do not feel drawn by desire for him. According to the Gospel of John, 'he came to his own and his own received him not' (Jn 1.10). And in some sense, now, no less than then, we refuse to receive him. At least, we find it hard to live the way he calls us to live, even while we say we love him.

Augustine teaches us that we fail to see the beauty of Christ because our loves are diseased. And he tells us to trust that as the Spirit enables us to open ourselves up to Christ in faith, and in him to the Father's love for us, our loves are being healed. Loving as he loves, we are beautified with his beauty. And that means we will live as he lived and suffer as he suffered – for the sake of those his Father loves.

Holiness as (In)Hospitality

Wesleyan theologian John Drury affirms the traditional Wesleyan claim that holiness is 'perfect love', but he maintains, correctly I believe, that by itself this claim bears no real theological weight.

---

[3] See Steven John Wright, *Dogmatic Aesthetics: A Theology of Beauty in Dialogue with Robert W. Jenson* (Minneapolis: Fortress Press, 2104), pp. 119-27.

[4] See Wright, *Dogmatic Aesthetics*, p. 121.

Somehow, the character of 'perfect love' must be shown. Drury suggests that a revelation of love's character requires a theological statement that conforms to the grammar of loving relationships as revealed in Christ, a statement that can be used to describe both divine and human relationships. That is, holiness must be defined in a way that makes sense of 'the logic of the command to be perfect *as* God is perfect'.[5] Given these assumptions, Drury says that a faithful description of holiness 'permits the subject, object, and verb of perfect love to be used consistently for both divine and human holiness'.[6]

The defining move in Drury's argument is his assertion that love is perfected in its object and not in its subject. Holiness, therefore, cannot be rightly understood as performance, intention, wholeness, or devotion, because all of these definitions assume that the lover and/or her loving must be perfect. But if holiness is understood as hospitality, then we see that 'holy living is not about *my* completeness or the completeness of *my love*, but rather the completeness of the *recipient* of my love'.[7] The mark of perfect love is the ineluctable desire to see to the good of the beloved. Love is perfected not in the one loving but in the one loved. The truly holy life, therefore, is one lived sanctifyingly – offered up, eucharistically, for the sake of the neighbor and the neighbor's world. This is exactly the love that we see in God's gospel-hospitality for us.

'To be holy according to the proclamation of Jesus is to be separated to God, and with God to be separated to the world.'[8] Loving Christ, and loved by him, we cannot help but come alongside those in need, doing what we can to bear their burdens for them, weeping with those who weep and at the same time rejoicing with those who rejoice, feeling their wounds as our own, even letting the consequences of their sins fall upon our heads. And we cannot stay near Christ and those he loves without suffering his fate for them. For his sake and theirs, we will be killed all day long. But precisely in those moments, we will be 'more than conquerors' – whether we realize it

---

[5] John L. Drury, 'Hospitality and the Grammar of Holiness', p. 8. Paper presented at 41st Annual Meeting of Wesleyan Theological Society (May 2-4, 2006), p. 1.

[6] Drury, 'Hospitality and the Grammar of Holiness', p. 1.

[7] Drury, 'Hospitality and the Grammar of Holiness', p. 8.

[8] Keen, *The Transgression of the Integrity of God*, p. 98.

or not (Rom. 8.36-37). It is this beauty, the beauty of holiness, that will save the world.[9]

Hospitality as Grace

Luke Bretherton also champions hospitality as the focal metaphor for holiness and sanctification. He gives attention to stories of hospitality in the OT and NT, but concentrates his reflections on Luke's stories of Jesus' table fellowship, especially the parable of the Great Banquet, and Jesus' provocative reconfiguration of Israel's 'purity boundaries'.[10] Bretherton argues that 'Jesus does not resolve the tension between hospitality and holiness present in the Old Testament', but radically re-works how the two imperatives relate to each other. In short, 'Jesus relates hospitality and holiness by inverting their relations: hospitality becomes the means of holiness'.

In Jesus' ethic, then, believers do not have to be 'set apart from or exclude pagans in order to maintain holiness'.[11] Instead, as believers are caught up in doing good to others in all of their impurity, God's holiness reveals itself. 'Instead of sin and impurity infecting him, it seems Jesus' purity and righteousness somehow "infects" the impure, sinners and the Gentiles.'[12] Pentecost assures us that the same purity, the same virtue, indwells our life together so that we are freed by the Spirit to engage others without fear of 'being assimilated to, colonized by, or having to withdraw' from the world.[13]

The Weight of Holiness

Drury and Bretherton rightly construe holiness as making room for the stranger, and creating the just conditions for living peacefully with our neighbors. But they only hint at what we might call the weight of holiness: its otherness, its glory.

---

[9] So Aidan Nichols (*Wisdom from Above: A Primer in the Theology of Father Sergei Bulgakov* [Leominster, UK: Gracewing Publishing, 2005], p.148) reminds us, '*Pace* Dostoevsky, who once famously (if, perhaps, ironically) declared that beauty would save the world, the beauty of holiness shown us by the Spirit [above all, in Mary] will save the world – save it not least from the false beauty that is alien to holiness and even antagonistic to it'.

[10] Luke Bretherton, *Holiness as Hospitality: Christian Witness Amid Moral Diversity* (Burlington, VT: Ashgate, 2010), p. 128.

[11] Bretherton, *Holiness as Hospitality*, p. 130.

[12] Bretherton, *Holiness as Hospitality*, p. 130.

[13] Bretherton, *Holiness as Hospitality*, p. 143.

Jean Luc Marion argues that the saint and the saint's holiness remain necessarily invisible to us. Holiness, he maintains, is by its nature inaccessible to all that is not of its own nature. But to say that holiness is invisible does not mean that it is ineffective. Holiness, unrecognizable as it may be in itself, nonetheless marks us, no less really because it is untraceable. The encounter with sanctity, however it comes, alters us inexorably: we find ourselves moved, impressed, marked. As holiness weighs on us, reordering our loves, reconstituting our desires, we begin to find ourselves at the mercy of compassion. We find we cannot not see – and see to – the needs of others. And as we are handed over in love to the care of our neighbor, we are being made available to the healing of the Spirit who cares for us as we are caring for others.

Returning, yet again, to the language of grace and nature, I want to say that grace perfects nature only by destroying all that has diseased it, by purging it from all that has rendered it unnatural.[14] Thus, in an effort to less misleadingly describe the ways of God's engagement with us, we have to insist that holiness entails judgment. God cannot forever endure sin and death, cannot finally leave us diseased with sin or enslaved to the powers. Therefore, God's holiness, even while bearing us and enduring the disorderdness of our world, must come as a consuming fire, an unconditional but all-conditioning presence that both promises – and, in a certain sense, even threatens – transfiguration. The divine ultimate Yes also necessarily entails a corresponding penultimate No, and the Spirit's welcome is always offered as an invitation to the joy that lies just on the far side of death.

Guests as Hosts, Enemies as Friends
Some perhaps fear that talk about hospitality as a form of judgment casts doubt on the very possibility of genuine openness to the stranger and the enemy. Such fear, however, arises from a basic misunderstanding. Judgment is not the denial of mercy but its perfection. Jesus is savior only as the coming judge and judgment of God, the enacting embodiment of the divine justice, the in-person-ness of the kingdom and its peaceful order. To call him 'savior' is to acknowledge him as the one who in his coming to us brings to bear the 'economy

---

[14] I am not sure we should buy Bonhoeffer's distinction in his *Ethics* between the creaturely and the natural, but I do think we can agree with him that 'the unnatural is the enemy of life' (p. 177).

of love' that 'aims always at the perfection and righting of relation'.[15] Even to brush up against the holy, then, is to be subjected, if only fleetingly, to the transcendence that puts our world graciously at hazard because it draws us into the authentic communion for which we are made.

In this way, we might say that holiness is (in)hospitable – hospitable and inhospitable both-at-once. We can see this (in)hospitality at work in Luke's story of Zacchaeus (Lk. 19.1-10). As the Gospel tells it, the wealthy chief tax collector seeks out Christ – 'he was trying to see who Jesus was' (Lk. 19.3) – but soon discovers that he is not so much the seeker as the sought and found. Jesus invites himself to be Zacchaeus' guest and Zacchaeus, suddenly, surprisingly cast in the strange role of invited host, happily receives him. The tax collector promises to make right his injustices just as he becomes Christ's host/guest, as the policies of God's economy triumph over and spoil the world as he has known it. Luke tells us that Jesus' acceptance of Zacchaeus drives 'all the people' to 'grumble' against him. They say, Jesus 'has gone to be the guest of a sinner' (19.7). Although of course they do not know what they are doing, by rejecting Jesus' acceptance of Zacchaeus, they bring themselves under judgment. But by entering into Jesus' (in)hospitality, Zacchaeus is freed to begin the long obedience of righting his injustices, the freedom to do God's will which is his right as a son of Abraham. Because he is forgiven, the past is not simply the past: it is open to him to make right his wrongs.

Later in Luke's Gospel (24.13-32), we come to another, similar story of (in)hospitality. Jesus, disguised, encounters a pair of disciples on the Emmaus road, and after a long, difficult conversation they invite him as a guest into their home, where he immediately assumes the role of host, blessing and breaking the bread.[16] Precisely in that instant, their eyes are opened so that they recognize him just as he 'disappear[s] from their sight' (Lk. 24.31), a disappearance that opens for them new horizons of awareness. Their shared encounter with Christ effected for them, as it had previously for Zacchaeus, the breaking down of accepted guest/host relations, and they too discovered in the disorderliness of that moment new imaginative and

---

[15] Graham Ward, *Christ and Culture* (Challenges in Contemporary Theology; Malden, MA: Blackwell, 2005), p. 82.

[16] See Arthur A. Just, *The Ongoing Feast: Table Fellowship and Eschatology at Emmaus* (Collegeville, MN: Liturgical Press, 1993), p. 261.

interpretive possibilities.[17] This, then, is the heart of St. Luke's testimony: 'through the stranger Jesus, God visits his people … [and] only when the stranger Jesus is received as a welcome guest, can God offer his salvation'.[18] If Jesus' (in)hospitality opened the past for Zacchaeus, it opened the future for these disciples, so that they could live again and with an unimaginable joy.

Baptized in the Spirit of Holiness

This Lukan theology of hospitality discloses so much of the character of Christ's holiness, and it also helps us to make faithful sense of Luke's theology of Spirit baptism. As Frank Macchia reminds us:

> In holiness, Jesus inaugurates the kingdom of God in power in solidarity with the sinner and the outcast. The righteousness of the kingdom is lived out in mercy and justice toward those who are broken and cast down. The spirit of holiness that raised Jesus from the dead also empowered him on his path toward the cross. The Spirit that Jesus pours out as the Spirit Baptizer makes us crucified with Christ living in newness of life in the power of the resurrection. It empowers us to bear one another's burdens and so to yearn and strive with all those who suffer for the liberty of God's grace.[19]

This is a question we do not ask ourselves often enough: What does it mean, really, to be baptized in the Spirit? It means we are empowered for living the life of Christ, a life of self-emptying intercession, a life of bearing others in their sin, suffering with and for them so they are borne along toward forgiveness, restoration, and

---

[17] According to Adelbert Denaux (*Studies in the Gospel of Luke: Structure, Language and Theology* [Münster: LIT Verlag, 2010], p. 102), '… in Luke's eyes, the relation between guest and host is not a unilateral one, as if hospitality only concerns what the host has to offer the guest'. For engagement with the themes of hospitality in Luke's Gospel, see especially Eugene LaVerdiere, *Dining in the Kingdom of God: The Origins of the Eucharist According to Luke* (Chicago: Liturgy Training Publications, 1994) and Brendan Byrne, *The Hospitality of God: A Reading of Luke's Gospel* (Collegeville, MN: St Benedict, 2000).

[18] Adelbert Denaux, 'Stranger on Earth and Divine Guest: Human and Divine Hospitality in the Gospel of Luke and the Book of Acts', in E. Van der Borght and P. van Geest (eds.), *Strangers and Pilgrims on Earth* (Leiden: Brill, 2012), p. 96.

[19] Macchia, *Baptized in the Spirit*, p. 143.

healing.[20] The fullness of the Spirit-baptized life is revealed in solidarity with the sinning and the sinned-against for whom Christ died and has been raised as saving Lord. Holiness does not so much make us sinless as it impels us to care for those who have been broken by sin.

According to John's Gospel, Jesus promised his apostles that a time was coming when they would pray to the Father in his name and that on that day he would not have to intercede for them (Jn 16.25-27):

> [25]The hour is coming when I will no longer speak to you in figures, but will tell you plainly of the Father. [26]On that day you will ask in my name. I do not say to you that I will ask the Father on your behalf; [27]for the Father himself loves you, because you have loved me and have believed that I came from God.

What are we to make of this promise? What would it mean for Jesus not to intercede for them/us? And how could that possibly be good news? The point, I think, is that we, like the apostles, have become so identified with Christ that we now share his identity-in-vocation, participating both in his intimacy with the Father and in his intercessory mission. He does not need to intercede for us in the same way because in the Spirit we have ourselves become one with his intercession. Praying what he prays, desiring what he desires, we are at-one-ed with him before the Father in the Spirit, co-operating with them in drawing others into that communion. 'Love has been perfected among us' so that 'as he is, so are we in this world' (1 Jn 4.17).[21] We are not merely his instruments. He does not use us, as we might use a tool. He is present with us and within us, so that we are truly his body, his presence. And he is truly our life.

Critics may worry that talk about theosis leads to confusing God and creature, but Jenson has it right, I think:

> God can be the creature's future, without absorbing the creature, in that God is not a monad: we can be brought into his life while

---

[20] For a critique of triumphalist readings of Luke-Acts, see Martin William Mittledstadt, *The Spirit and Suffering in Luke-Acts: Implications for Pentecostal Pneumatology* (JPTSup 26; London: T&T Clark, 2004).

[21] This is why we must affirm the departed saints' participation in Christ's ongoing intercession for us and for the world. If we do not, then we imply that conformity to Christ, sharing in his divine-human holiness, has a character other than hospitable, kenotic intercession.

becoming neither Father nor Son nor Spirit. God can himself be the purpose of his own act to create, without absorbing or abolishing his creation, in that God who is his own future is another person than God who has this future.[22]

Holiness as Transparency

'Sainthood is a matter of transparency.'[23] The saints live with an unrelenting openness to God, a constant readiness to be 'interrupted' by God. Most of us 'spend so much of our lives patrolling the borders, making sure no one breaks in on us, no one takes us unaware, no one robs us of ourselves'.[24] But the saints, freed by collaboration with the Spirit from 'restless distrust' and self-absorbed, self-protecting anxiety, live with a reckless openness, an unanxious readiness to lose their own lives in receiving God's. And in this availability to God, their lives shine with the light of God. Transparent, their lives bear witness to a reality that is not of their own making. And this divine-human beauty is visible not through but as their humanity.

Those who are marked by God's holiness embody a kind of 'hard-won consciousness' that allows the experiences of life to stream through them clearly, without 'getting slowed and clogged up in the drift waste of ego or stagnating in little inlets of despair, envy, rage'.[25] Unashamedly aware of their emptiness and brokenness, they live with no concern for self-protection. And their lives transfigure suffering into beauty, 'like a ramshackle house on some high, exposed hill, sings with the hard wind that is steadily destroying it'.[26]

Why does such transparency reflect God so wonderfully? Because God is transparent. If the saints' glory is for God to be visible in them, then God's glory is for the saints to be seen for who they are. Unlike the prince in the classic fairy tales, Christ does not disguise himself as a beggar. Instead, he identifies himself with the 'least of these' (Mt. 25.31-46) because he does not want to be known apart

---

[22] Robert W. Jenson, *Systematic Theology Vol. 2: The Works of God* (New York: OUP, 1999), p. 26.

[23] John Webster, *The Grace of Truth* (Farmington Hills, MI: Oil Lamp Books, 2011), p. 204.

[24] Webster, *The Grace of Truth*, p. 204.

[25] Wiman, *My Bright Abyss*, p. 150.

[26] Wiman, *My Bright Abyss*, p. 150.

from them. He would rather not be God at all than to be God without us.

Readers of the Fourth Gospel are introduced to Jesus as 'the Word' who was with God before all beginnings (Jn 1.1), the one who is so near the Father's heart (Jn 1.18) as to be himself God. This shows us that God, as Trinity, is essentially roomy.[27] And because God is roomy in the way that God is, 'God can indeed, if he chooses, accommodate other persons in his life without distorting that life …'[28] When Jesus promises to prepare a 'place' for his disciples 'that where I am, there you may be also' (Jn 14.3), readers immediately recognize – even if the disciples in the story do not – that the 'place' Jesus goes to prepare is nothing less or other than room fashioned within the Son's own eternal intimacy with the Father, the embrace he eternally has and is.[29] We know that he is promising his disciples – and of course with them, us – that they and we together are to be incorporated into his own intimacy with God. In the language of the Apocalypse, Jesus gives us, with them, a place with him on his throne (Rev. 3.21).

Jenson affirms that God is jealous, as well as roomy.[30] Indeed, jealousy is his name (Exod. 34.14). We have to move carefully here to avoid misunderstanding. God is not jealous of us, resenting our freedom and the ways we abuse it in betraying him. Instead, God is jealous for us, desiring above all things for us to know the fullness of joy intended for us in Christ. And the truth is, that joy can be ours only if we are at-one-ed with God in Christ, made partakers of his nature and partners in his mission.

Given that we are created in the image of *this* God, we cannot truly be happy until we are conformed to the image of Christ, God's fullness. And Jesus' death and resurrection make it plain: God is determined not only to draw us into that room prepared for us but also to make us roomy. Over time, as we by the Spirit avail ourselves to God's transfiguring presence, we become, like Jesus, roomier and roomier, more and more zealous to enfold others into the joy that embraces us. We find ourselves compelled, as Paul was, to open our lives wider and wider for the sake of others – so wide in the end as

---

[27] Jenson, *Systematic Theology Vol. 1*, p. 226.

[28] Jenson, *Systematic Theology Vol. 1*, p. 226.

[29] The same logic is apparent in the Christ hymn of Philippians 2.

[30] Jenson, *Systematic Theology Vol. 1*, p. 226.

to become 'all things to all people' (1 Cor. 9.22). At their most perverse, the holiness traditions have been fractious and schismatic. But where holiness is truly at work there is a hospitality, an unusual eagerness to make more and more room for unexpected guests.

Holiness as Endurance

And precisely because holiness is hospitable, it makes possible a way of living in time differently.[31] We might even go so far as to say that the saints are strange because they live at a different speed from the rest of us. They live 'in step with the Spirit', and just for that reason they are out of rhythm with what seems to us ordinary. In one sense, I suppose, this is just another way of saying that the saints are *patient*. But that is not quite the whole of it, because they are also the quickest to act when the time is right. The saints have a keener sensitivity to the moment than the rest of us do. They discern when to speak and when to be silent, when to laugh and when to mourn. They have become, in Hauerwas' phrase, 'friends of time', knowing what we forget: 'we have all the time we need in a world that doesn't think it's got much time at all'.[32] And because they have befriended time, they know how to be truly, fully present in the given moment with God and neighbor.[33] They know that Christ is 'the end of the way', and that to become like him 'requires time'.[34]

The Pentecostal practice of 'tarrying' in prayer witnesses to this relationship of holiness and time. As Daniel Castelo says, 'tarrying on the Lord' in agonizing prayer 'beckons eschatological time' to intersect and disrupt ordinary time, sensitizing us to the 'in-breaking presence of the Spirit' in the midst of the day-to-day.[35] In whatever form, prayer is 'the suspension of time' in 'waiting for the stirrings of God', a waiting that requires 'stepping out of the current of activities' that

---

[31] J. Alexander Sider, *To See History Doxologically: History and Holiness in John Howard Yoder's Ecclesiology* (Grand Rapids: Eerdmans, 2011), p. 209.

[32] Quoted in John Swinton, *Dementia: Living in the Memories of God* (London SCM Press, 2012), p. 252.

[33] See Williams, *Where God Happens*, p. 108.

[34] *LRE* 1.3 (Dec 1908), p. 11.

[35] Daniel Castelo, 'Tarrying on the Lord: Affections and Virtues in Pentecostal Perspective', *JPT* 13.1 (2004), pp. 31-56 (50).

we call 'the present'.[36] Praying, we are borne into a different kind of time altogether in which past, future, and present are, in a sense, liquefied by the Spirit like glass in the furnace.[37]

The patience required to pray is sustained, at least in part, by the theological conviction that time itself is God's mercy, a way God has made for us to know him.[38] If we are going to pray in faith and in hope, we have to be convinced that God can and does act timefully for us. We can commit ourselves into God's care only because we know that our 'times' are in God's hands (Ps. 31.5, 15). We are, in that patience, able to find the 'middle voice' of prayer in which we act and are acted upon.[39]

Ricoeur points out that because human be-ing is essentially temporal, it is necessarily narrated, and admits of different – and, sometimes, conflicting – interpretations. We understand ourselves 'in light of the possibilities that have been chosen in the past, are being contemplated at present and projected for the future',[40] and, therefore, we make sense of ourselves in the making and making sense of narratives. We are 'nourished by memory and hope' and therefore are bound to the crafting and interpretation of 'stories and histories that remind us and encourage us towards possibilities'.[41]

If, then, we hope to craft and interpret these stories and histories rightly, Ricoeur insists, we must: (a) bear faithful witness to the past; (b) 'make present those who are absent' by remembering those who are forgotten and paying attention to those others have ignored, learning to empathize with those who are strange to us, including those whom we have abandoned or oppressed; and (c) imagine a

---

[36] Michael K. Duffey, *Be Blessed in What You Do: The Unity of Christian Ethics and Spirituality* (New York: Paulist Press, 1988), p. 38.

[37] See Robert W. Jenson, 'The Holy Spirit', in Carl E. Braaten and Robert W. Jenson (eds.), *Christian Dogmatics Vol. 2* (Minneapolis: Fortress Press, 2011), pp. 101-82 (170-73).

[38] See Cheryl Bridges Johns, 'Yielding to the Spirit: A Pentecostal Understanding of Penitence', in Mark J. Boda and Gordon T. Smith (eds.), *Repentance in Christian Theology* (Collegeville, MN: Liturgical Press, 2006), pp. 287-306 (301-303).

[39] See Eugene Peterson, *The Contemplative Pastor: Returning to the Art of Spiritual Direction* (Grand Rapids: Eerdmans, 1993), pp. 103-104.

[40] Kevin J. Vanhoozer, *Biblical Narrative in the Philosophy of Paul Ricoeur: A Study in Hermeneutics and Theology* (Cambridge: Cambridge University Press, 1990), p. 276.

[41] Vanhoozer, *Biblical Narrative in the Philosophy of Paul Ricoeur*, p. 281.

future that is more just than what we have yet known.[42] In other words, our stories must show that the same God who has been with us from the beginning has promised to be with us until the end – and beyond it.

Ricoeur's model brings to light oft-unseen aspects of the relation of holiness and the saintly life to space-and-time. The saint's life moves at a different speed just because the saint narrates her life and the life of her neighbors differently. She bears faithful witness to the past, creates room in the present by her loving presence to 'the other', and imagines in hope a future where justice is at home. If Ricoeur is right to say we are 'prophets of our own futures' because 'we can imagine future possibilities',[43] then the saints are prophets in that they imagine not their own futures but ours. We might even say that the saints are holy just insofar as they free us to read our lives in hope for what God's salvation means for us, now and in the End. Their words spoken for us to God and to us from God open a future for us we could not imagine for ourselves, and in that way they create in us the character to enter that future filled with hope. Jesus reads Peter's future in just this way: he does not merely predict Peter's betrayal – 'the cock will not crow today before you have denied me three times' – but invokes the restoration that is to follow: 'I have prayed for you that your faith may not fail, and when you are converted, strengthen your brothers' (Lk. 22.32). This is what it means to prophesy: not so much to know beforehand what is to happen, but to speak of what has happened and is happening in ways that prepare hearers to meet what is coming in good faith.

Holiness as Transgression

The resurrection of the crucified one not only fulfilled the nature of the priestly vocation but also utterly transformed it. Israel's priests were known 'by virtue of their separation from others' – especially the dead. Under the Law 'God had been perceived as the source of all life and holiness precisely in his separation from death', so that

---

[42] See Richard Kearney, 'On the Hermeneutics of Evil', in David M. Kaplan, *Reading Ricoeur* (Albany, NY: State University of New York Press, 2008), pp. 47-88 [81]. See also Richard Kearney, *Poetics of Imagining: Modern to Post-Modern* (New York: Fordham University Press, 1988), pp. 241-55.

[43] Vanhoozer, *Biblical Narrative in the Philosophy of Paul Ricoeur*, p. 234.

Israel's 'purity regulations' were designed to create and maintain 'the maximum distance between the corpse and the Holy of Holies'.[44] The corpse, therefore, was 'the ultimately impure object, "the father of the fathers of impurity"', and the priest was bound to remain clear of the dead at all costs. No exceptions were allowed: 'the High Priest was not allowed to mourn even his closest relatives, follow behind their coffins or touch their corpses, lest he be unable to enter into the Holy of Holies on the day of Atonement'.[45] The logic is clear: the holy ones are kept holy by keeping themselves free from the dead.

According to Hebrews, Christ's priesthood transgresses this code of separation, unimaginably and irrevocably. In the cataclysmic newness of his resurrection as the crucified one, the Spirit effects an absolute reversal of this order. Jesus' priestly work takes place not in separation from the dead, but in utter solidarity with them – separating them from the powers of evil that had separated them from each other and from God. In fact, Christ is consecrated to his priesthood just by the entrance into suffering and death; 'he is ordained by immersion in the impure'.[46] As Heb. 13.11-12 says,

> For the bodies of those animals whose blood is brought into the sanctuary by the high priest as a sacrifice for sin are burned outside the camp. So Jesus also suffered outside the gate in order to sanctify the people.

What could this mean? Why compare Christ suffering for us 'outside the camp' to the burning of the discarded bodies of the already-sacrificed animals? Because only so can we grasp the irony that is at the heart of the good news: Levirate priests were defiled by contact with a corpse, but we are made holy by communion with the broken body and shed blood of Christ, a sacrifice offered in solidarity with us in our defilement and godforsakenness. In the giving of his body, Christ defiles defilement itself, negating the negation.

> For the author of Hebrews, the holiness of God revealed in the death of the Son of God is a holiness offered, ironically and paradoxically, through the profanity and defilement of a corpse. Now, that which sanctifies is precisely the dead corpse outside the camp.

---

[44] Radcliffe, 'Christ in Hebrews', p. 499.
[45] Radcliffe, 'Christ in Hebrews', p. 499.
[46] Radcliffe, 'Christ in Hebrews', p. 500.

Holiness as separation – of life and death, male and female, priest and lay, Jew and Gentile, purity and impurity – is displaced by *holiness as solidarity*: the solidarity of Jesus the great high priest in sharing human nature as flesh and blood and, above all, in accepting the defilement of death.[47]

Having made this outlandish claim about the sanctifying power of Jesus' defiled body, Hebrews immediately calls us to 'go to him outside the camp' (Heb. 13.13). Does Hebrews not also say that Christ, having offered the atoning sacrifice once for all, 'sat down at the right hand of God' (Heb. 10.12)? If so, then what sense does it make to say he can be found now 'outside the camp' with the other discarded, mutilated bodies? Because Christ remains, even now, immersed in the impurities of our world, identified with the defiled. Resurrected in glory, Christ remains nonetheless the crucified one.[48] Lord of the cosmos, he is nearest to the least and to the most unholy among us. Therefore, his bruised and bloodied body, which by the Spirit is present to us sacramentally, calls us into the presence of the holy God precisely for the sake of the unholy 'outsiders' he loves so relentlessly, so completely.

Against all our expectations, then, we find that the 'holy of holies' is found only 'outside' the boundaries drawn by our religions and moral systems. We 'enter the sanctuary' through the 'new and living way that he opened through the curtain (that is, through his flesh)' (Heb. 10.19-20) only by going to him 'outside the camp to bear the abuse he endured' (Heb. 13.13). Therefore, in our worship we focus our attention and gather our bodies around the proclamation in preaching and the Eucharist of Christ, the alienated and crucified one whose alienation is in fact his solidarity with us in our forsakenness.

For us the most holy object is the 'father of the fathers of impurity', a corpse. The focal point of our cultic space, that around which the community gathers, is not, as in the Temple, that which is farthest from death, but that which is closest, the cross.[49]

---

[47] Stephen C. Barton, *Holiness: Past and Present* (London: T&T Clark, 2003), p. 206.

[48] So Jürgen Moltmann, *The Crucified God* (Minneapolis: Fortress Press, 1993), p. 182, insists that Christ's resurrection '"does not evacuate the cross" (1 Cor. 1.17), but fills it with eschatology and saving significance'.

[49] Radcliffe, 'Christ in Hebrews', p. 499.

God's holiness breaks forth in the heart of defilement, so that the place of desecration becomes holy ground.[50] So now, we, like Christ, 'sanctify the world by going out'.[51] As the Lord's co-sanctified co-sanctifiers, we give ourselves in service to the broken and defiled. And that very giving becomes our sanctification, by grace.

Holiness as Strangeness

The saintly life is transparent, but that does not mean that it makes sense to us. Saints 'are not typically balanced, well-rounded people'.[52] They are not, as a rule, 'healthy'. In fact, they, like Jesus, are invariably strange – and often estranging:

> That is why we ourselves are knocked off balance when we en-counter a holy life: we reel in the presence of sanctity, just as we might reel before the strangely distorted lines of perspective in a Russian icon. The perspective of the saint's life seems skewed – but only because it is really *our* world that is bent out of shape. In the weirdness of the saint, we are glimpsing the geometry of an-other world'.[53]

This strange shape is the shape of Jesus' life, and because he is the light that enlightens everyone who comes into the world, many times it appears in the lives of people who have never heard his name or in the lives of people who reject the uses Christians have made of his name. In other words, although it is tragic that not all Christians are saints, we should be reassured by the fact that not all saints are Christians. As Jesus himself said, he has sheep that is not of our fold.

Hans Trüb, the Swiss psychotherapist, visited the dying Franz Rosenzweig, the author of a masterwork of modern Jewish philoso-phy, *The Star of Redemption*. Afterward, he wrote to a mutual friend, Martin Buber, about his encounter.

> In his room something in me was touched that I cannot name … That day is ever again present for me. I see Rosenzweig physically before me, walled in in his crippled body … Day after day he

---

[50] Radcliffe, 'Christ in Hebrews', pp. 500, 503.

[51] Radcliffe, 'Christ in Hebrews', p. 500.

[52] Ben Myers, *Christ the Stranger: The Theology of Rowan Williams* (London: T&T Clark, 2012), p. 77.

[53] Myers, *Christ the Stranger*, p. 77.

places himself in his suffering and gives us report of the imperishable life of the human person.[54]

Trüb acknowledges that Rosenzweig has been severely weakened by his illnesses, but he is startled to realize that somehow the suffering had not diminished Rosenzweig's humanity:

> I dwell with this dying man wholly from my heart. I recognize the unshakable fact of the progressive course of his illness and am deeply sad because of it. But in my whole depths I am shaken by the fact that with all of this the person himself remains undiminished, present in full value.[55]

He goes so far as to suggest that even death will not efface Rosenzweig's spirit:

> Will he from the moment when he closes his eyes, when he can no longer give any sign, be any less present than earlier when he could still walk and speak, or than now, when only a thin thread of possible communication joins him to us? I love Rosenzweig for the sake of his cross. He will continually work good in my life.[56]

Days after Rosenzweig died, Buber spoke about his friend's long bout with sickness: 'In those eight years Rosenzweig confirmed in the Face of God the truth he had seen. Lamed in his whole body, he fought for the truth through being true'. Years afterward, Buber was asked if Rosenzweig had been a saint, and he responded that the term was inappropriate, because it was 'too Christian'. But he quickly added, 'he was, I believe, a suffering servant of the Lord'.[57]

Those who let themselves be loved by God, who have, as Rosenzweig did, placed themselves in their suffering and in the suffering of others, are strange because they find themselves incapable of just playing by the rules, mindlessly submitting to the expectations and demands of the status quo. Submitted to the 'law of Christ' (1 Cor. 9.21), whether they call it by that name or not, their lives are by all worldly standards transgressive and disruptive. In defiance of the

---

[54] Quoted in Maurice Friedman, *Martin Buber's Life and Work* (Detroit: Wayne State Press, 1988), p. 90.

[55] Friedman, *Martin Buber's Life and Work*, p. 90.

[56] Friedman, *Martin Buber's Life and Work*, p. 90.

[57] Friedman, *Martin Buber's Life and Work*, p. 92.

principalities and powers that order and disorder life as we know it, they are, like Paul, 'free from everyone and everything' (1 Cor. 9.19) – a freedom that subverts in small and large ways the overblown claims of the powers-that-be. As a result, the truly sanctified life is lived mostly at odds with 'common sense'.

Or, to say the same thing another way, the holy life is a cruciform life, a life lived always under the sign of the cross. We are bound, by Christ's word, to carry our cross daily (Lk. 9.23), bearing both the otherness, the strangeness, of the God (the vertical beam) and the strangeness of our sisters and brothers outside and inside the church, and all the difficulties their strangeness cause for us and for them (the horizontal beam). Only as our lives are crowded by strangers and enemies and neighbors in need can we find the rest of Christ. This is true in a double sense: we find we can rest in him only as we welcome his fullness, which comes to us through those who are unlike us. We know him. But there is always more to be known. And we will receive this 'more' only as we receive those who have known him differently than we do. This is why it is 'essential to our humanity that there should always be foreigners, human beings from another community who have an alternative way ...'[58]

But hard as it may be for us to hear, Bonhoeffer is right: 'Only as a burden is the other really a brother or sister and not merely an object to be controlled'.[59] We are called, above all, to 'bear one another's burdens' (Gal. 6.2), for only in that bearing are we borne along by the Spirit. To quote Bonhoeffer again,

> ... the law of Christ is a law of forbearance. Forbearance means enduring and suffering. The other person is a burden to the Christian, in fact for the Christian most of all. The other person never becomes a burden at all for the pagans. They simply stay clear of every burden the other person may create for them. However, Christians must bear the burden of one another ... the community of the body of Christ that is here realized, the community of the cross in which one must experience the burden of the other.

---

[58] Oliver O'Donovan, *Desire of the Nations: Rediscovering the Roots of Political Theology* (Cambridge: Cambridge University Press, 1996), p. 268.

[59] Bonhoeffer, *Life Together*, p. 100.

If one were not to experience this, it would not be a Christian community.[60]

It is only when we are burdens to one another that it becomes possible for us to bear one another's burdens. It is only when I feel the weight of your otherness, and you feel the weight of mine, that we are able truly to care for one another as we need to do.

Troubling 'God'

The saints are strangest and heaviest in how they speak to God and of God. Because they see more truly than we do, they recognize how easily God is confused with 'God' and how tragic this confusion inevitably turns out to be. The saints distrust nothing so much as conventional wisdom about God and the nature of the good life. Enlightened by God's wisdom, they see how the socio-economic, cultural, political, and religious structures that seem to give our lives meaning and purpose seek to impose their will on us through various regulations (e.g. matters of food and drink, dress, and holy days) that dictate the form of our conscience and so determine the shape of our day-to-day lives and the limits of our loves. As Paul says, these regulations have 'an appearance of wisdom': they even promote a kind of piety. But they are, in the final analysis, 'simply human commands and teachings' that prove worthless for true transformation into Christ (Col. 2.20-23). Again, morality is often at odds with holiness. And good people are the first to persecute others, almost always in the name of defending God's name and God's laws.

The saints see through the lies and false promises that hold up our worldly systems, however. Therefore, like Israel's prophets, they live among us as icons and iconoclasts, challenging the idols we have made for ourselves, calling us to revoke our false allegiances. Like Christ, they are always saying, in one way or another, 'You have heard it said, but I say …' (Mt. 5.38). Thanks to their intercession, and the pressure of the weight of holiness bearing down on us, we begin to find our own lives upset and reordered, set free from the oppression of forces we had not known even to resist.

Estranging Presence, Strangely Present

The fact that we can so easily lose sight of God and fall out of rhythm with the Spirit again points to the need for both ordered and

---

[60] Bonhoeffer, *Life Together*, pp. 100-101.

disordered worship. Worship has to be sanctified before it can be sanctifying. And, as I have already argued, it is the role of liturgy to bind us to faithful witness, ordering our bodies into a posture of sacred awareness of and openness to the Spirit. And it is the role of the prophetic to free us from those bonds when they keep us from living lovingly.

But we must not limit ourselves to talking only of the formative power of the liturgical forms or the prophetic critique. We have learned from our mothers and fathers in the faith that it is the encounter with the presence of God that truly transfigures us. Worship does not change us. The God we worship does.[61]

We talk often about our longing for the presence of God. But perhaps at times we forget that the God who is present to us is the holy one, which means his presence is always necessarily strange to us, never familiar. Or, to say the same thing another way, God is infinitely unique, not an object among other objects, or an agent in competition with other agents. This is why Scripture says his ways are not our ways (Isa. 55.8) and his love is 'beyond all we can ask or imagine' (Eph. 3.20). God is present to us, always. And in some sense, we are always experiencing it, although we only rarely if ever realize it. But the good news is his presence is our good, even if we do not yet know how to open ourselves to him.

Deeper Crucifixions

As people who take joy in the presence of God, we must never forget the danger of fixating on the experience of God's presence. Rowan Williams finds in the mature reflections of Teresa of Avila a warning against just this temptation. Over time, reflecting on her own experiences and those of her Carmelite sisters, Teresa became 'suspicious of interiority pursued for its own sake'.[62] She worried especially that 'the delight that is felt when God begins to be sensed by the soul' would hinder her and her sisters from true spiritual progress into union with God, which, she writes in *The Interior Castle*, 'does not lie in thinking much but in loving much'. Loving, for Teresa, has nothing

---

[61] Henry H. Knight III, 'Worship and Sanctification', *Wesleyan Theological Journal* 32.2 (1997), pp. 5-14 (12).

[62] Rowan Williams, *Teresa of Avila* (London: Continuum Books, 2003), p. 141.

to do with 'the inner sensation of delight in God' but with the 'concrete task of good community life – obedience and service'.[63]

To be sure, Teresa knew very well the sweetness of the experience of God's presence. But she also realized that the reluctance to leave the enjoyment of that sweetness betrayed a tare-like 'self-indulgence' that had grown up with the wheat of genuine devotion. Therefore, as Williams explains, she came to believe that the goal of the prayerful life is 'to find delight in the will of God – not, that is, in the sensed presence of God but in doing gladly what God (and especially God in Jesus Christ) does'.[64]

In the light of Teresa's teaching, we can see that the true goal of the prayerful life is to become like Jesus on the cross, where he is 'left without any perceptible consolation or sense of support from the Father'.[65] Jesus, as he is dying, finds that the Father 'has ceased to be in any way a graspable other' for him. Nevertheless, it is precisely in this 'emptying out of the sense of the Father as the term of any kind of gratification' that Jesus accomplishes 'total reconciliation of humanity with God'. It would seem, therefore, that when we pray we may rest in the confidence that 'the negation of all determinate consolation'[66] leaves us at-one-ed with the will and activity of God in and through and around us.

J.H. King, one of the most gifted theologians in the early Pentecostal movement, argued along strikingly similar lines. Via a typological reading of the story of Abraham and his firstborn sons, King suggested that the casting out of Ishmael typified 'purification', while the sacrifice of Isaac represented 'consecration'.[67] Framed in this way, King concluded that the truly consecrated life would receive the 'richest blessings and the deepest experiences' in God only by way of the most intense 'crucifixions'.[68]

We shall be crucified in our emotional nature, largely. There are times when God plays upon the emotions and it is delightful, for

---

[63] Williams, *Teresa of Avila*, p. 140.

[64] Williams, *Teresa of Avila*, p. 140.

[65] Rowan Williams, 'The Deflections of Desire: Negative Theology in Trinitarian Discourse', in Oliver Davies and Denys Turner (eds.), *Silence and the Word: Negative Theology and Incarnation* (Cambridge: Cambridge University Press, 2002), p. 121.

[66] Williams, *Teresa of Avila*, p. 140.

[67] J.H. King, 'Abraham Rejoiced to See My Day', *LRE* (Sept. 1910), pp. 11-12.

[68] King, 'Abraham Rejoiced to See My Day', p. 12.

whatever God does is delightful, and we shall be lifted into the ecstasies of joy, into the peace of heaven, and we feel this is essential to our living acceptably before God and overcoming Satan in all his attacks upon us, but we shall come to the point where God will lead us away from these ecstasies, where He will wholly crucify them, and we shall not be depending upon them as an evidence of salvation or acceptance with God, and as a result we shall sink deeper into Him, become more sober in our minds and spirits and thus hideaway in God where the deepest things may be revealed to us. This is a great deprivation to many individuals, but it is God's way to the deepest peace that He has to impart.[69]

Like Teresa, King desired more than anything complete conformity to God's nature and character. Teresa speaks for King as well as herself when she says to her sisters that she wants them to know union with the will and act of God: 'this is the union that I desire and would want for all of you, and not some absorptions, however delightful they may be'.[70]

To be sure, these warnings should not deter us from pursuing God, or squelch our desire for the 'things of God'. But they should remind us that what we need most is not merely to be with God but to become like God. Having acknowledged his yearning 'to depart and be with Christ' (Phil. 1.23), Paul insists that what he wants above all is 'to know Christ and the power of his resurrection and the sharing of his sufferings by becoming like him in his death', so that through them he might 'attain the resurrection from the dead' (Phil. 3.10-11). What Paul wants, deepest down, is not merely to be in God's presence but to be made to share in God's nature and character. He wants, whatever the cost, to be conformed to Christ. He wants to be sanctified. We were made for holiness, for living with God's own relationality; therefore, nothing less or other can satisfy.

Holiness as Intercession

We must not think that the strangeness of the saint is an abandonment of the world. The saint is nothing if not in love with the world, just as God is (Jn 3.16). In fact, true holiness shows itself as essentially

---

[69] King, 'Abraham Rejoiced to See My Day', p. 12.
[70] Quoted in Williams, *Teresa of Avila*, p. 141.

paracletic. The Spirit Jesus sends is the Paraclete: that is, the one who comes alongside. Hence, those who are filled with this Spirit are moved to come alongside their neighbors in unrelenting compassion and unstinting care. 'The saint doesn't stand at a distance from ordinary human experience but is more deeply involved in it, since the saint stands closer to the source of what it means to be a full human being.'[71] Therefore, holiness, under the conditions of this world in its fallenness, reveals itself always best in intercession, in our self-denying participation with others in their sins and in their repentance, in their joys and in their sorrows, in their life and in their death.

We are, I suspect, always underselling the responsibility gifted to us in our co-operation with Christ's intercession. We have a responsibility, in and with Christ, to intercede for those who have been sinned against, as well as for those who are sinning: 'If you see your brother or sister committing what is not a mortal sin, you will ask, and God will give life to such a one' (1 Jn 5.16). Above all, we have a responsibility to intercede for those whose hearts are condemned, for those who labor under the unbearable burden of a distorted sense of who God is and what God expects from them. Bearing that call, we do all that we can to help one another put our hearts at rest, driving out the terrorizing fear of the unloving 'gods' Christ reveals as false.[72] At the heart of our vocation is the passion to say, 'No! God is *not* like that! God is like *this!*' – as we point to the crucifix.

Living such a paracletic, intercessory and forbearing life often strains us to and (seemingly, at times) even beyond our limits. Craig Keen is at least partially right: *agape* – the love we find in Jesus – opens wounds more than heals them, and tears down whatever walls we have erected for our security.[73] Compelled by this love, we find ourselves emptied, opened up astonishingly and agonizingly to our neighbors and enemies. We have to say, therefore, that holiness, as the perfection of love, is

> ... an openness that prevails even when one can no longer cope with the chaos of another day, cannot say how the events of one's life are steps on a journey. *Agape* is perfection, holiness, because it

---

[71] Myers, *Christ the Stranger*, p. 75.
[72] Cf. 1 Jn 3.19-21 and 4.18.
[73] Keen, *The Transgression of the Integrity of God*, p. 152.

is a kind of ek-stasis that unravels every communitarian fabric, every story, every virtue, every habit.[74]

Theotic sanctification, in other words, carries us out, ecstatically and eccentrically, past whatever goodness we might want for ourselves or achieve by our own efforts. Or, to put it the other way, holiness comes to us as transformative grace, which is always more than we naturally can handle. The truly holy life is a life so radically devoted to others in God, so kenotic in its love for God and neighbor, that it runs the risk of not being a recognizable life at all. When Jesus said that we would have to die to live, perhaps this is what he meant?

The character and aim of Christ's intercession is revealed paradigmatically in his life and death, witnessed to us by the Gospels. But because Christ is never known apart from his saints, we also see it in the lives of God's people – in Abraham interceding for Lot and Sodom, Stephen praying for his torturers, and Paul convincing Philemon to welcome Onesimus home. In other stories, such as Balaam's and Jonah's, we see it by virtue of its opposite. But no story narrates the truth more forcefully for me than that of Moses' and Aaron's intercession in Numbers 16.

Envious of Moses' appointment of Aaron and his sons to the priesthood, and disillusioned by his failure to lead Israel into the land 'flowing with milk and honey' as promised, four of Israel's elders – Korah, Dathan, Abiram, and On – gather two-hundred and fifty others from among Israel's leaders to confront Moses. Their accusations against him are rooted in a truth of Israel's call – 'All the congregation is holy, every one of them, and the Lord is among them' (16.3) – but their purposes are anything but good. Moses falls on his face in prayer, invoking the Lord to judge between him and his accusers. The

---

[74] Keen, *The Transgression of the Integrity of God*, p. 152. In my judgment, Keen's disagreement with Hauerwas' doctrine of holiness runs the risk of reducing the work of *agape* to self-denial, even self-negation. But in truth, the love the Spirit is and gives is kenotic just in the sense that it moves us to give ourselves ecstatically, delightedly. To be sanctified, then, is to be moved to give ourselves to others in the ways God gave and gives himself to us. We are called not merely to die to ourselves, but to live lovingly with and for others as we have been loved by the Father who shares his life with us. Put bluntly, God's love does not only always unmake us and our world; it also always works to remake us, drawing us into the beauty from which we came and for which we are made. Nonetheless, Keen rightly reminds us that we come to share in that remaking only as we give ourselves over to the unmaking.

next day, at the moment of truth, the earth is rent apart to devour the rebels with all their households, and fire rages out from the sacred tent to consume the two-hundred and fifty elders standing with them. Moses' authority and Aaron's holiness, his set-apart-ness for the priesthood, are decisively confirmed.

If we stopped reading at this point, it would seem that 'holiness' has to do entirely with chosenness, with the set-apart-ness of the righteous. But the story continues, subverting the very conclusions it seems to have given us. On the next day, the text says, 'the whole congregation of the Israelites rebelled against Moses and against Aaron' (Num. 16.41). Stunningly, the sudden, cataclysmic destruction of the rebels, far from provoking repentance, has only inflamed the insurrection smoldering in the hearts of the people. In response to this latest rebellion, God commands Moses and Aaron to stand apart from the people 'so I can consume them in a moment' (16.44). Instead, the prophet and the priest fall on their faces in intercession, and Moses, flatly ignoring the divine command, directs Aaron to run, armed with fire taken from the altar, into the midst of the congregation 'where the plague had already begun among the people' (16.46). Aaron takes his stand 'between the living and the dead, and the plague was stopped' (16.48). He stands with Moses against God's judgment for the salvation of the judged, and in that way they together embody God's righteousness, prefiguring the prophetic and priestly ministries of Christ, the just and justifying judge. As they together intercede for those dying under the judgment of God, the true splendor of holiness breaks forth, providing a glimpse of the true character of the thrice-holy God.

As with Moses and Aaron, so with us: the divine-human holiness God is and gives to us reveals itself to and through us only in our intercession for others. Sanctification moves us always deeper in, more toward the center of the church-community, and so into the heart of the world. Therefore, we take up our prophetic and priestly task not by withdrawing from the world, but by running into its midst, standing with all of those 'children of wrath' who in their estrangement seem to stand condemned under the judgment of God (Eph. 2.3). We are so bold because we know we are sinners too, and that God's judgment falls on them as it falls on us – as grace. We know that they are loved, inescapably, and that we are called to be the form that God's love takes for them, here and now, as they, with us, are drawn together toward that sanctifying life for which all of us are made and in which we find at last our truest joy.

PART THREE

SCRIPTURE

6

READING FOR CHRIST: INTERPRETATION AND (TRANS)FORMATION

Introduction

I have tried to make the case (in Part One) that we are called to share in Christ's vocation, joining him in bringing to bear God's holiness for the good of all creation, and (in Part Two) that we cannot live out our vocation unless and until we dramatically reimagine the character of holiness and the sanctified life, seeing our set-apart-ness not as an end in itself, but as a call to live together with Christ in his radical openness to and intercession for our neighbors. Here (in Part Three), I want to explore how our readings of Scripture work to draw us into that holiness, transforming us for our vocation as Christ's co-sanctified co-sanctifiers.

Holy Scripture and Divine-Human Vocation

As a rule, evangelical theologies of the Scripture are made to fit within larger, encompassing accounts of divine revelation. In these models, claims about the Scriptures' nature and purpose, as well as the making and enacting of rules for interpretation, arise from and give expression to claims about how and why it is that God reveals Godself.[1]

---

[1] As John Webster (in paper presented at 2009 Annual Meeting of T.F. Torrance Society in Montreal) says,

> Most theological accounts of Scripture and its interpretation treat three topics: the economy of divine revelation, the nature of the biblical writings and their place within that economy, and the nature, acts and ends of interpreters ... questions about the nature and interpretation of Scripture are subordinate to

But what if we were to take a different approach? What if we began, not with a theory of divine revelation, but with an account of human vocation? What if, instead of asking 'How does God use the Scriptures in making God known?' we were to ask 'How does God use the Scripture in readying us to fulfill our calling?'[2]

Just to be clear, I of course do believe that God uses the biblical texts in the ongoing divine work of revelation. Scripture, faithfully received, gives us knowledge of God. But I am also convinced that Scripture has the deeper purpose of making us wise, for only in wisdom are we able to fulfill our vocation and enter fully into the salvation made known to us in the Scripture's witness to Christ.[3] In other words, Scripture, read with and in the Spirit, actually works to conform us to Christ, materializing his character in us, incorporating us into his identity. So we need not only to confess what Scripture is – 'inspired by God'; inerrant; infallible, or whatever – but also to let it do what it is meant to do: 'teach ... reprove ... correct ... and train [us] in righteousness, so that [all of us] who belong to God may be proficient, equipped for every good work' (2 Tim. 3.16). As Lewis Ayres, drawing on Henri de Lubac's account of Patristic and medieval exegesis, insists, 'the Scriptures are a providentially ordered resource for the shaping and reformation of the Christian's imagination and desire'.[4] Just as we are reformed by the Scripture's wisdom, we

---

questions about divine revelation; bibliology and hermeneutics are derivative from principles about the active, intelligible presence of the triune God to his rational creatures.

[2] The emphasis must fall on God's work for us in our reading, as J. Todd Billings says, 'The practice of interpreting Scripture [happens] in the context of the triune activity of God, the God who uses Scripture to reshape the church into Christ's image by the Spirit's power ...' (*The Word of God for the People of God: An Entryway to the Theological Interpretation of Scripture* [Grand Rapids: Eerdmans, 2010, p. xiii).

[3] Gregory L. Jones insists that 'developing habits of wise and faithful readings of Scripture ... will enable us to address issues of biblical method and biblical authority in more life-giving ways'. These habits 'will not preclude ongoing disagreements' but they will enable us to disagree gracefully – for our good and the good of others ('Formed and Transformed by Scripture: Character, Community, and Authority in Biblical Interpretation', in William P. Brown (ed.), *Character and Scripture: Moral Formation, Community, and Biblical Interpretation* [Grand Rapids: Eerdmans, 2002], pp. 18-33 [27]).

[4] Lewis Ayres, 'The Soul and the Reading of Scripture: a Note on Henri de Lubac', *Scottish Journal of Theology* 61.2 (2008), pp. 173-90 [189].

rediscover our 'mission and true end as *imago Dei* within the body of Christ'.[5]

We should be careful not to miss the point: the Scripture does not merely tell about salvation. By the Spirit's grace, the Scripture works salvation, renewing our vision of the world by transforming us at the depths of our being. So transformed, we begin to discover our place in the mission of God entrusted to the church, and to bring his goodness and justice to bear in the lives of our neighbors and enemies.

(Mis)Reading Scripture, (Mis)Apprehending God

Luke 10 tells the story of a lawyer who tests Jesus by asking what must be done to inherit life in the everlasting kingdom. Jesus responds by asking him to answer two interrelated questions: 'What do the Scriptures say and how do you read them' (Lk. 10.26)? I think that story has much to teach us about what it means to find Christ in the Scriptures and to share in his 'eternal life'. Like the lawyer, we come to Jesus (again and again, throughout our lives) with questions that are shaped in us by unrecognized pretensions and confused assumptions. As he did for the lawyer, Jesus graces us by directing us to the Scriptures, pressing us into the work of interpretation, which begins bit by bit somehow to lay bare the secrets of our heart.

Matthew 9 describes a similar encounter between Jesus and some troubled Pharisees. They see Jesus eating with tax collectors and sinners and are scandalized. As he does with the lawyer in Luke 10, Jesus directs them to the Scriptures. To save them from their foolishness, Jesus instructs them to 'Go and learn what this means, "I desire mercy, not sacrifice"' (Mt. 9.13). Later, he encounters (the same?) Pharisees again (Mt. 12.1-8), and he again directs their attention to some troubling scriptural texts (troubling for us, as well as for them):

> At that time Jesus went through the grainfields on the sabbath; his disciples were hungry, and they began to pluck heads of grain and to eat. [2]When the Pharisees saw it, they said to him, 'Look, your disciples are doing what is not lawful to do on the sabbath'. [3]He said to them, 'Have you not read what David did when he and his companions were hungry? [4]He entered the house of God and ate the bread of the Presence, which it was not lawful for him or his

---

[5] Ayres, 'The Soul and the Reading of Scripture', p. 189.

companions to eat, but only for the priests. [5]Or have you not read in the law that on the sabbath the priests in the temple break the sabbath and yet are guiltless? [6]I tell you, something greater than the temple is here. [7]But if you had known what this means, "I desire mercy and not sacrifice", you would not have condemned the guiltless. [8]For the Son of Man is lord of the sabbath'.

What should we learn from these stories? First, we should learn that our misapprehensions of God's purposes are bound up with and revealed in our misreadings of Scripture. The Pharisees cannot understand what Jesus is doing because they have misunderstood how to read Scripture as the people of God. Their misapprehension of the kind of community God's people are called to be also blinds them to the truth and perverts their readings of Scripture.

We also see in these stories that coming to know Jesus depends on coming to be like him, and that coming to be like him depends on grappling with the difficulties of Scripture. The effort required to search out the meaning of 'I desire mercy, not sacrifice' (and other such difficult texts) is the effort of ever-deepening repentance, the ascetical and deifying work of faith as its moved toward maturity by God-awakened love. In this sense, everything comes down to how we read the Scriptures. We can read them in ways that sustain and validate our self-righteousness, our wish-dreams of community, our pretensions to meaning and purpose. Or we can read them in ways that nurture our shared sanctification and bring about faithful witness to the triune holiness of God. As Bonhoeffer warns us, 'God hates … wishful dreaming', because it sets up a false ideal that makes living in authentic community impossible.[6]

Pentecostals and the Scriptures

As a rule, Pentecostals, at least those in the Classical traditions, have held and continue to hold to Evangelical models of Scripture. For much of our history, anyway, we have been concerned with establishing Scripture's divine origins and insisting that it provides a complete and errorless revelation of God and God's purposes. But, following Billy Abraham, I am convinced that these models work mischief on our imaginations and our habits, generating unnecessary

---

[6] Bonhoeffer, *Life Together*, p. 36.

problems that obscure Scripture's deepest purposes and distract us from the real work of interpretation. Abraham is right, I believe: we need to shift away from epistemological accounts to soteriological ones, developing models of inspiration and interpretation that emphasize the way God works in and through our readings of Scripture to form us into Christlikeness.[7]

It is not enough, therefore, simply to hold a 'high' view of Scripture. The question is not so much what we believe about the nature of the Scriptures, and not at all whether we read them or not. What matters is how we read. As I have said, we have to do more than confess what Scripture is – 'inspired by God'; inerrant; infallible, or whatever. We have to let it actually work on us. We have to let God use it to do to us what it is meant to do. Only as we are taught, reproved, and corrected are we trained for righteousness, drawn into sanctifying communion with God and given a share in Christ's work of mediating that holiness to the world (2 Tim. 3.16).

What would such a re-conceiving entail? Pentecostals, due in part to the work of my colleagues in the so-called 'Cleveland school', have developed and continue to develop new hermeneutical models.[8] I affirm what has already been worked out, and it will be obvious that I assume much of that work in the model I am trying to sketch here. As Cheryl Bridges Johns has recently remarked, however, we still have 'a way to go'.[9] She argues that over the last twenty years or so, many Pentecostals have found an escape from fundamentalism through post-foundationalist accounts of Scripture. But she holds that these accounts, for all their strengths, tend to leave us with 'centrifugal' readings of Scripture that 'pull the text inward', subsuming the biblical text into our own cultures so that 'the otherness of the text is entirely lost' and we find ourselves trapped in 'textual tribalism'. Reading Scripture in these ways, we hear only our own voices speaking back to us in self-determined cadence.[10] Hence, both

---

[7] Abraham, *The Bible*, pp. 36-46.

[8] For an introduction to some of the developments, see Chris E.W. Green, *Foretasting the Kingdom: Toward a Pentecostal Theology of the Lord's Supper* (Cleveland, TN: CPT Press, 2012), pp. 182-94. See also Lee Roy Martin (ed.), *Pentecostal Hermeneutics: A Reader* (Leiden: Brill, 2013).

[9] Cheryl Bridges Johns, 'Grieving, Brooding, and Transforming: The Spirit, the Bible, and Gender', *JPT* 23.2 (Fall 2014), pp. 141-53 (142).

[10] Johns, 'Grieving, Brooding, and Transforming', p. 143.

fundamentalism and post-foundationalism have effectively subverted the efficacy of the biblical texts, each in their own way. In her words,

> The Bible has become a book that speaks in 'cadences that sound strangely like our own'. It has become a text that describes our world and not one that has the power to disrupt, re-describe or reorient it.[11]

I believe Johns rightly sees that what we need is 'a new Bible, one that can speak to us as Holy Scripture and pull us outward in centripetal force into new worlds'.[12] In other words, we need deeper reflection emerging with and from (re)new(ed) and reimagined models of interpretive praxis that let Scripture be more fully God's Word to us, disrupting us gracefully, upending and overwhelming us for our good and the good of all. We need to 'unleash' the Scriptures again.

Re(dis)covering Early Pentecostal Hermeneutics

I believe a close, critical reading of early Pentecostal hermeneutics can stimulate our reflections on the significance of scriptural interpretation.[13] Two interpretive habits stand out: first, they came to the Scriptures expecting to encounter *Christ*; and, second, they came to the Scriptures expecting to *encounter* Christ. Arguably, this is most evident in their reading of the narrative portions of the OT and the Psalms, although of course the same instincts and habits show themselves in their readings of the NT, and perhaps especially the Gospels, Acts, Hebrews, and Revelation.

Seeking and Finding the (Pre)Figured Christ

Early Pentecostal readings of the OT were shaped to a large extent by the imitation, conscious or not, of the hermeneutics of the NT, as seen for example in 1 Corinthian 9-10 and Hebrews 4. And early Pentecostal readers, on the whole, were convinced that the OT Scriptures find their meaning and purpose in the making known of Jesus

---

[11] Johns, 'Grieving, Brooding, and Transforming', p. 144.

[12] Johns, 'Grieving, Brooding, and Transforming', p. 144.

[13] For a different, but not necessarily contradictory account of early Pentecostal hermeneutics, see Kenneth J. Archer, *A Pentecostal Hermeneutic: Spirit, Scripture, and Community* (Cleveland, TN: CPT Press, 2009). At the risk of oversimplification, I would say the difference is that Archer emphasizes the way early Pentecostals read for the development of doctrine while I am emphasizing the way they read for formation.

and his story, so that the OT speaks everywhere of and to Christ – exactly as the risen Lord himself demonstrated to his apostles before his ascension (Lk. 24.27, 44). As a result, they held that the whole of the OT, in all its diversity, as well as in each of its parts – down to and including the strangest, minutest detail – was believed to remain fully apt for the Spirit's work of speaking the gospel by testifying of Christ. G.F. Taylor asserts the point axiomatically: 'All the Bible points to Jesus on the cross. We may not be able to see Jesus in it all, but He is there just the same'.[14]

Another, unnamed contributor states it with a bit more force, 'everything in the Word from Genesis to Revelation speaks of Christ the Messiah – Jesus the Saviour (sic), the Sanctifier, the Baptizer (with the Holy Spirit), the Healer and coming Bridegroom and King'.[15] They agreed with the ancient dictum: 'The New Testament lies concealed in the Old, and the OT is revealed in the NT'.[16] And they shared with pre-critical readers a basic conviction:

> Jesus Christ brings about the unity of Scripture because he is the endpoint and fullness of Scripture. Everything in it is related to him. In the end he is its sole object. Consequently, he is, so to speak, its whole exegesis …'[17]

Reading for Christ took place most often through figural interpretation of the OT 'types and shadows' that in figure 'represent what NT believers are now receiving in reality'.[18] Early Pentecostal interpreters expected to find 'New Testament truth encouched (sic) in the Old Testament fact and figure', providing the best possible illustrations of the good news that makes plain the purposes of God.[19] In G.F. Taylor's words, 'all the types and shadows of the Mosaic Covenant' point to Jesus.[20]

---

[14] *PHA* 1.9 (June 28, 1917), p. 1.

[15] *WE* 197 (July 7, 1917), p. 2.

[16] *WE* (Dec 9, 1916), p. 13.

[17] Henri de Lubac, *Medieval Exegesis Vol. 1: The Four Senses of Scripture* (Grand Rapids, Eerdmans, 1998), p. 237.

[18] *AF* 1.9 (June-Sept 1907), p. 2. For other instances, see *TBM* 5.98 (Nov 15, 1911), p. 4; *Pentecostal Evangel* 366-67 (Nov 13, 1920), p. 1; *LRE* 11.10 (July 1919), p. 2.

[19] *WE* (Dec 9, 1916), p. 13.

[20] *PHA* 4.3 (May 17, 1920), p. 8.

In a series entitled 'Pictures of Pentecost in the Old Testament',[21] Alice Luce considers the figure of the tree growing by the well described in Gen. 49.22-24, taking the tree as 'a type of Christ, the Tree of Life' and the well as an image of 'the Holy Spirit who is the River of the Water of Life'.[22] In another place, Luce takes up the triplexed figure of grain, wine, and olive oil from Jer. 31.12, discerning that the wheat speaks of Christ 'by whom we are to live moment by moment, feeding on Him in our hearts by faith', while the wine typifies 'the manifestations of the Holy Spirit in joy, strength, and a superhuman exaltation, a lifting out of ourselves into the Spirit-life, which is contrasted with the false counterfeit exaltation of drunkenness', and the oil speaks to the church of the 'graces of the Spirit, of His guidance, His adjustment of the members and their respective ministries in the one body of Christ, and of His healing power'.[23] The story of Isaac and Rebekah,[24] the brass serpent,[25] the layout and furniture of the Tabernacle,[26] the ritual sacrifices,[27] the burning bush, the fiery furnace,[28] the bitter waters and the purifying tree,[29] the shepherd's comforting rod and staff (Psalm 23)[30] all in various ways prefigure Christ and the spoils of his cosmic victory.

Early Pentecostals shared the conviction that the OT and NT belonged together as one Word of God. And because they believed the Scriptures were God's Word, they understood that interpretation is impossible without divine illumination and guidance, and that the meaningfulness of Scripture is inexhaustible and irrepressibly manifold. This experience led some of them to delineate multiple 'senses' in the biblical texts (again, in ways similar to the claims of ancient and medieval interpreters). Alice Luce, for example, assumes that the OT Scripture has (at least) two different senses: a historical sense and a spiritual sense. And within the spiritual sense, readers might find a

---

[21] Later, these articles were published with the same title as a booklet by the Assemblies of God publishing house in Springfield, MO.

[22] *WE* 183 (Mar 31, 1917), p. 5.

[23] *WE* 206 (Sept 8, 1917), p. 4.

[24] *TBM* 16.240 (Oct 1922), p. 1.

[25] *LRE* 9.7 (Apr 1917), p. 21.

[26] *COGE* 5.5 (Jan 31, 1914), p. 6.

[27] *PT* 2.1 (Jan 1912), p. 8; *PHA* 3.38 (Jan 15, 1920), p. 4.

[28] *PHA* 1.28 (Nov 8, 1917), p. 7.

[29] *PHA* 3.34 (Dec 18, 1919), p. 2.

[30] *PHA* 4.37 (Jan 13, 1921), p. 3.

multitude of significations. So, as she reads it, the account of the river gushing from the rock (in Exod. 17.16) prefigures both the atonement and the Pentecostal experience of baptism in the Spirit.[31] This is so, she believes, because of the ways that God's works take shape within time. She observes that Scripture says that 'all these things happened to [wandering Israel] by way of example ...' (1 Cor. 10.11), which for her is proof that what God did anciently in and for Israel was even then intended for the purpose of God's work in the church and the world 'in later dispensations'. She also hears in the Isaianic promise of deserts-becoming-gardens two promises: one that will be 'literally fulfilled when the Lord Jesus sets up His throne on this earth' and another that is even now 'fulfilled in a spiritual sense in every individual believer who crowns His King and submits entirely to His sway'.[32]

The effort to discover the mystery of Christ in the figures of the OT required Pentecostal exegetes as it had ancient and medieval readers to read past the 'letter' to the 'spirit' of the text. The Scriptures can do what God means them to do only if 'the letter [is being brought to] life by ... a superabundance of the Spirit'.[33] Only the inspiring Spirit can 'open up' the Scriptures in ways that make a saving difference for the readers.[34] Only through the aid of the Spirit can the Scriptures 'unfold' their endless significances.[35] In the words of

---

[31] *WE* 185 (Apr 14, 1917), p. 2.

[32] She reads the promises of Zechariah 12 and Joel 2 in the same way:

All these promises will be literally fulfilled to the Jewish nation, restored to their own land, and converted by the vision of their once-crucified Messiah, returning in the clouds of heaven, with power and great glory'. She finds that 'Peter's quotation from Joel on the Day of Pentecost shows us that though the literal fulfillment of the promises is still future, yet they have a spiritual application to us in this dispensation of the Holy Ghost (*WE* 185 [Apr 14, 1917], p. 2).

[33] *WE* 172 (Jan 13, 1917), p. 3.

[34] *PHA* 5.39 (Jan 26, 1922), p. 13.

[35] *PHA* 4.10 (July 8, 1920), p. 9. At times, this conviction seems to have led to an interpretive overconfidence. For example, one contributor boasts that 'Men's opinions and theories fall to the ground under the brilliant blazing light of the Holy Ghost as He reveals Scripture', *COGE* (5.9 [Feb 28, 1914], p. 3). Now, as then, this hyper-confidence is a manifestation of a peculiar kind of revivalist subjectivism. Andrew Davies describes the confidence some Pentecostals have in reading Scripture as subjectively rooted:

Elizabeth Sexton, the coming-in-power of the Spirit lifts the 'veil' that obscures the readers' vision so that the sanctifying 'types and symbols and figures' in the text are revealed.[36] In some ways, the more difficult it proved to be to find Christ in a particular passage, the better. As D. Wesley Myland put it, the 'paradoxes' and 'seeming contradictions' in the biblical text provide 'the greatest illumination of truth' once they are put in 'right relations' and seen from 'the right angle'.[37] And citing the church fathers, William Schell contended that divine inspiration has deliberately obscured some truths in Scripture in order 'to prevent the carnal-minded man from illegally obtaining a correct understanding of the holy Scriptures'.[38]

Reading-as-Hearing: the Voice of the Scriptural Christ

At its best, I have argued, early Pentecostal hermeneutics were concerned not only with reading for Christ, but with encountering Christ in and through their reading. But what does that mean? And is it something we can and should imitate?

In an early essay, Jamie Smith argues that the earliest Christians were not so much 'people of the Book' as 'people of the Spirit', concerned less with the scriptural texts and more with the living Word. Their communities gathered not around scribes but prophets, and they emphasized 'hearing' rather than 'reading'.[39] Smith insists that contemporary   Pentecostal/charismatic   spirituality   is   similarly

---

the ultimate guarantor is the internal one, which, simple though it is, cannot be faked or fabricated – our own sense of conviction as to the significance of the text for ourselves ... In other words, what makes any reading of the biblical text a 'correct' reading is simply that it has meaning to me ('Reading in the Spirit: Some Brief Observations on Pentecostal Interpretation and the Ethical Difficulties of the Old Testament', *Journal of Belief and Values* 30.3 [Dec 2009], pp. 303-11 [309]).

This approach to the Scriptures becomes especially troublesome, I believe, when it loses touch with the *regula fidei* and the history of interpretation.

[36] *TBM* 3.51 (Dec. 1 1909), p. 1. Also, some considered the 'exposition and application of Scripture under the power of the Holy Ghost' a particular form of prophesy. See for example *PHA* 5.3 (May 19, 1921), p. 8.

[37] See *LRE* 4.8 (May 1912), p. 14.

[38] William G. Schell, *The Ordinances of the New Testament* (Guthrie, OK: Faith Publishing House, 1902), pp. 5-6.

[39] James K.A. Smith, 'The Closing of the Book: Pentecostals, Evangelicals, and the Sacred Writings', *JPT* 11 (1997), pp. 49-71 [49-50].

oral/aural and similarly committed to the role of prophecy alongside the interpretation of biblical texts.[40]

Smith arguably overplays the difference between reading and hearing, basically turning the evangelical model inside out. But, drawing on John Behr's account of pre-Nicene Christianity,[41] we can perhaps develop a similar, but more nuanced account. We can, I think, construct an authentically Pentecostal hermeneutics and theology of Scripture that holds together in the tightest interplay the Spirit's work in prophecy and scriptural interpretation. In other words, instead of privileging reading over hearing or holding reading and hearing in 'balance', we can integrate them, so that reading becomes hearing. Because Scripture is the Spirit-enlivened witness to the living Word; because there exists a 'vital connection' between Christ, the Eternal Word, and the Scriptures as 'written Word';[42] because the missions of the co-equal Word and the Spirit are perfectly intermutually determined; we can expect that faithful readings bring us effectively into the presence of the living Word in the life-giving Spirit.

The Anglican theologian Ephraim Radner shows us a way forward. Engaging the work of an obscure 18th century Jesuit theologian, Jacques-Joseph Duguet, Radner argues that 'the way we read Scripture is itself the form of our life'.[43] Because of the power of the biblical texts to 'order the passions of the human soul into a receptive openness to God's own character', Radner holds 'Scripture is designed to change us into God's image, given in Christ'; therefore, 'reading the Bible a certain way changes the heart'.[44]

But what is this certain way of reading, this 'consistently conversionary task', that changes the heart? Radner argues that it is 'figural reading': the searching of the biblical texts for hidden figures of Christ.[45] He gives an example:

---

[40] For a remarkably similar account although constructed in different terms, see Rick D. Moore, 'Canon and Charisma in the Book of Deuteronomy' *JPT* 1 (1992), pp. 75-92.

[41] Behr, *Formation of Christian Theology Vol. 1*, pp. 11-16.

[42] *LRE* (Apr 1910), p. 7.

[43] Ephraim Radner, *Hope Among the Fragments: The Broken Church and Its Engagement with Scripture* (Grand Rapids: Brazos, 2004), p. 95.

[44] Radner, *Hope Among the Fragments*, p. 95.

[45] So Paul J. Griffiths, *Song of Songs* (BTC; Grand Rapids: Brazos Press, 2011), pp. lvii–lviii.

When in Leviticus 12, for instance, we hear of the laws governing the purification of women after childbirth, we are invited into a search for Christ amid the details of birth, blood, and sacrifice, whose traverse must inform the depths of our souls ... Creation, fallenness, incarnation, humiliation, sacrifice, and finally divine love are all found to be bristling within these legal verses, disengaged only with the most patient and hopeful care.[46]

In ways remarkably similar to early Pentecostals, Radner envisions the biblical texts as a kind of labyrinth: readers trace along their way through the 'figural pathways of a biblical text' by following the 'scarlet cord'[47] that winds like Ariadne's thread through the maze. In a real sense, the tracing is what makes scriptural interpretation a transfiguring event.[48] Finding Christ figured in such texts, Radner argues, believers encounter the risen Christ himself. Reading faithfully, they undergo 'exposure to the divine presence, literally, through the instrumentality of an ordered text'.[49]

He is right, I believe, in arguing for the absolute bound-togetherness of 'divine presence' and 'ordered text', and in advocating a return to a kind of hermeneutics that seeks to hear Christ's word in Scripture. Understood in this way, the canonical Scriptures are recognized as made by the Father for us the word of the living Word, so that our reading avails us to the Spirit's transfiguring work. In the words of Steve Land, 'as the Spirit formed Christ in Mary, so the Spirit uses Scripture to form Christ in believers'.[50] Reading Scripture prayerfully, we trust that God draws near to us to do in us what only God can do.

He trains our judgment. He schools our understanding. He disciplines our inner spirit. He opens the eyes of our hearts (Eph. 1.18). He teaches us what to pray for, and how to pray, and – even more – how to pray persistently.[51]

---

[46] Radner, *Hope Among the Fragments*, p. 97.

[47] Radner, *Hope Among the Fragments*, p. 92.

[48] Radner, *Hope Among the Fragments*, p. 108.

[49] Radner, *Hope Among the Fragments*, p. 96.

[50] Land, *Pentecostal Spirituality*, p. 100. See also, Green, *Foretasting the Kingdom*, pp. 184-88.

[51] *LRE* (Nov 1912), p. 12.

The Gospel of John says that Jesus is 'the true light, which enlightens everyone' (Jn 1.9). And that means every character in Scripture bears his likeness, just as we do. To read Scripture for Christ, then, is to look for that likeness, to seek out the distinctive pattern of his life wherever it appears, including, of course, the stories in Israel's Scriptures. We see that pattern in the days of creation, for example, in the movement of light and darkness, the heavens opened wide for us, the seed that dies and springs to life, the beast that covers and feeds us, the ground from which we are made, the rest of God. We see it, too, in Adam, sweating drops of blood, making blessed bread from cursed soil. And in Eve, bringing forth her children in unimaginable pain. We see the pattern not only in Abel's blood darkening the ground, but also in Cain's banishment from the Presence. We see it in Moses and Aaron, of course, but also in their sister, Miriam, whose song frees the captives and draws even the oppressor into her dance. We see it even in the Red Sea itself, its body rent for the sake of deliverance, its depths drowning all that once enslaved. We see it not only in Rachel, the altogether desirable one, but also in her sister, Leah, who has no beauty that we should desire him.

More often, we see this image reversed. We see him doing the opposite of what others said and did. So, for example, we see he is the better Jephthah, offering himself instead of another not in bargain to God but in love for his enemies. We see he is the better Levite, longing for the one he loves and has lost, his body broken and given out to all as a sign of his devotion to her. We see he is the better Abraham, becoming the one just man in Sodom so that the city is spared. We see he is the better Idit, Lot's wife,[52] who does not seek to escape the judgment of God, but turns back to die with her children.

Christ is figured not only in these OT characters and their stories, but also in the laws and in the Psalms, in the voices of the Psalmists. What Bonhoeffer says of the Psalter as a whole is true of each particular Psalm, as well:

> It is the incarnate Son of God, who has borne all human weakness in his own flesh, who here pours out the heart of all humanity before God, and who stands in our place and prays for us. He has

---

[52] The name of Lot's wife is not stated in Scripture, but the rabbis referred to her as "Idit" (*Tanḥuma Vayera* 8).

known torment and pain, guilt and death more deeply than we have. Therefore it is the prayer of the human nature assumed by Christ that comes before God here. It is really our prayer. But since the Son of God knows us better than we know ourselves, and was truly human for our sake, it is also really the Son's prayer. It can become our prayer only because it was his prayer.[53]

This holds true even for Psalm 88, the only lament that does not at some point turn toward repentance or praise. Indeed, as Brueggemann reads it, it is a confession of the loss of faith. 'Nothing works. Nothing is changed. Nothing is resolved. All things deny life. And worst of all is the "shunning"'.[54] How can this be the voice of Jesus? Because it witnesses uniquely to his agonies, profiling him for us as the one most acquainted with grief.

Jesus' 'hour' of suffering carries him from the garden to the cross and into the grave. And Psalm 88 voices not only his cries in Gethsemane but also his wail from the Calvary and his silence in Joseph's tomb. In the garden, he, like the psalmist, stretched his hands out unavailingly to God. On the cross, he offered up the psalmist's complaint in his own words: 'Why do you hide your face from me?' (88.14). Afterward, he is buried hastily in a borrowed grave. In fulfillment of his mission, he is 'numbered among those who sink into oblivion' (88.4). And in spite of what our teachings sometimes suggest, he was in every sense truly dead – 'finished' (88.15). The Psalmist knew only to fear being 'left alone among the dead' (88.5). But Jesus does not leave the dead alone: he dies in order to be dead with the dead, so they are never alone. Reading this Psalm that way, we can see God has made room for our sufferings inside his own, and therefore we can reimagine the Spirit-filled life not as a life lived apart from sorrow, but a life in which joy and sorrow are held together, a life lived in the presence of God and in the presence of those who are godforsaken.[55]

---

[53] Dietrich Bonhoeffer, *Life Together and Prayerbook of the Bible* (DBW 5; Minneapolis: Fortress Press, 2004), pp. 159-60.

[54] Walter Brueggemann, *A Theological Commentary on the Psalms* (Minneapolis: Augsburg Fortress Press, 1994), p. 78.

[55] See Chris E.W. Green, 'I Am Finished: Christological Reading(s) and Pentecostal Performance(s) of Psalm 88', *Pneuma* 40.1-2 (2018), pp. 150-66.

The shape of Jesus' life is given in the laws, stories, and prayers of the OT, but also, and especially, in the lives of the prophets and apostles. The life of the apostle Paul, for example, was, in the words of the early Pentecostal pastor and teacher William H. Piper, a life of 'protracted martyrdom'. And just so, his life teaches Christ to us. As Piper says, that does not mean we all have to suffer just as Paul did. But it does mean that the depth of our spirituality is somehow bound up with the depth of our suffering – not our own troubles, only, but our participation in the pain and loss of others. Hence, 'the baptism in the Holy Spirit means something more than glory and ecstasy … It is fellowship with Christ in His humiliation and in His sufferings as well as in His glory'.[56]

But if the OT is truly about Jesus, then it is also truly about us, because he refuses to be known apart from us. And so the lives of the apostles and prophets, the figures of the patriarchs and kings, and the voices of the psalmists all witness to the co-reality of Christ with us, and us with one another. So, we can say, as Archbishop Lazar Puhalo does, that the OT is 'the story of each one of us, of our own spiritual, emotional, psychological and physical struggles.'[57] In these narratives, if we can resist the temptation to think we already know them too well, we can find the same 'depths of love and hate, the corrosive effects of egoism, bitterness, malice, envy and self-focus, but also the heroic struggle of mankind, the presence of hope and joy' that make human life recognizable anywhere, anytime. These stories are told in sparse detail, but they never spare the characters themselves – including, most of all, the God character. On every page, from beginning to end, we find 'the chaos and destructive energy of unconstrained desires and passions', which are present in our own lives, day to day. And so, we have to admit that these stories are nothing if not 'realistic' in that sense.

It is always a shock to readers who are finally convinced to pay attention: against all expectations, the stories in the Hebrew Scriptures are almost invariably stories of overwhelming frailty and failure, terrible harm, tragic confusion – even madness. Beginning with

---

[56] *LRE* 1.8 (May 1909), p. 23.

[57] Lazar Puhalo, *The Mirror of Scripture: The Old Testament Is about You* (Abbotsford, Canada: Macrina Press, 2018) p. vii.

Abraham and Sarah, and continuing through Isaac and Jacob and their wives and children, Moses and Aaron and Miriam and their children, the judges and the kings and their wives, and the prophets who are killed by those kings and their wives, the OT tells us story after story after story that leaves us more or less completely at a loss. And yet, when it is all said and done, we believe, as the Jewish people have taught us to believe, that those stories are the training we need in order to learn to be truthful about ourselves and our world in relation to God. So, the Archbishop concludes:

> Even the best are often defeated by their own ego and self-love. The birth of such ego and self-centredness is revealed in the fall of Adam and Eve, and carried to its terrible depth when brother murders brother. Wars and horrifying cruelty are manifestations of national ego headed by the ego and self-love of rulers and warriors. Power and lust for power – manifestations of great ego and self-focus – are shown in all their destructive force. Perhaps this is the central theme of our study. Ego and self-love are the main elements of our pride, and pride, where false or real, whether individual, tribal or national, bring such great grief upon mankind and every level of human interaction, even the destruction of the earth's life support system through the wanton misuse of the earth's resources. These are themes that are an integral part of our own lives, and we realise that the Hebrew Scripture is a mirror into which we gaze and see the reflection of our own selves.[58]

I add only one quibble: the OT is not merely a mirror. Whatever we might wish, we never merely see our own reflection, because our reflection is itself already an image of another's face. If we read rightly, then, the mirror, we might say, sparks a fire in the dry grass – a fire that burns away the darkness that had convinced us we were alone and under threat.

Making Peace with the Warrior God

But, needless to say, talking about the ways that the OT stories trouble us, and the darkness that seems to hang threateningly over it,

---

[58] Puhalo, *The Mirror of Scripture*, p. 208.

forces us to face the stories of violence, including the accounts of Canaanite genocide. What are we to do with these stories? Or, better, what are we to let them do for us? Puhalo suggests that the violence arises always from egoism and self-regard, never from God's purposes. And yet the text does repeatedly attribute violence – and the call to do violence – directly to God. God is said to kill, as in the Flood (Genesis 7) and the burning of Sodom and the cities of the plain (Genesis 19). And God is said to require others to kill; for example, Samuel says the word of the 'Lord of hosts' is that Saul is to 'go and attack Amalek, and utterly destroy all that they have; do not spare them, but kill both man and woman, child and infant, ox and sheep, camel and donkey' (1 Sam. 15.3). God is said to deceive (Jer. 20.7), and to make others lie (1 Kg. 22.22). What are we to do with these passages?

We might simply ignore them, and pray no one notices them. As I once overheard someone say, 'The OT is someone else's mail'. Or we might say that we have no right to question what God has done. God is the maker, and we are the made, so we should refrain from engaging with 'things too wonderful' for us (Job 42.3). Or we might say that God takes time to show us the fullness of the truth, so that over time he allows the people of God to misunderstand what he means, as they grow toward understanding, and in the meantime to act in ways that they are convinced are in keeping with his will but are in fact at odds with what he desires.

The first is obviously a mistake, but there is wisdom in these last two approaches. Read these ways, the OT reveals either a God whose wisdom so exceeds our own that we really can know nothing about the ways he orders our lives or a God who is humble and clever enough to let himself be misrepresented in the short run so he can care for his representatives for the long haul. In this latter approach, God is happy for a time not to be known rightly, even by his own people, if eventually he can make himself known fully both to them and through them to the world. In the former approach, God is happy for his providence always to remain unsearchable.

But there is a fourth approach, one which is essentially Patristic, and which I think also fits with the best of Pentecostal interpretations. It insists that there is a spiritual sense to every text, and that we must press past the literal sense, 'the letter', to grasp or be grasped by 'the spirit'. Read this way, the violence in the OT actually means something besides what it seems to mean at the literal level. Origen, for example, argues that the calls for Israel to wipe out the people of the land as described in Joshua are a parabolic way of calling for the churches to put to death their sinful appetites. In his own words, 'a kingdom of sin was in every one of us before we believed. But afterwards, Jesus came and struck down all the kings who possessed kingdoms of sin in us, and he ordered us to destroy all those kings and to leave none of them'. And he concludes: 'Unless [Israel's] physical wars bore the figure of spiritual wars, I do not think the books of Jewish history would ever have been handed down by the apostles to the disciples of Christ, who came to teach peace, so that they could be read in the churches'.[59]

> For what good was that description of wars to those to whom Jesus says, 'My peace I give to you; my peace I leave to you', and to whom it is commanded and said through the Apostle, 'Not avenging your own selves', and, 'Rather, you receive injury', and, 'You suffer offense?' in short, knowing that now we do not wage physical wars, but that the struggles of the soul have to be exerted against spiritual adversaries, the Apostle, just as a military leader, gives an order to the soldiers of Christ, saying, 'Put on the whole armor of God, so that you may be able to stand firm against the cunning devices of the Devil'. And in order for us to have examples of these spiritual wars from deeds of old, he wanted those narratives of exploits to be recited to us in church, so that, if we are spiritual – hearing that 'the Law is spiritual' – 'we may compare spiritual things with spiritual' in the things we hear.[60]

Needless to say, many of us find this 'allegorical' or 'spiritual' way of reading disorienting and strange. But I think David Steinmetz is essentially right: 'the medieval theory of levels of meaning in the biblical text, with all its undoubted defects, flourished because it is true, while the modern theory of a single meaning, with all its demonstrable virtues, is false'. Peter Leithart has argued that we need the 'fourfold sense' of Scripture or something close to it. He gives the example of the rock of Horeb and the water that flowed from it. That event happened as the text describes, but it also foreshadowed another

---

[59] Origen, *Homilies on Joshua* 15 (TFOC; Washington, DC: Catholic University of America Press, 2002), p. 138.

[60] Origen, *Homilies on Joshua*, p. 138.

event: the death of Jesus. 'God orchestrates history so that the real rock and the watery water foreshadow the temple rock of Ezekiel from which water flows, the Rock on the cross whose side is opened by a spear, who was the Rock that followed Israel.'

He assumes, obviously, that all events described in the OT actually happened. The literal sense is a historical sense and it is true both historically and theologically. But not every proponent of spiritual exegesis has held that assumption. Some argue that there are events described in the OT which are simply unworthy of God. In those cases, they argue, we should recognize that these things could not have happened, even though they have been conveyed to us as in-spired stories. The question, then, is not about what God did then with them but about what God intends to do now with us. The same was true for the original hearers, as well. And will be true for readers after us. The question, then, is not what only God then did with them but what God intends to do now with us.

Some protest that it is misleading for God to take time to reveal his will fully, or that it would be deceptive for him to give us texts we are meant not to take at face value. But as I have argued, Jesus, re-vealing God, tells parables. It is fitting, then, that the OT should be parabolic. And in some ways, we are already aware that this must be true. For example, we know that God does not travel from place to place, as depicted in the Sodom story, or change his mind, as de-scribed in the flood story. He does not tempt David to sin, or send lying spirits into the mouths of his prophets. These things, as many of the Fathers would say, are simply unworthy of him. They do, of course, put us as readers in a difficult place. How could we ever know what is and is not worthy of God? The good news is that God means to put us in that difficult place.

Where does all of this leave us, then? I say we need to integrate the final three approaches, with the weight falling on the last. Jesus, the crucified, living Lord, is the canon of the canon. We cannot come to understand his teachings or the meaning of his life without careful study of the Scriptures. But we can only study the Scriptures rightly in the first place if we come to them as a word about him. The whole of the OT, as well as the NT, including the most troubling passages, and perhaps especially the stories of divine violence, are about Jesus, and about the grace he brings to bear on us. We should read them, then, as gospel, remembering that even the 'dark' passages are light to God, and that in him there is no darkness at all.

Take, for example, God's command, given through Samuel, for Saul to destroy the Amalekites (1 Sam. 15.1-3):

> Samuel said to Saul, 'The LORD sent me to anoint you king over his people Israel; now therefore listen to the words of the LORD. ²Thus says the LORD of hosts, "I will punish the Amalekites for what they did in opposing the Israelites when they came up out of Egypt. ³Now go and attack Amalek, and utterly destroy all that they have; do not spare them, but kill both man and woman, child and infant, ox and sheep, camel and donkey"'.

Saul gathers warriors and goes to battle, defeating the Amalekites (1 Sam. 15.7). He took King Agag alive, 'but utterly destroyed all the people with the edge of the sword'. After the slaughter, he and his warriors decide to keep 'the best of the sheep and of the cattle and of the fatlings, and the lambs, and all that was valuable, and would not utterly destroy them'; but 'all that was despised and worthless they utterly destroyed' (1 Sam. 15.9).

Before Saul returns, the Word of the Lord comes again to the Samuel: 'I regret that I made Saul king, for he has turned back from following me, and has not carried out my commands' (1 Sam. 15.10). When the king returns, joyful, the prophet immediately rebukes him for his failures. At first, Saul defends himself, twice contending that he had in fact fulfilled his mission. But Samuel is relentless (1 Sam. 15.22-23):

> Has the Lord as great delight in burnt offerings and sacrifices, as in obedience to the voice of the Lord? Surely, to obey is better than sacrifice, and to heed than the fat of rams. For rebellion is no less a sin than divination, and stubbornness is like iniquity and idolatry. Because you have rejected the word of the Lord, he has also rejected you from being king.

Finally, Saul relents. But Samuel offers no mercy: 'I will not return with you; for you have rejected the word of the LORD, and the LORD has rejected you from being king over Israel'. (1 Sam. 15.26). Saul begs, tearing Samuel's robe. But the prophet reiterates the irreversibility of the judgment: 'The LORD has torn the kingdom of Israel from you this very day, and has given it to a neighbor of yours, who is better than you. Moreover, the Glory of Israel will not recant or change his mind; for he is not a mortal, that he should change his mind' (1 Sam. 15.28-29).

Saul turns to prayer, sincere or not, but Samuel calls for the soldiers to bring the prisoner, Agag, to him. He speaks over the king a final curse – 'As your sword has made women childless, so your mother shall be childless among women' – and then hews him to pieces 'before the Lord in Gilgal' (1 Sam. 15.33). After that day, the king and the prophet never saw each other again. And the story ends with these words: 'And the Lord was sorry that he had made Saul king over Israel' (1 Sam. 15.35).

In his autobiography, Martin Buber tells how one day, seated on the train by a man he knew as a devout Jew, he found himself confessing to this man his horror at the passage, which had terrified him since he was a boy. He confided in the old man that he found the story simply unbelievable: 'I have never been able to believe that this is a message of God. I do not believe it.' And he recounts how the man's glance 'flamed into my eyes'. The man sat quietly, for a long time, obviously troubled. At last, he asked Buber, haltingly, 'So, you do not believe it?' Buber said he did not. A few moments later, the man asked again, this time almost threateningly. Buber again said he did not believe it. 'So, what do you believe?', the man asked, exasperated, and Buber answered, without reflection: 'I believe that Samuel has misunderstood God'. Again, they fell into silence. And after a long time, the man asked if that is in fact what Buber believed. 'So, you believe that?' 'Yes.' Suddenly, the man's anger vanished, and he looked up at Buber and smiled, 'Well, I think so, too'.

Reflecting on this experience Buber observes how it surprises him, even years later: 'There is in the end nothing astonishing in the fact that an observant Jew of this nature, when he has to choose between God and the Bible, chooses God: the God in whom he believes, Him in whom he can believe. And yet, it seemed to me at that time significant and still seems so to me today.'

As he continues to reflect, he admits that the conversation returns to him often. He finds himself rehashing it, wondering each time if he answered the man's questions rightly. He says he always returns to the assurance that he did in fact say what he had to say. And that point, turns to a brief meditation on misunderstanding:

What is involved here is not ultimately the fact that this or that form of biblical historical narrative has misunderstood God; what is involved is the fact that in the work of throats and pens out of which the text of the Old Testament has arisen, misunderstanding has again and again attached itself to understanding, the manufactured has been mixed with the received. We have no objective criterion for the distinction; we have only faith – when we have it. Nothing can make me believe in a God who punishes Saul because he has not murdered his enemy. And yet even today I still cannot read the passage that tells this otherwise than with fear and trembling. But not it alone. Always when I have to translate or to interpret a biblical text, I do so with fear and trembling, in an inescapable tension between the word of God and the words of man.[61]

I, too, heard this story when I was a young – frequently, in fact, and always as an illustration of sin that is left undealt with in the Christian's life. I was always deeply troubled by it, in part because it reminded me so much of the story of Achan, which nearly destroyed me when I first heard it, as a child of six or seven or eight. I still remember where I was when I first had these lines read to me, and my response, which was a mix of fury, shock, terror, and panic:

> Then Joshua and all Israel with him took Achan son of Zerah, with the silver, the mantle, and the bar of gold, with his sons and daughters, with his oxen, donkeys, and sheep, and his tent and all that he had; and they brought them up to the Valley of Achor ... And all Israel stoned him to death; they burned them with fire, cast stones on them, and raised over him a great heap of stones that remains to this day. Then the LORD turned from his burning anger (Josh. 7.24-26).

Like Buber, I find these stories simply unbelievable. They are so obviously unworthy of God. I cannot believe that God would require actions like these of anyone, no matter the circumstances. But I do not want to choose between God and the Bible. So, I am left to say that these stories are inspired by God, but not to tell us about something God once did and made his people do. They are not reports on

---

[61] Martin Buber, *Meetings: Autobiographical Fragments* (New York: Routledge, 2002), pp. 62-65.

an evil that we must accept as good because God required it. They are not even reports on something Israel wrongly believed God had required. Instead, they are stories, true in the ways only God's stories can be, true like a measurement, like a cut, dividing the bone of the soul from the marrow of the spirit, laying bare the hearts of our hearts (Heb. 4.12).

Do not let anyone tell you that to read in this way is to do violence to the text or to show a lack of faith in God. Just the opposite is true, in fact. This story, carefully read, read as it was intended to be read, is a story that calls into question not Saul, but *Samuel* – and in this way catches those of us who side with Samuel in our reading, exposing our complicity in what he does and fails to do.

Notice how the story ends: 'And the Lord was sorry that he had made Saul king over Israel' (1 Sam. 15.35). Of course, God does not disappoint himself, and is never caught off guard by our failures. So, when the text tells us that God is disappointed, it is an invitation for us to reflect on the seriousness of what has gone wrong. That is, the text is urging us to read the story again, asking why God would be left in such a state by what has happened. In this case, the line calls back to the events of the flood: 'And the Lord was sorry that he had made humankind on the earth, and it grieved him to his heart' (Gen. 6.6). But, as thoughtful readers remember, the flood does not settle God's unease. After he has 'blotted out every living thing' (Gen. 7.23), God says to himself: 'I will never again curse the ground because of humankind, for the inclination of the human heart is evil from youth; nor will I ever again destroy every living creature as I have done' (Gen. 8.21). Having made this commitment to himself, God blesses Noah as the new Adam, and Noah, like Abel, Adam's son, is said to be 'a man of the soil' (Gen. 9.20). He plants a vineyard, drinks himself to sleep, and that night his son, Ham, 'sees his father's nakedness' – probably a euphemism for sleeping with his father's wife, his mother, or step-mother (Gen. 9.21-25).

Strikingly, the same story plays out later in Genesis. God hears that Sodom and the other cities of the plain are depraved, and he comes down to see for himself if the rumors are true (Gen. 18.21).[62]

---

[62] Again, this should be obvious: we know that God does not travel, and that God does not depend on rumors for his knowledge of creation. So, we have no choice but to accept that these stories are told in ways that present God as a

In spite of Abraham's intercession, 'The Lord rained down fire on Sodom and Gomorrah ...' (Gen. 19.24). Lot's wife looks back, 'and she became a pillar of salt' (Gen. 19.26). But Lot escapes, and lives in a cave with his two daughters. And they conspire to do to him what Ham had done to his father: 'And the firstborn said to the younger, "Our father is old, and there is not a man on earth to come in to us after the manner of all the world. Come, let us make our father drink wine, and we will lie with him, so that we may preserve offspring through our father"' (Gen. 19.31-32).

Obviously, Genesis provides us with a pattern: human beings sin grievously, and God pours out wrath on them. And yet, those who survive quickly return to their wickedness, so that God comes to regret what he has done to his creatures in his disappointment with them. This same pattern appears later, long after the story of Samuel and Saul, in the prophecies of Jeremiah, who delivers this word to Israel: 'If you will only remain in this land, then I will build you up and not pull you down; I will plant you, and not pluck you up; for I am sorry for the disaster that I have brought upon you' (Jer. 42.9-10).

All to say, when we read that God regrets having made Saul king, we know that the judgment that falls on him will fail. And this is made all the clearer by the fact that Samuel 'hewed Agag to pieces', which hearkens back to what the Levite does to his concubine after she was raped and left for dead (Jud. 19.29), an act of unspeakable violence, and one that issued in civil war. Strikingly, Samuel takes this task on himself even though the Lord does not command him to do it. Earlier, Saul had offered a burnt offering to the Lord in Samuel's absence. Seven days late, the prophet arrived the moment the offering was complete, and immediately condemned Saul's rashness, and says to him that if he had not offered the sacrifice, God would have established his kingdom forever, but now, because of his impatience, God would appoint another ruler over Israel (1 Sam. 13.13-14).

This story is made all the stranger by the word of judgment first spoken against the people of Amalek, long before Agag became king. According to Exodus, in their wilderness journey, Israel is attacked without provocation by the Amalekites, taken by surprise at Rephidim. In the ensuing battle, Joshua leads Israel to victory, as Moses,

---

character, trusting us to figure out why. A 'literal' reading is one that accepts the nature of the literature as it is given to us. In this case, it is given to us as 'legend'.

Aaron, and Hur interceded in prayer. After the victory is won, the Lord commands Moses to 'Write this as a reminder in a book and recite it in the hearing of Joshua: I will utterly blot out the remembrance of Amalek from under heaven'. Moses builds an altar near the battle site, which he names The Lord is My Banner, and he prophesies that 'the Lord will have war with Amalek from generation to generation' (Exod. 17.14-16). The irony is impossible to miss: if the intention is to 'blot out the remembrance of Amalek', then why have Moses write the threat and why have Israel repeat the story? And how can God make war with Amalek 'from generation to generation' if he succeeds in destroying them entirely?

The history of Jewish and Christian readings of this passage, at least as I know it, shows that our best readers realized that there must be 'something more' at work in the story of Amalek. And many of them came to see it as a warning against self-righteousness and the use of God's name to justify violence. For both Jews and Christians, 'Amalek' personifies evil. And the strange stories about Amalek, including this one in 1 Samuel, come to serve as a warning that evil must not be resisted in ways that are themselves evil. As Rabbi Arthur Waskow puts it, 'The Torah is teaching us that even as we face the danger of an Amalek without, we must also blot out the urge to Amalek within ourselves, by turning that urge toward compassion'.[63]

If we follow the trajectory, we can see that this moment of conflict leads only to loss. Samuel, angry that the king he loved has failed, yet again, to do what God required of him, takes matters into his own hands at last, rejecting Saul and executing Agag. But in so doing, he does not end evil or make peace. Saul is destroyed by the rejection. From this moment, he is portrayed as mad (1 Sam. 16.14; 18.10; 19.9, 24). And at the end of his life, when even the Lord ignores his cries for help, he hires a necromancer to bring Samuel back to him. But that too ends in disappointment and terror (1 Sam. 28.21). Samuel himself, after this moment, recedes to the background of the story, and dies without fanfare: 'Now Samuel died; and all Israel assembled and mourned for him. They buried him at his home in Ramah. Then David got up and went down to the wilderness of Paran' (1 Sam.

---

[63] Arthur Waskow, *Godwrestling – Round 2* (Woodstock, VT: Jewish Lights, 1995), p. 218.

25.1). Both he and Saul and Saul's sons end in the same place of unrest (1 Sam. 28.19).

When all is said and done, then, Samuel's penultimate exchange with Saul, like so many other stories in Scripture, is a cautionary tale, one that warns us against the corrupting effect of religious zeal, but more importantly also reminds us that what we do to others in the name of God not only may not heal them but actually may do irreparable harm. Instead of blotting out the name of Amalek forever, we may become Amalek, our violence generating a new cycle of failure and failed judgment. If we truly want to make peace with the warrior God, then we have to learn to read these stories in ways that 'make for peace' (Lk. 1.79; 19.42). These are, after all, Jesus' stories.

Scripture as Sacrament, Interpretation as Encounter

If we hope to receive more of the fulness offered in the Scriptures, we need deeper and wider theologies of Scripture, which can help make intelligible the claim that reading the Scriptures is a form of listening to the Word. Cheryl Bridges Johns, in conversation with Telford Work, John Webster, and Cathrine Mowry LaCugna, offers just such a framework, proposing an ontology of Scripture that is centered in the Spirit's power to make Christ present through the faithful readings of the written Word.[64] In her words,

> Pentecostals understand the Bible as married to the work of the Spirit in actualizing the presence of the Living Word in actualizing the work of God in the healing of creation. In this work the Bible brings about the real presence of Jesus.[65]

Johns is careful to maintain a distinction between Christ and the Scriptures: 'The Bible does not have the same ontological status as the Incarnate Word. It is not divine.' Nonetheless, she insists that Scripture does have 'its own genuine reality, one that is fit to enter into the divine service'. Scripture is 'a sanctified, Spirit-filled vessel in service of restoring creation', possessed of the power 'to mediate the presence of the triune God'. In Work's phrasing, Scripture is 'a means of divine presence and grace in a fallen world ... a participant in the

---

[64] Johns, 'Grieving, Brooding, and Transforming', p. 144.
[65] Johns, 'Grieving, Brooding, and Transforming', p. 147.

life that God has and offers creation through the Word made flesh'.[66] As a result of the Spirit's presence, 'the scriptures are not just pregnant with meaning; they are pregnant with the eternal life of God'.[67]

A careless reading might infer otherwise, but John's ontology of Scripture refuses any distinction between what the texts of Scripture are in themselves and what they are for us in the event of interpretation. In other words, what she seems to claim for the Scriptures is in fact a claim about what God does with the Scriptures as they are interpreted and enacted. By God's grace, the Spirit rests upon the interpretive moment in such a way that a 'space' is created for us, engendering our redemption and the renewal of all creation. 'Performance of the Bible creates a thin space where the veil between the supernatural and the natural world becomes transparent', and we enter by the Spirit into 'eschatological time' where 'the past draws near and the future bends toward the present'.[68] 'Reading the text is, therefore, an eschatological experience, a trans-temporal journey that brings participants into the eternal presence of God.'[69] If, in fact, a sacrament is a sign that by the Spirit does what it signifies, then the interpretation of Scripture is sacramental, because as we are interpreting it, we are made interpreters with and in Christ. In Johns' words,

> The space that is created by the Holy Spirit within the sacred vessel of the scriptures is abounding with real presence. It is a space that offers potential for re-orientation of existence. It is transforming space, alive and radiated by the Holy Spirit. Not static, scriptural space offers a truth that seizes us, captures us in its holy power. Not unlike the realm of the Holy of Holies in the temple, sacred scriptural territory is, at the same time, both wonderful and dangerous. It is wonderful because in it we find the delights of the triune life offered to us out of God's ecstatic self-giving. It is dangerous because this space offers to us God as the living subject. Here we are known and read more than we know and read.[70]

---

[66] Work, *Living and Active*, p. 19.
[67] Johns, 'Grieving, Brooding, and Transforming', p. 148.
[68] Johns, 'Grieving, Brooding, and Transforming', p. 148.
[69] Johns, 'Grieving, Brooding, and Transforming', p. 149.
[70] Johns, 'Grieving, Brooding, and Transforming', p. 149.

In a more recent article, Rickie Moore, reflecting on Johns' paper, the first version of this book, and an article by Walter Brueggemann, argues that readings of Scripture, if they are truly Spirit-led engagements with the Word and not merely self-directed interpretations of biblical texts, lead inevitably to the altar and to our altering. Given that this is so, the question of biblical authority does not hinge on 'our capacity to explain or to explain away Scripture's many limitations, tensions, complexities, dissonances, incoherencies, contradictions, obscurities, ethical difficulties, and so forth'. Instead, what matters is Scripture's God-given and God-used power to transform us. In Moore's own words, since 'God's goal and end in giving us Scripture is less about conveying knowledge than about facilitating and transacting a salvation that surpasses knowledge' we can trust that 'all of the problematics that confront us in Scripture can be seen as intended precisely to do just that – to confront us' in ways that

> expose our vested interests, the fears beneath them, and the deep, unresolved wounds underlying and underwriting these fears – to expose them so that we will then have the chance to spread them out before the altar of God and give the God of the altar an opportunity to transform us.[71]

As a child, I was taught an old children's song: 'Read your Bible and pray every day, and you will grow, grow, grow'. That's true, but not because reading the Bible and prayer 'work'. Holiness does not happen in us automatically. We cannot devise techniques that guarantee our sanctification. We can only draw near to God and stay near him, even when, sooner than later, he requires us to keep company with people we do not like. Reading the Bible and praying every day only matters if we know how to do that in ways that show the love of God to those who have not been loved as they should have been. After all, if holiness is a name for God's own way of relating, then our readings of Scripture can be sanctifying only if they actually change our lives so we become more and more strangely roomy and inviting.

---

[71] Rickie D. Moore, 'Altar Hermeneutics', *Pneuma* 38.1-2 (2016), pp. 148-59 (156).

SCRIPTURE AS DIVINE AND DEIFYING FOOLISHNESS

Introduction

I have already argued that the crucial matter is not that we read Scripture but how we read it. And this has always been true: 'Christians became the scriptural community that they did not merely by choosing books and marking distinctions between those books and others, but also by choosing to use and read those books in a certain way, by means of certain reading practices'.[1] Precisely for that reason, we have to learn to read and reread in ways that trouble and thwart us into participation with Christ, into the wisdom God is and gives.[2] That is, we have to read Scripture so we that we are made wise with God's own wisdom, transformed as Christ's co-sanctified co-sanctifiers, mediators with him of God's divine-human beauty. As Jenson says, 'The knowledge of God is knowledge-in-action, or it is not knowledge of God at all'.[3]

Despite what we might wish, the reading of Scripture, instead of ending or saving us from the discerning process, returns us to it, again and again, in always deepening and widening ways. 'The Scriptures serve as the template for reading the world. It is in the light of Scripture that the patterns of life are recognized and woven into the

---

[1] Lewis Ayres, '"There's Fire in That Rain": On Reading the Letter and Reading Allegorically', in Hans Boersma and Matthew Levering (eds.), *Heaven on Earth: Theological Interpretation in Ecumenical Dialogue* (Malden, MA: Wiley-Blackwell, 2013), pp. 33-51 (35).

[2] David F. Ford, *Christian Wisdom: Desiring God and Learning in Love* (Cambridge Studies in Christian Doctrine; Cambridge: Cambridge University Press, 2007), p. 69.

[3] Jenson, *The Knowledge of Things Hoped For*, p. 45.

divine-human narrative. Through the Scriptures human critical reflection is judged, negated, transformed and/or enhanced, producing a new perception of reality.'[4] By God's grace, the shared work of faithful interpretation over time effects in us, corporately and individually, an increased capacity for and readiness to bear with others in their weaknesses, sins, and immaturity. Held in that process, we find that we are being taken up into our calling, being drawn along toward God, one another, and all things in Christ by the Spirit. In the agonies of interpretation – whether in preaching, study, prayer, or meditation – we are made apt for the work of the Spirit who impels us toward ever-deepening communion and ever-widening collaboration with God in mediating Christ's divine-human holiness to the rest of creation. Struggling to read Scripture faithfully, we find ourselves doing exactly what we are made to do.

Sanctifying Troubledness

How does our co-sanctification happen? Among other things, it takes place as we are forced into the process of discernment by the difficulties of making faithful sense of the biblical texts,[5] a process that trains us for making faithful sense of our lives together before God in the world. In fact, I am convinced that we can talk about Scripture as God's 'living and active' Word (Heb. 4.12) just inasmuch as we acknowledge its power to bewilder and trouble us, dividing bone from marrow, soul from spirit, evoking from us 'cries, calls, appeals, and shouts',[6] throwing us on the mercy of God in our neighbors' wisdom.

Or, said differently, trying to make sense of Scripture necessarily 'tears us apart' so that 'through those wounds, if we have tended them, love may enter us'.[7] Scripture does more than merely prefigure Jesus' death or explains its effects. Read in the Spirit, Scripture brings us into participation with Christ in his sufferings. Wrestling with Scripture, and being wounded by it, alters us savingly, because

---

[4] Jackie D. Johns, 'Yielding to the Spirit: The Dynamics of a Pentecostal Model of Praxis', in Murray W. Dempster, Byron D. Klaus, and Douglas Peterson (eds.), *The Globalization of Pentecostalism: A Religion Made to Travel* (Carlisle, CA: Regnum, 1999), pp. 70-84 (79).

[5] See Williams, 'Language, Reality and Desire', p. 143.

[6] Ford, *Christian Wisdom*, p. 65.

[7] Wiman, *My Bright Abyss*, p. 159.

Scripture does not merely tell the story of the cross: reading it requires our crucifixion.[8]

St. Jerome long ago acknowledged what any serious reader of the Bible discovers soon enough: 'Even things that seem clear in the Scriptures give rise to a mass of problems'.[9] Why would God give us such an endlessly problematic gift? For at least a couple of reasons, I believe. First, some of what seems to us wrong or strange in the Scriptures is in point of fact simply a reflection of what is wrong and strange in *us*. As the raven says to Mr. Vane in MacDonald's *Phantastes*: 'Indeed you are yourself the only riddle. What you call riddles are truths, and seem riddles because you are not true.'[10]

But there are other things in our sacred texts that are indeed wrong and dangerous, and they are there for us as Scripture because God has purposed them to generate difficulties for us, difficulties that test our patience and frustrate our expectations. These include not only ambiguous texts – ambiguities due, for example, to translation problems or opacity of metaphors – but also, and perhaps especially, those texts that horrify us, as well as those that strike us as out and out bizarre. And we should not shy away from this truth, ugly as it may appear at first, because God means to use them for our good, training us through interpretation for the work of mediation. As James says, the Spirit uses these dense and disturbing texts to provoke responses from us, and in order to mirror back to us our images of ourselves and others, exposing what otherwise remains hidden from us in the darkness of our hearts (Jas 1.23-24).

Tragically, many of us have been taught to read Scripture in ways that confirm our biases, reassuring us our hearts are pure and our thoughts true. Perhaps the surest sign that our interpretations of Scripture are self-directed and not led by the Spirit is that they leave us believing we are the faithful remnant who hold the line against all of those who have compromised or lost faith. We need, then, to let these strange and troubling texts be what God means them to be, and not what we have made them to be to protect ourselves from God.

---

[8] As Walter Brueggemann says, 'it belongs to Bible reading to live in crisis and to spend our energy adjudicating that crisis' (*A Pathway of Interpretation: The Old Testament for Pastors and Students* [Eugene, OR: Cascade, 2008], p. 9).

[9] Jerome, *Commentary on Matthew* (trans. Thomas P. Scheck; Washington, DC: The Catholic University of America Press, 2008), p. 179.

[10] George MacDonald, *Phantastes* (Grand Rapids: Eerdmans, 1981), p. 45.

All to say, so long as we do quench or stifle the Spirit, the Spirit uses Scripture to trouble us in any number of ways – wowing us, disturbing us, provoking us, puzzling us, boring us. The sacred texts 'instruct us for salvation' (2 Tim. 3.15) not so much by delivering sacred knowledge to us, but by 'training us in righteousness' (2 Tim. 3.16), driving and nudging and leading us into the imaginatively and affectively transformative experience of interpretation as the different kinds of difficult Scriptures work on our affections and imaginations in different ways. By the Spirit's art, we find ourselves encountering Christ where we would not expect him and failing to find him where we expected him to be, and these moments occasion the formation of certain personal and corporate virtues, the wisdom that is vital to the work of faithful priestly mediation.

The Humiliated, Humbling Word

By and large, evangelical models emphasize what we might call the 'glory' of the Scriptures: their majesty, their beauty, their power. But the Scriptures are at-one-ed with Christ as the living Word of the gospel's God only insofar as they share in his ongoing humiliation, in his weakness and foolishness that subverts worldly power and wisdom (1 Cor. 1.18-25). And so, Scripture's glory is nothing but its ordinariness, its humility.

This should not surprise us if we know the story of the gospel. God's glory is revealed above all in God's humility, as the events of creation, the call of Israel in Abraham, the Incarnation, Passion and Ascension, and the Eucharistic gathering of the Church testify. And the same holds for the Scriptures. They are holy just in that they are 'low and despised', chosen to expose the pretensions of the wise and the strong, 'to reduce to nothing' our assumptions about God, ourselves, and the world (1 Cor. 1.27-28). The sacred texts, in Hamann's words, are like the 'old rags' twisted together into ropes to draw Jeremiah from his pit.[11] Receiving them in all of their humanity, we find ourselves humanized, made that much more transparent, opened in small and odd ways toward God in our neighbor and our neighbor in God. Perhaps, in the end, we devise glorious theologies of Scripture because we hope to avoid the humiliation of simply being ordinary?

---

[11] See John R. Betz, *After Enlightenment: the Post-Secular Vision of J.G. Hamann* (Malden, MA: Wiley-Blackwell, 2009), pp. 43-45.

God against Us for Us

This reveals one of the strangest strangenesses in the Christian life: on the one hand, we cannot even begin to read the Bible as Scripture unless we have some sense of who God is and what God is like, but, on the other hand, we never read the Scripture faithfully without having our sense of what God is like in some way dramatically upended and altered. We can be sure, for example, that God is not capricious or cruel. We can know that God is not in any sense unfaithful. But the awful truth is that even in knowing God's faithfulness we often misperceive what that faithfulness means for us and requires of us at any given time. Therefore, we have to let the Spirit rescue us from readings of Scripture that distort the image of God. Reading faithfully, our idolatrous misapprehensions of God are graciously wrecked, again and again, as we are drawn toward Christlikeness.

John 5 shows that many of Jesus' contemporaries rejected him because they believed his actions on the Sabbath violated the Scriptures. But he responds by insisting that they are in fact misreading the sacred Scriptures. 'You pore over the scriptures', he warns them, 'believing that in them you can find eternal life' (Jn 5.39a NJB). Tragically, they cannot see how these very texts witness to Christ. 'It is these scriptures that testify to me, and yet you refuse to come to me to receive life!' (Jn 5.39b-40 NJB). Therefore, in the End, they stand accused by the very texts they claim to understand and wield in judgment against Jesus.

> [45]Do not think that I will accuse you before the Father; your accuser is Moses, on whom you have set your hope. [46]If you believed Moses, you would believe me, for he wrote about me. [47]But if you do not believe what he wrote, how will you believe what I say?

Jesus not only rebukes them for failing to keep the Law given by Moses (Jn 7.19), but also insists that they in effect have re-written the Law in their own terms. Twice he tells them, 'In *your law* it is written …' (Jn 8.17; 10.34), and in his last words to his disciples he says he has been hated without cause 'to fulfill the word that is written in *their* law' (Jn 15.25). Tellingly, at Jesus' trial 'the Jews' tell Pilate, 'We have a law, and according to that law he ought to die' (Jn 19.7), and Pilate gives them their way: 'Take him yourselves and judge him according to your law' (Jn 18.31). Similarly, Paul differentiates 'the Torah of sin and death' from 'the Torah of the Spirit of life' (Rom. 8.2), a difference determined by how we read – and live in response to – the Scriptures.

Like those who opposed Jesus then, we can, and no doubt often do, search the Scriptures, to our own and others' hurt. We can so distort the Scriptures that we make God's Word unfaithfully our own. We need to be saved from these unsanctified and unsanctifying readings, and that salvation takes place only as we allow the Spirit to uses texts to threaten and overthrow our misreadings. Said differently, Scripture sanctifies us by overthrowing the unfaithful uses we have made of Scripture, by being a Word not of our own making, a Word that is for us by first being against us. It is as we struggle with texts that wreak havoc with our interpretive grid that we, like Jacob, are seized by the unnamed one who speaks the saving blessing.

God Against 'God' for Us

God uses the Scripture to overthrow our false conceptions of God. Paul was deeply committed to the Scriptures before he encountered Jesus on the road outside Damascus. But after that encounter, he was differently and more faithfully biblical, because he saw God differently – in the face of the resurrected crucified Jesus of Nazareth.

We can see the effect of Paul's transformation in his reading of the stories of Phinehas and Abraham. In the OT, both men are said to have had their acts 'counted to them as righteousness': Phinehas for his 'zeal' and Abraham for his 'faith'.[12] It seems, then, that Paul experienced in his 'conversion' a dramatic turn away from a Phinehas-centered view of covenantal fidelity to an Abraham-centered view. Imitating Phinehas had led him to persecute Christ, but Paul tells the Philippians that he now counts his former Phinehas-like zeal, expressed in persecuting the church, as 'loss in order to gain Christ' (Phil. 3.6-8). And seeking to be one with Christ requires him to imitate the faith of Abraham, a faith in a God who does the impossible.

Paul's life teaches us that in spite of the fact that Numbers and Psalms speak of God's approval, Phinehas' zeal does not reflect the virtues required to follow Christ faithfully. So how can we take at face

---

[12] See Num. 25.6-13; Ps. 106.28-31; Rom. 4.1-3. See also N.T. Wright, *Paul and the Faithfulness of God* (Minneapolis: Fortress Press, 2013), pp. 80-89; Dane C. Ortland, *Zeal Without Knowledge: The Concept of Zeal in Romans 10, Galatians 1, and Philippians 3* (London: T&T Clark, 2012).

value the praise for that zeal the Scriptures put in God's mouth? If we cannot take that praise at face value, then what are we to make of it?

I am convinced that Paul discovered in Christ that the Abraham story can and should take theological precedence over the Phinehas story,[13] and that in the exchanging of 'zeal' for 'faith', Paul models for us the way to read all of the Scriptures faithfully. But we should not take that to mean the Phinehas story and other stories of 'zeal' have no significance for us. How are we to read them, then? Unquestionably, we are not supposed to read them as Paul did before his encounter with Christ. We should instead read them in 'faith'; that is, in the light of the good news of Christ's victory over sin and death and the promise of New Creation. In this way, we can see that we are called to be both like and unlike Phinehas, and all others zealous to defend God's reputation and Israel's purity: like him, we should be zealous for God's holiness; but, unlike him, we know that that holiness is brought to bear not by violence against sinners but by intercession for them.

Making Peace with the Warrior God

I have already acknowledged that Scripture presents us with different kinds of difficult texts. But for most of us, I suspect the most difficult are the 'texts of terror' that characterize God as vindictive, bloodthirsty, malevolent.[14] The God we think we find in the OT is difficult to stomach, never mind adore. What are we to do in the face of these difficulties? We cannot ignore them, or dismiss them by using Jesus' ethic as a trump card, playing the NT off against the OT. And we cannot explain these difficulties away by saying the OT texts merely witness to an earlier phase of God's self-revelation and the moral development of God's people. According to Jesus' own teaching, how we read the OT is itself God's judgment of us. The OT is nothing other than Jesus' testimony, the Spirit's prophecy (Rev. 19.10); therefore, to refuse Moses' witness is to turn away from Christ.[15] But to

---

[13] Paul makes a similar argument in Galatians 3, contending that 'the promise of the Spirit through faith' (3.14) precedes and supersedes law and circumcision.

[14] Phyllis Trible, *Texts of Terror: Literary-Feminist Readings of Biblical Narratives* (London: SCM Press, 2002).

[15] *TBM* 3.51 (Dec. 1 1909), p. 1. Davies rightly maintains that 'any interpretation that claims to be Spirit inspired has to be read in line with (and in the light of) the entire testimony of the seamless robe of Scripture' ('Reading in the Spirit', p. 308).

receive that testimony faithfully is to be indwelt by the Word that glorifies us with God's own glory (Jn 5.36-47). Turning toward Jesus as he is embodied in 'Moses and all the prophets' (Lk. 24.27), we make ourselves apt for God, availing ourselves to the transformative Spirit who makes all things new – our lives no less than the texts of sacred Scripture.

That is well and good, you might say, but how should it determine our reading of horrifying texts? We must begin, I believe, with a clarification, distinguishing the God who inspires and interprets the OT texts from the one described in the texts themselves. The inspiring, interpreting God is of course the Triune God revealed in the life, death, and resurrection of Jesus the Nazarene. But the narrated God, the God who is a character in the biblical stories God has inspired, is sometimes an entirely or almost entirely false image of the true God. In the Scriptures, God humbly takes on the guise of a character, one character among others – sometimes even a bad, or at least conflicted, one.[16] As Rowan Williams argues, one way of understanding Scripture is as 'a parable or a whole series of parables' in which God says of himself: 'This is how people heard me, saw me, responded to me; this is the gift I gave them; this is the response they made', requiring us to respond in kind.[17]

I would say it just a bit differently than Williams does. In the 'parables' of the OT, God is not reporting to us how people understood and misunderstood his ways then and there. Instead, God is here and now putting us to the test by describing himself at least somewhat

---

[16] See for example Casey S. Cole, 'Taking Hermeneutics to Heart: Proposing an Orthopathic Reading for Texts of Terror via the Rape of Tamar Narrative', *Pneuma* 39.3 (2017), pp. 264-74.

[17] Williams, *Being Christian*, p. 28. He continues (pp. 28-29):

> One of the great tragedies and errors of the way people have understood the Bible has been the assumption that what people did in the Old Testament must have been right 'because it's in the Bible'. It has justified violence, enslavement, abuse and suppression of women, murderous prejudice against gay people; it has justified all manner of things we now cannot but as Christians regard as evil. But they are not there in the Bible because God is telling us, 'That's good'. They are there because God is telling us, 'You need to know that that is how some people responded. You need to know that when I speak to human beings things can go very wrong as well as very wonderfully'. God tells us, 'You need to know that when I speak, it isn't always simple to hear, because of what human beings are like'. We need, in other words, to guard against the temptation to take just a bit of the whole story and treat it as somehow a model for our own behaviour.

misleadingly. 'Everything written long ago was written to teach us' (Rom. 15.4). In Scripture, God presents himself to us in various disguises — sometimes in story, sometimes in legal codes, sometimes in prophecy — and in these ways works to draw out of us responses that lay bear our hearts, opening us to the possibility of transformation. And so we have to read/hear Scripture discerningly, knowing that some of what God seems to be saying in Scripture, and some of what Scripture seems to be saying about God, is meant to test us. It is not only a window, but also a mirror, revealing not only God's character, but also our own.

I want to be careful here. I do not mean that God tries to deceive us with Scripture, at least not in the ways we fear. We have an enemy who does that. I mean God 'tests' us precisely in order to save us from deception. To say that God tests us is to say that he teaches us discernment — and discernment cannot be learned any other way. As we come to know the character of the God who speaks to us, we can, like Jonah, discern the Word beyond the words: 'this is why I fled to Tarshish at the beginning; for I knew that you are a gracious God ...' (Jon. 4.2). Recognizing the justice of God in the face of Jesus Christ, we are bold to argue with God as Abraham did, interceding for the forgiveness of the wicked (Gen. 18.22-33). Filled with the Spirit of Christ, we are compelled, as Moses was, to identify ourselves with those who have alienated themselves from God: 'But now, if you will only forgive their sin — but if not, blot me out of the book that you have written' (Exod. 32.32).

(Mis)Understanding Jesus

If what I have just been describing seems too strange to believe, take a moment to consider the way Jesus taught and how people responded to his teaching. The Evangelists show us that he spoke mostly in parables, riddles, and symbolic acts, and read the Scriptures subversively and troubled traditional practices. In response, some of his contemporaries think they have understood him when they in fact have not. Others, like the rich young ruler (Mt. 19.16-22), understand him just well enough to be enraged or saddened by what he has said. A few are intrigued enough to follow him in spite of their lack of understanding. Most are left in complete bafflement.

To make matters stranger, Jesus tells us that he intended such responses: 'I speak in parables, so that "looking they may not perceive, and listening they may not understand'" (Lk. 8.10). Why would he do that? Rickie Moore offers what I take to be the pathbreaking insight:

> Jesus told parables for one reason: in order to 'throw' people. Jesus threw people for one reason: in order that they might be broken. And Jesus became the wildest parable of all when He became broken. Everybody was thrown by that.[18]

Here, then, is the critical point. The same Jesus whom we find teaching in the Gospels is the Word who speaks in Scripture. And his pedagogy remains the same. He continues to tell parables, and for the same reason. He means to throw us, too.

The Endurance of the Scriptures

Obviously, talking in these ways troubles traditional Protestant notions of Scripture's clarity. I do not want to dismiss those notions too quickly, however. John Webster has provided an excellent model of the Reformed notion of Scripture's perspicuity, first, by placing it in 'a soteriological context' and, second, by insisting that Scripture's clarity belongs to the intervening work the Spirit and not to the text itself, isolated from faithful readings and the Spirit's guidance. In his words, 'Scripture is clear because through the Spirit the text serves God's self-presentation'. So, 'it is not Scripture which is self-interpreting but God who as Word interprets himself through the Spirit's work'.[19]

We should have no problem affirming the claim that the Spirit (at times) clarifies the Scriptures savingly for us. But we should also insist, I believe, that the Spirit at times obscures the Scriptures sanctifyingly for us. If the Spirit hid Jesus from the Emmaus disciples so he could teach them what the Scriptures say about him, then it makes sense to say the Spirit keeps us, for a time, from seeing clearly the meanings of Scripture so we too can begin to learn Christ, taking on his nature. We are learning to speak to, for, and about God just as we in fact give ourselves to meditation and contemplation, silence and prayer, prophecy and testimony. And we are learning to listen to/for God as we are wrestling with the Scriptures – and especially with our

---

[18] Shared with me via personal email.

[19] John Webster, *Holy Scripture: A Dogmatic Sketch* (New York: Cambridge University Press, 2003), p. 94.

neighbors' readings and performances of the Scriptures, neighbors living and dead, from our own and other traditions – as well as helping them to discern the faithfulness of their testimonies and prayers, their praise and their witness. Because we are creatures who have been spoken into being, made for dependence on God's Word and the words of one another, listening is where our interpretive task begins, and the Christian life is always necessarily a life that finds its center in the determination to hear together the Word of God in the Scriptures.[20]

Given that God comes to us always only surprisingly, gracefully mystifying and troubling us, we must read the Scriptures always 'with an eye to tensions within the text, to the voices on its edge, to which it opposes or suppresses', attending carefully to how the scriptural texts are 'unsettled, made "tense", driven into contradiction'.[21] In other words, we have to pay attention to what is strange in the text, what seems incongruous, unexpected. 'The sacred text thus enacts its sacred character not by its transparency but by its nature as unresolved, unfinished, self-reflexive or self-questioning. It is through these things that its "excess" appears …'[22] That 'excess' is the sanctifying touch of Christ's presence, the way he, as Word, gets to us and does his work on us.

While we often claim that the Spirit in the manifestations of the charismatic gifts will never contradict the Scripture, we often fail to see that if we hope to come into alignment with 'the mind of Christ', then the Spirit must at least sometimes contradict us – and that includes, perhaps above all, our readings of Scripture. Without that contradiction, sanctification simply cannot take place. As Bonhoeffer says,

> The entire Bible, then, is the Word in which God allows himself to be found by us. Not a place which is agreeable to us or makes sense to us *a priori*, but instead a place which is strange to us and contrary to our nature. Yet, [that is] the very place in which God has decided to meet us.[23]

---

[20] See Webster, *Word and Church*, pp. 227-29.

[21] Rowan Williams, 'Historical Criticism and Sacred Text', in David F. Ford and Graham Stanton (eds.), *Reading Texts, Seeking Wisdom: Scripture and Theology* (Grand Rapids: Eerdmans, 2003), pp. 224-25.

[22] Williams, 'Historical Criticism and Sacred Text', p. 227.

[23] Bonhoeffer, *Meditating on the Word*, p. 45.

God not only meets us there – at the point of our troubledness and bewilderment and wonder and awe – but also there transfigures us. That is, sanctification is possible because of the contrariness of the Word, because the Spirit makes these texts 'hard' for us. It is difficult for us who have been raised in a Christianized culture – or even a 'Christ-haunted' post-Christian one – to recognize how strange Scripture really is. We have a familiarity with the 'body' of these texts that numbs us to their 'spirit', their odd liveliness. But, in T.F. Torrance's words, we mature into our knowledge of God 'only as we allow what we learn of God to strip us of our own inventions and presuppositions …' And that means we must somehow encounter the Scriptures anew, stripping away as best we can the layers of familiarity that have clouded our vision.[24]

Read in this way, Scripture inculcates habits of what Sarah Coakley calls 'un-mastery',[25] which keeps us endlessly 'open to the possibility of risk and challenge'.[26] To borrow an image from Israel's story, the Spirit uses the Scriptures to lead us on 'the roundabout way' (Exod. 13.18), like Israel in the wilderness, to prove what is in our hearts. Or, to change the image yet again, the Spirit uses the difficulty of reading Scripture to press us into service, as the Roman soldier forced Simon of Cyrene to bear Jesus' cross. And just in this way the Spirit brings us into contact with Christ, availing us to the suffering that will impress on our affections and imaginations the character of the God Jesus makes known.

Frustration as/and Redemption

Why would the Spirit obscure the Scriptures? Because we are constantly at risk of 'premature closure', endlessly tempted to seek out a kind of 'instant clarity and transparency' that fulfills our desires and puts all of the ambiguity of human experience and language behind us. But, to borrow Paul's phrasing, learning Christ comes over time as a process – not always or even usually in a single, epiphanic

---

[24] Thomas F. Torrance, *The Hermeneutics of John Calvin* (Edinburgh: Scottish Academic Press, 1988), p. 164.

[25] Sarah Coakley, *God, Sexuality, and the Self: An Essay on the Trinity* (Cambridge: Cambridge University Press, 2013), p. 43.

[26] Coakley, *God, Sexuality, and the Self*, p. 49.

moment of 'penetration and mastery'.[27] The complexity and impenetrability of the language of the Scriptures, therefore, affords us sanctifying adversity. We find, as we struggle with and against the Scriptures, that the fulfillment of our deepest desires – to delight in all things in God – is deferred into hope, and in that state of frustrated, enflamed desire we also find our first love renewed in us.[28]

Paul says of Scripture that 'all these things which were written so long ago were written so that we, learning perseverance and the encouragement which the Scriptures give, should have hope' (Rom. 15.4 NJB). But, again, we have to ask how this happens? The Scriptures teach us endurance not so much by providing us with examples of patience as by requiring us to persevere in the work of interpretation. In the suffering that comes in seeking to interpret Scripture faithfully we begin to learn endurance, and to develop the character that grounds authentic, sustaining hope in the God who does not disappoint (Rom. 5.3-5). In other words, it is only as we learn to endure the oddity and contrariness of the biblical texts that we learn to endure our neighbors whom the Lord of Scripture calls us to serve.

We hear an echo of this truth in Romans 8, which sings of God subjecting creation to 'frustration' (Rom. 8.20). God does so, Paul avers, 'in hope' – a hope not fulfilled until our incorporation into Christ's final appearing and the 'manifestation of the sons and daughters of God' (Rom. 8.21). As I argued in the first part of this book, we are called as mediators to the creation of God's divine-human holiness. And we cannot do our work without knowing that unless and until our work is perfect, the creation remains subjected to 'futility', bound in 'frustration'. Therefore, the Spirit leads us into our vocation precisely by frustrating us, and our ambitions to make meaning of God's Word, subjecting our interpretive work to futility. Only so God awakens us to the true hope that opens our eyes to Christ hidden in the text and in our neighbor. To that end, 'the Spirit's work in [our reading of] Scripture is not unlike the Spirit's work in creation,

---

[27] Williams, 'Language, Reality and Desire', p. 142.
[28] Williams, 'Language, Reality and Desire', pp. 142-43.

namely, groaning over the brokenness, brooding over the chaos, and calling forth new worlds'.[29]

The (Trans)Formation of Desire

Speaking of frustration reminds us that our sanctification is bound up with the alteration, the righting of our desires. 'To move into the divine life is to find desire reconstituted.'[30] Sanctification alters our desiring absolutely and entirely, although of course that takes all of our lives – and more. It does so in three ways: by putting our unnatural desires to death; by re-ordering our natural desires, and by awakening in us 'supernatural' desires for God.

St Augustine argues that God uses Scripture to purge our minds of untruth by suiting the language of Holy Scripture to our immaturity and building into that same language depths of meaning. As a result, the more and more deeply we understand these truths, the more we find ourselves drawn up into communion with the divine transcendence:

> For, from the things which are found in the creature, the divine Scripture is wont to prepare enticements, as it were, for children. Its purpose is to arouse the affections of the weak, so that by means of them, as they were steps, they may mount to higher things according to their own modest capacity, and abandon lower things.[31]

Following Augustine's lead, Matthew Levering proposes that we think of interpreting Scripture as a 'task that at its best is a participation in God's own teaching', a task that ushers us into the transforming experience of God that re-orders our loves.[32] The work of reading Scripture, in other words, is for us grace, sanctifying us as we give ourselves to learning divine wisdom and 'training in righteousness' (2 Tim. 3.17). Romans 8 suggests the salvation of creation waits on and is somehow mediated through our salvation: the whole creation

---

[29] Johns, 'Grieving, Brooding, Transforming', p. 144.
[30] Williams, 'The Deflections of Desire', p. 120.
[31] Augustine, *The Trinity* I.1.2 (Washington, DC: Catholic University of America Press, 2010), p. 5.
[32] Matthew Levering, *Participatory Biblical Exegesis: A Theology of Biblical Interpretation* (Notre Dame, IN: University of Notre Dame Press, 2008), p. 68.

groans, in travail, longingly anticipating 'the manifestation of the children of God'. So, our salvation, and the salvation of all things, is bound up with the re-ordering of our loves in sanctification, in our coming to love God and neighbor perfectly – that is, in our coming to love with God's own love in a fittingly human way. Scripture, faithfully received, works to that end, not only by witnessing to Jesus Christ as the one Word of God, but also by becoming through the Spirit his interceding word to us and about us. As we are submitting ourselves to the Scripture in prayer, in preaching, in study, in meditation, we are inviting God to transform our loves into Christlikeness, so that in loving as he loves we can fulfill our calling as bearers of the *Imago Dei* and mediators of God's divine-human holiness.

Daniel Castelo makes a helpful distinction between the affections and the virtues, arguing that the affections are formed from above to below by divine initiative, and that the virtues are formed from below to above by human response.[33] That means that only as our affections are transformed by the Spirit can Christ's divine-human virtues be formed in us. And the church's ministerial practices provide the 'active forms of waiting' for God's graceful self-presentation, while the waiting itself also proves formational:

> … the spiritual senses are awakened and the fruit of the Spirit flourish. Over time, believers 'see' and 'hear' with greater acuity and attentiveness what God is doing, and as such they increasingly mature and grow in conformity to the divine image.[34]

Along similar lines, Rowan Williams suggests that our 'longing for communion with the Word' is not strictly a desire to know Jesus alone, but is 'a desire for the desire of the Word'.[35] In other words, we long to love the Father as Jesus loves the Father and the Spirit, and with them, all things. As we are 'incorporated into [Jesus'] relation to the Father', we come to share 'the "deflection" of the Son's desire towards the Father's excess of love'. That is, we come to share

---

[33] Daniel Castelo, *Revisioning Pentecostal Ethics: The Epicletic Community* (Cleveland, TN: CPT Press, 2012), pp. 60-61.

[34] Castelo, *Revisioning Pentecostal Ethics*, p. 53.

[35] Williams, 'The Deflections of Desire', p. 119.

in 'the movement of the Spirit',[36] which is the movement of God's own desire.[37]

What, you ask, does that have to do with reading Scripture? Following Castelo's and Williams' lead, I think we can begin to see how the faithful reading of the Scriptures belongs to the nexus between the awakening of the affections and the response of the virtues.[38] Reading the Scriptures serves as an 'active waiting' that troubles and bewilders us, comforts and awes us, awakening and re-directing our desires, inflaming our affections, engendering and nurturing the virtues in us. Reading Scripture with desire for Christ and his desire for the Father in the Spirit, we begin, by that same Spirit, to participate in the desire of Christ. We become, as Jackie Johns writes, 'participant[s] in God's affections'.[39] In other words, we begin to be Spirit-filled, and just so empowered for our vocational participation in Christ's mission.[40]

Living and Dying by the Word

Borrowing language from the Reformed tradition, we can say that as we are engaging these texts under the Spirit's influence, we undergo

---

[36] Williams, 'The Deflections of Desire', p. 119.

[37] Williams draws this understanding of Scripture from his reading of Augustine's hermeneutics. In *De Doctrina*, Augustine describes Scripture as 'arous[ing] in us an appropriate love and delight when read properly'. See Williams, 'Language, Reality and Desire', pp. 141-42.

[38] See Eugene F. Rogers, 'How the Virtues of an Interpreter Presuppose and Perfect Hermeneutics: the Case of Thomas Aquinas', *Journal of Religion* 76.1 (Jan 1996), pp. 64-81.

[39] Johns, 'Yielding to the Spirit', p. 81.

[40] See Verna E.F. Harrison, 'Allegory and Asceticism in Gregory of Nyssa', *Semeia* 57 (1992), pp. 113-30 (124). As Martin Laird, 'Under Solomon's Tutelage: The Education of Desire in the *Homilies on the Song of Songs*', *Modern Theology* 18.4 (Oct 2002), pp. 507-27 (516), explains, the three Solomonic books serve as a focus of Gregory's hermeneutical model. Through spiritual readings of Proverbs and Ecclesiastes, believers are enflamed with desire for virtue and the invisible, immaterial realities of the heavenly world. But the 'ineffable mysteries' embodied in the erotica of the Song of Songs draw readers beyond desire into communion with the one desired, into 'union with God beyond all image and concept', the 'holy of holies' of the divine being. Through the pedagogy of allegorical interpretation, moving beyond the literal sense of the texts to the underlying, spiritual senses, readers move toward godlikeness, their passions overcome in virtues. See also Hans Boersma, *Embodiment and Virtue in Gregory of Nyssa: An Anagogical Approach* (New York: OUP, 2013), p. 6.

mortification and vivification. In Webster's words, 'to read Holy Scripture is to be gathered into the divine work of reconciliation in which we are slain and made alive'.[41] We do not merely 'apply our interpretive skills to one more set of texts'. Instead, reading in faith by the Spirit, we avail ourselves to the God we have always over-looked or resisted.[42] Rapt by the Spirit in the interpretive event, we 'keep company with the holy God',[43] and keeping that company means we begin to be healed from the corrupting disease of sin and freed from bondage to the powers, delivered into the kingdom of the beloved Son (Col. 1.13), even if this transformation does not come as quickly and powerfully as we might wish.

Webster is surely right: faithful reading of Scripture is 'an escha-tological activity'.[44] But what does that mean, really? It means, as he says, that God's Word is nothing we can possess or manage. It is not a thing at our disposal to use as we like. Instead, it happens to us as we hear these texts and try to hear them rightly.[45] The divine sancti-fying work re-situates us within the newly-constituted order of God's hidden, heavenly reign so that we come to live, move, and have our being 'in the presence of, in response to, and under the tutelage of the new reality which has been established definitely in Jesus Christ'.[46] Crucially, because the act of interpreting the Scripture brings us into contact with the End in which all things are made holy as God is 'all in all', the interpretive act necessarily alters us by opening us up to a hidden – but not secret! – reality that calls into question, among other things, our moral common sense and our political realism.

What we see in Scripture tells us not only the truth about how we imagine God, but also the truth about how we see our neighbors and ourselves and our responsibilities for their well-being. Therefore, the effort to read the Scriptures faithfully, in the context of our experi-ences and interactions with one another, forces us into a crisis where it becomes possible for us to develop the character and skills needed for faithful interpretation and graceful mediation. Not to put it too

---

[41] John Webster, 'Reading Scripture Eschatologically (1)', in David Ford and Graham Stanton (eds.), *Reading Texts, Seeking Wisdom* (London: SCM Press, 2003), pp. 245-56 (249).

[42] Webster, 'Reading Scripture Eschatologically (1)', p. 249.

[43] Webster, 'Reading Scripture Eschatologically (1)', p. 246.

[44] Webster, 'Reading Scripture Eschatologically (1)', p. 248.

[45] Billings, *The Word of God for the People of God*, p. 204.

[46] Webster, 'Reading Scripture Eschatologically (1)', p. 248.

simply, but God gives us Scripture so that in our efforts to make sense of these texts we might learn how to interpret one another and our shared experiences of God and the world, experiences which are every bit as difficult to read as the hardest parts of Scripture. Thus, we find ourselves caught up more completely in Christ's mediating work.

Perhaps, in conclusion, I can offer an extended reading as an example. As I have argued elsewhere, 1 Corinthians 11.2-16 is one of the more troubling texts the Spirit has given us. And the closer we read it, and the more we read others' readings of it, the more the trouble intensifies. The passage opens with a word of praise: the Corinthians have remembered Paul by keeping the traditions he has handed on to them. He then quickly offers a word of clarification: 'But I want you to understand that Christ is the head of every man, and the husband is the head of his wife, and God is the head of Christ' (11.3). Men must be unveiled and women must be veiled as they speak to God in prayer or for God in prophecy; otherwise, they 'disgrace' their 'head' (11.5).

Paul anticipates the question that is sure to arise, and answers that the man must be unveiled because he is 'the image and reflection of God', and the woman must be veiled because she is 'the reflection of man' (11.7). Having stated his case in one way, apparently tracing the logic of the incarnation, the apostle takes another tack in which he seemingly draws on Israel's creation story: 'Indeed, man was not made from woman, but woman from man. Neither was man created for the sake of woman, but woman for the sake of man' (11.8–9).

If women unveil themselves in worship, they bring an overwhelming disgrace on themselves and others. It is as if their heads were shaved (11. 5-6). Not only that, but women are also to be veiled 'because of the angels' or for the angels' sake (11.10). Having said that, Paul seems to alter course abruptly: 'nevertheless, in the Lord woman is not independent of man or man independent of woman' (11.11). Man comes from woman just as surely as woman came from man, and, in the final analysis, all come from God (11.12).

On the basis of these claims, the apostle goes on to insist that the Corinthians need to judge for themselves: is it fitting for a woman to pray with her head uncovered? Or for a man to pray with his head covered? He asks, rhetorically, 'Does not nature itself teach' that these things are wrong or inappropriate (11.14)? Does not nature itself teach that long hair on a man is a shame, but that a woman's hair is her 'glory', given to her as a natural veil or 'covering'? Apparently, he assumes that his readers know the answer to these questions and that those answers convincingly support what he has been arguing. So, he heads off any remaining disagreement with a final word: contentiousness is not a custom among the people of God (11.16).

This text generates a storm of difficulties. What Paul wants to say is far from clear, not only to us but to readers from the beginning, including, almost certainly, the first readers. We can only guess why he felt the need to say it at all. In Francis Watson's judgment, the text is marked by 'flaws, obscurities, and illogicalities'.[47] And Lucy Peppiatt has argued that it gives us nothing less than an interpretive litmus test:

> First, it is abundantly clear that the passage itself is one that commentators, without exception, claim is obscure. The total lack of consensus on the passage, and the wide range of readings clearly demonstrate that the church has been unable to 'make sense' of this passage of Scripture ... [What is more,] a traditional reading creates for us an embarrassment in terms of Paul's own thought, both with respect to his own argumentation in the passage, which remains convoluted, and with respect to his wider theology, which he appears to contradict in this passage. Was Paul really so muddled or so hypocritical or so tyrannical? [Finally], there is a clear agreement among commentators that this passage contains within it an 'apostolic ruling'. If this is the case, then surely the church needs to make a decision as to what should be enforced for all churches everywhere.[48]

All kinds of questions arise: why does Paul begin by speaking of the husband as head of the wife, only to talk about man and woman together from that point on? Does he mean to talk only to married men and women? Does he mean for the woman or wife to be veiled, or only to keep her hair uncut? Does he want the man or husband to be unveiled, or only to keep his hair cut short? What does Paul mean by 'nature'? Is it a reference to cultural custom in Roman culture, to

---

[47] Francis Watson, 'The Authority of the Voice: A Theological Reading of 1Cor 11:2–16', *NTS* 46 (2000), pp. 520–36 (522).

[48] Lucy Peppiatt, *Women and Worship at Corinth: Paul's Rhetorical Arguments in 1 Corinthians* (Eugene, OR: Cascade Books, 2015), p. 108.

the natural law inscribed in human conscience, to the condition of the world 'in Adam', or something else? And what does any of this have to do with the angels?

What are we, as readers of Christian Scripture, supposed to do with the parts of this text that seem hopelessly indecipherable? And how are we to handle the dissonances, the contradictions it creates with other biblical texts? In a startling passage, Jacques Derrida observes that 'The one who wanted to veil the heads of the women and unveil those of the men, that very one later denounced Moses and the children of Israel for having been veiled – 'the veil over the face of God, the veil over the covenant, the veil on the heart'.[49] How could Paul have missed the contradiction of requiring women in his communities to veil themselves when Christ's work accomplished the unveiling of all?

Of course, not everything in the passage is unclear. And, truth be told, the apparently clearer statements create the most trouble. First, Paul seems to write subordination into the divine life. Then, he ascribes that same subordination not only to marriage and civic life, but also to human be-ing itself. Finally, the appeal to nature, regardless of what it means, opens a Pandora's box of theological troubles. To put it bluntly, what sense does it make to say that in Christ 'All things have become new' or that 'There is now no longer Jew or Gentile' if 'nature' is simply another name for God's will? And if the Father is head of Christ in the same way that the man is head of woman, does that not mean that the Son is less divine than the Father and that the woman is less human than the man? If Christ is less than the Father, then how can we trust that he fully and truly reveals God? In the same way, if the woman is less than the man, then does that not mean the woman must be saved differently from the man? Indeed, does it not suggest that she must be saved through a man? Even if it is possible somehow to explain what the text says about the subordination of Christ to God, it is even harder to know how to deal with the way it speaks about the subordination of women to men or wives to their husbands and its appeal to 'nature' as support for this subordination.

The history of interpretation, at least as much of it as I have been able to read, suggests that until the last few decades, nearly every

---

[49] Jacques Derrida, *Acts of Religion* (New York: Routledge, 2002), pp. 346-47.

reading of this passage in the Christian tradition has used it to reaffirm patriarchy. Readers not only take Paul's words as an avowal of androcentrism and male superiority, but also contend that everything depends upon the truth of this establishment. What are we to do, if we are unsatisfied with this interpretation? We might simply accept the text's apparent meaning, whatever that happens to be, even if we cannot reconcile it with other beliefs that we hold or with other readings of other biblical texts. Or we might outright reject what it says as false and oppressive. Or we might ignore both the text and its history of interpretation, choosing not to be troubled by it all. Or we might use a historical-grammatical strategy to establish an unlikely but still plausible 'original meaning' of the passage that seems to us less offensive or problematic. Or we might try to discern the 'redemptive spirit' in what Paul has said, and extrapolate from it a moral or theological wisdom. Or we might, as Peppiatt does, contend that the patriarchalism in the text belongs not to Paul, but to the Corinthians.

At some point, it becomes tempting to dismiss the passage as simply too troublesome. Why bother with it? But we should resist this temptation. We can and should bother with it, I believe, because, as I have already said, God means to save us by interpretation, not from it. Therefore, whenever we find a text resisting us, as this one does, we need to ask how the Spirit is using it to trouble us toward the truth. It may be that this text is simply unreadable for us. But even so, it can serve as a reminder both of the limits of our understanding and the limitlessness of God's power to speak to others in ways they need to hear. And it may be that the text is patriarchal and hierarchical. But it does not follow that it therefore reveals God's desires for us. Perhaps, instead, it simply exposes our all too familiar readiness to submit to what seems 'natural' – the unquestioned and seemingly unquestionable customs and conventions of our particular worlds. If even an apostle succumbs to these temptations, or accepts them as unavoidable, as almost all Christian theologians from the ancient world to the modern world accepted slavery as unavoidable, then how much more are we likely to give in to them?

Even if all of that is true, more needs to be said. And if we follow Paul's line of thought to its end, we can hear at least something of what he must have wanted us to hear. In the essay on the resurrection, which comes at the very end of the letter, Paul promises that after Christ has sanctified and glorified creation with his own holiness and glory, he too will be 'subjected to the one who put all things in subjection under him, so that God may be all in all' (15.28). Here, we find the same pattern of rule and subjection. But now, the subjection is performed as an intra-Trinitarian gift-exchange and it accomplishes a perfectly mutual fulfillment through a perfectly mutual co-participation.

This should not surprise us, at least not if we confess the creed. If the Son is truly very God from very God, then his subjection cannot mean that he is somehow less than the Father or subordinated to him in any way. Jesus' identification with creatures does not alter his oneness with the Father and the Spirit. He is not demeaned by the incarnation. Instead, his identification with us is such that through the Spirit we become one with him in his oneness with the Father. Far from being reduced to a subordinate of the Father, therefore, his 'subjection' is our elevation into a shared enjoyment of his communion with the Father in the Spirit.

We can conclude, then, that the pattern of authority and submission described in 1 Cor. 11.2–16 is purposed for a fulfillment that both completes it and ends it. If maleness and femaleness come from God in creation (11.12), and so exist 'in Adam', then they are meant to be returned to God in and as new creation 'in Christ'. And in that light, we can see that the traditional readings fail to take the text's 'nevertheless, in the Lord' with necessary seriousness.

In Christ the male/female order 'in Adam' is fulfilled and relativized, and as testament to that reality we need both males and females to stand in Christ's stead at the Table. As George Hunsinger insists, the claim that only males can represent Christ at the Eucharist

> … contradicts basic elements in the doctrines of the incarnation and the new order of creation, the virgin birth, which sets aside male sovereignty and judges it as sinful, the hypostatic union of divine and human natures in the one Person of Jesus Christ who is of the same uncreated genderless Being as God the Father and God the Holy Spirit, the redemptive and healing assumption of complete human nature in Christ, the atoning sacrifice of Christ which he has offered once for all on our behalf, in our place, in our stead, and therefore it conflicts also with the essential nature

of the Holy Eucharist and the communion in the body and blood of Christ given to us by him.[50]

It follows, then, that we need both men and women serving together in the work of preaching and teaching, celebrating the sacraments, providing spiritual direction and pastoral care, working for social and political justice and peace, nurturing community and culture. If, indeed, the role of the priest is 'to confront me with God's incarnate word in such a manner that I can be sure that it is not I who am making use of it', then surely the ordination of women is not only prudent but actually necessary. Not to ordain them is to assure that 'nature' and not grace, this present age and not the Eschaton, has the first and last word on what it means for us to be priests of God for the sake of the world.

On this, the tradition has certainly always been right: our bodies and what we do with them matter. But we must not unreflectively accept whatever has been said about sex and gender in the church's history, or simply acquiesce to the majority opinion held by Christians down through the years. In this, as in everything else, the normal is not inherently normative. We should instead separate as well as we can the wheat of familiar Christian teaching about what it means to be male and female from the chaff of androcentrism, misogyny, and patriarchy. We should affirm Gregory Nazianzen's formula: 'One same Creator for man and for woman, for both the same clay, the same image, the same law, the same death, the same resurrection' – and then actually follow through on the social and political changes required by the truth of such a claim. We should affirm Aquinas's statement about women's full equality 'in the Spirit' – and then remove his and all other qualifications. In fact, his statement about women in religious orders should apply to all of us equally: they are free from the dominion of men because they, like their brothers, are subject to Christ, and subjection to Christ is radically different from and at odds with subjection as practiced in all 'natural' orders of society.

All to say, we are meant to know maleness and femaleness through the 'nevertheless' to nature that is spoken by grace 'in the Lord'. Through baptism, men and women alike share in the one new

---

[50] George Hunsinger, *Eucharist and Ecumenism: Let Us Keep the Feast* (Cambridge: Cambridge University Press, 2008), pp. 235, 240.

humanity of Christ (Gal. 3.26; Eph. 2.15). They cannot, therefore, be known 'after the flesh' any more than Jesus himself can be (2 Cor. 5.16). They are 'hidden' in him (Col 3.3) and just so revealed as new creations (2 Cor. 5.17). These convictions must continuously both shape and be shaped by the way we read 1 Cor. 11.2–16. The Spirit has given us this perplexing, troubling text, one that surfaces deep-seated presuppositions about maleness and femaleness. We should, therefore, receive it as a gift, trusting that the Spirit guides our troubled readings into the untroubled heart of the God who always meets us in the heart of our troubles.

The Spirit, the Seed, the Soils

Most, if not all that I have argued in the book to this point comes clearest in Jesus' parable of the seed and the soils in Mt. 13:3-9.[51]

> Listen! A sower went out to sow. And as he sowed, some seeds fell on the path, and the birds came and ate them up. Other seeds fell on rocky ground, where they did not have much soil, and they sprang up quickly, since they had no depth of soil. But when the sun rose, they were scorched; and since they had no root, they withered away. Other seeds fell among thorns, and the thorns grew up and choked them. Other seeds fell on good soil and brought forth grain, some a hundredfold, some sixty, some thirty. Let anyone with ears listen!

This deceptively simple parable reminds us that God is a story-teller and that his stories require attentive, careful interpretation. 'Listen!' is Christ's first and last word in this passage. His parable reminds us, too, that interpretation is from beginning to end a matter of the heart, a matter of radical, unconditional vulnerability before God and receptivity to God. 'Deep' readings, then, are not deep because they go over our heads. They are deep because they reach all the way down to the bottom of our heart of hearts. As it relates to interpretation, aptitude, skill, and expertise matter, of course. But they are not what matters most. What matters most is the readiness, the willingness to let the truth be the truth. And, as the parable tells us, so long as our

---

[51] Thanks to Lee Roy Martin for pointing this out to me.

hearts are hardened by superficial religiosity or by worldly cares and acquisitiveness, we can never truly receive the gift God wants to give.

In the reading and preaching of the Scriptures, 'deep calls out to deep'. So, we must never settle for superficial meanings, for the first pleasant or surprising interpretation that 'speaks' to us. And we must not let ourselves think, even for a moment, that the Word given is a resource to be used for our own purposes. In spite of what so many have been told, there are no 'biblical principles', secret or otherwise, that we can follow to make for ourselves the lives we think we want. On the contrary, the Spirit uses Scripture like a plow to dig at us, to break us open, to turn us inside out. God is a farmer who does not wait to find good ground. He makes it good. But that making good requires uprooting and plowing open our hearts. He wounds only in order to heal. But make no mistake: he wounds. It is not for no reason that Hebrews compares the Word of God to a sword (Heb. 4.12) and the prophet Jeremiah compares it to a hammer (Jer. 23.29). We become 'good soil' just in that we are opened and deepened, broken open and beaten down, stripped bare of anything that would choke the grace seeded into our spirit.

But the Gospel does not leave us only with this parable and its interpretation. Matthew tells us that after Jesus gives it, the disciples are confused – not only by what he said but also, but even more so – by why he speaks to the crowds in this way. His answer, like the parable itself, is deceptively simple:

> [11]To you it has been given to know the secrets of the kingdom of heaven, but to them it has not been given. [12]For to those who have, more will be given, and they will have an abundance; but from those who have nothing, even what they have will be taken away. [13]The reason I speak to them in parables is that 'seeing they do not perceive, and hearing they do not listen, nor do they understand'. [14]With them indeed is fulfilled the prophecy of Isaiah that says:
>
> > 'You will indeed listen, but never understand,
> >   and you will indeed look, but never perceive.
> > [15]For this people's heart has grown dull,
> >   and their ears are hard of hearing,
> >   and they have shut their eyes;
> > so that they might not look with their eyes,

and listen with their ears,
and understand with their heart and turn –
and I would heal them.'

[16]But blessed are your eyes, for they see, and your ears, for they hear. [17]Truly I tell you, many prophets and righteous people longed to see what you see, but did not see it, and to hear what you hear, but did not hear it (Mt. 13:11-17).

On the face of it, Jesus' answer suggests that the apostles know all the secrets. It suggests that they, unlike the crowds, are 'blessed', because they have heard and seen what all the prophets and saints longed to see and to hear but did not. His answer also suggests that he wants the crowds not to understand. He says, quite bluntly, that he gives them only riddles and dark sayings precisely in order to keep them from grasping the truth that would lead to their salvation.

But if we have been paying attention, we know we must not take the first interpretation, the easy one. And we must not take any reading that appeals to our 'flesh', our desire to be superior to others, to have an advantage with God over them. The disciples do not see and hear as clearly as they think they do, because as soon as Jesus tells another parable, they again require an explanation (Mt. 13.36). And at the end of his response, he says to them exactly what he had said to the crowds at the first: 'Let anyone with ears listen!' (Mt. 13.43). But they continue to misunderstand him, as can been seen in Peter's rebuke to Jesus after Jesus tells the disciples – ever so plainly! – that 'he must go to Jerusalem and undergo great suffering at the hands of the elders and chief priests and scribes, and be killed, and on the third day be raised' (Mt. 16.21). And in the request of James' and John's mother for her sons to be enthroned beside him once his rule begins (Mt. 20.20-23). Amazingly, the ones who understand Jesus best are a Canaanite woman who falls at Jesus' feet, pressing him, even after he has harshly dismissed her, until he heals her daughter (Mt. 15.21-28), and the woman in Bethany at the house of Simon the leper who anointed Jesus' head with a costly ointment (Mt. 26.6-13).

Paradoxically, then, those whom Jesus at first says do not understand him, do, in fact. And those he said at first did understand him, do not. He points to this enigma in a later parable (Mt. 21.28-32):

[28]What do you think? A man had two sons; he went to the first and said, 'Son, go and work in the vineyard today.' [29]He answered,

'I will not'; but later he changed his mind and went. [30] The father went to the second and said the same; and he answered, 'I go, sir'; but he did not go. [31] Which of the two did the will of his father? They said, 'The first'. Jesus said to them, 'Truly I tell you, the tax collectors and the prostitutes are going into the kingdom of God ahead of you. [32] For John came to you in the way of righteousness and you did not believe him, but the tax collectors and the prostitutes believed him; and even after you saw it, you did not change your minds and believe him.'

All to say, we must not come away from the parable of the seed and the soils with a cheap understanding of it. Especially as we are thinking about what it means to read the biblical texts faithfully, we must be careful not to let ourselves think we can work out a technique that produces the outcomes we desire – not even techniques that promise to show us the deep things of God. We have to engage these texts in the spirit of the woman with the alabaster jar, and in the spirit of the Canaanite woman who refused to go away without a fight. The woman in Simon's house knew something the disciples, somehow, did not: Jesus is bound to suffer. And so, she suffers for him and with him. The Canaanite woman knew not only that Jesus was the only one who could heal her daughter. She also knew that nothing would stop him from doing so – and she cared for her daughter too much to accept no for an answer, anyway. That is what we have to know, too, if we hope to read Scripture sanctifyingly. These sisters of ours embody love for God and love for neighbor, and this, as Jesus himself said, is the only way in which we can hear and understand the Word given to us. Without that love, the texts remain dead letters.

It is the 'implanted word' that saves us (Jas 1.21). But Christ is not only the seed sown by the Father. He is also the soil cultivated by the Spirit. He is 'plowed' (Ps. 129.3) so that we may be 'rooted' in him (Col. 2.7). And he is the water that nourishes the new life growing within our new nature. He gives us himself so that we can be ourselves fully. This is the promise of the gospel: 'A new heart I will give you, and a new spirit I will put within you; and I will remove from your body the heart of stone and give you a heart of flesh. I will put my spirit within you' (Ezek. 36.26-27). When all is said and done, then, Christ is God to us and us to God, the Word given and the Word received, so that we grow up just as he did, like a tender plant from what we had thought was barren ground. 'We are not a law to ourselves; the Lord is our law, and the law he writes on our hearts he writes by the same Spirit who wrote the scriptures'.[52]

---

[52] East, *The Doctrine of Scripture*, p. 138.

8

Praxis: The Ways of Sanctifying Interpretation

Introduction

Hopefully, by this point it is clear that I believe we are called to share in Jesus' priestly ministry, embodying God's own way of relating, bringing his overwhelming goodness to bear in the world. And I hope it is also clear that I am convinced the Scriptures have been given to us not only to identify the God who has called us to live his way of life and to teach us what this calling requires of us, but also to shape our minds and our hearts for that work. As I have said, these texts are purposed to do more than simply tell us the truth: they are purposed to make us true. In conclusion, then, I want to describe an array of interpretive practices that helps us attend to the canonical texts wisely, sanctifyingly.

What I am proposing should not be mistaken for a method, if by that is meant 'a self-sufficient set of rules' for reading the Bible.[1] What I am offering, instead, is a style of interpretation, characterized by a set of practices, which are galvanized by a spiritual posture or disposition of openness to the teaching of the Spirit.

Hearing the Whole Counsel of God

Everything depends on whether or not we actually give ourselves to the Scriptures. We need to saturate our hearts and minds with these texts – in our worship, in our devotions, in our scholarship. As Jenson insists, we need to 'privilege this book within the church's living

---

[1] Jeffrey Stout, *Ethics After Babel: The Languages of Morals and Their Discontents* (Boston: Beacon Press, 1988), p. 296.

discourse'.[2] And the reason for that privileging is obvious: God can use Scripture to sanctify us only as we actually attend to it. 'The first and foremost doctrine [about Scripture] is therefore not a proposition about Scripture at all. It is rather the liturgical and devotional rubric: let the Scripture be read, at every opportunity and with care for its hearing …'[3] So, when all is said and done, what matters most is not that we hold a 'high' view of Scripture, but that we become intimately familiar with its depths. We should know by now that 'honorific propositions about Scripture' are no evidence that we know the Word, or even that we know how to read the texts caringly and in the right spirit.[4]

We can give ourselves to reading and hearing and studying of Scripture because we trust God and therefore trust that he is at work. This is how Augustine heard the promise for us: as we devour God's words, we are eaten up by our desire for him, which, it turns out, is nothing less than his desire for us.[5] Practically, we should intentionally incorporate readings from the OT and NT into our weekly worship services, as in fact we are instructed to do (1 Tim. 4.13). In far too many of our services, the preacher's text is the only Scripture read, although, to be fair, songs or testimonies may also use language drawn from Scripture. And the hard truth is that a congregation simply cannot be sustained for very long on the strength a pastor's devotional life, however deep she might be. We can also commit to praying and singing the Scriptures together – corporately and individually, in community and alone. We could, at the very least, commit to praying the Lord's Prayer and at least one Psalm daily, in our time

---

[2] Robert W. Jenson, 'The Religious Power of Scripture', *Scottish Journal of Theology* 52.1 (1999), pp 89–105 [90].

[3] Jenson, 'The Religious Power of Scripture', p. 89.

[4] Jenson, 'The Religious Power of Scripture', p. 90.

[5] In Augustine's own words (*Confessions* VII.10),

When I first knew You, You lifted me up, that I might see there was that which I might see, and that yet it was not I that did see. And Thou beat back the infirmity of my sight, pouring forth upon me most strongly Your beams of light, and I trembled with love and fear; and I found myself to be far off from You, in the region of dissimilarity, as if I heard this voice of Yours from on high: 'I am the food of strong men; grow, and you shall feed upon me; nor shall you convert me, like the food of your flesh, into you, but you shall be converted into me'.

alone, as well as weekly in our worship gathering.[6] Who knows what good those habits would work in us and do for others over the long haul? As Merton says, 'If we use the Psalms in our prayer, we will stand a better chance of sharing in the discovery which lies hidden in their words for all generations. For God has willed to make himself known to us in the mystery of the Psalms.'[7]

I have said that we are bound to attend to all of the Scriptures. But we are also bound to attend to them as a whole.[8] Many of us are drawn back, again and again, to the same texts. But we must be careful not to fixate on those selections that we find most suitable or meaningful. On this, our mothers and fathers in the faith were right: we become a people formed in the Spirit just as we give ourselves to what they called 'the whole counsel of God'.[9] In the words of Elisabeth Sisson, 'it takes the Word, only the Word, all the Word to reveal to us fully and hold us wholly in Christ'.[10] Or, as Radner says, the faithful reading of Scripture is a 'particular discipline of hearing the whole Bible, Old and New Testaments together, speak of Christ'.[11]

We can only read the Scriptures as a whole if we read them under the rule of faith.[12] The unity of the Scriptures is not self-apparent; so, unless the Spirit forms in us the awareness required to discern how these texts hold together, we cannot hope to hear them as belonging

---

[6] N.T. Wright suggests three ways to use the Lord's Prayer:

First, there is the time-honoured method of making the Lord's Prayer the framework for regular daily praying … Second, some people use the Lord's Prayer in the same way that some use the Orthodox Jesus-prayer. Repeat it slowly, again and again, in the rhythm of your breathing, so that it becomes as we say second nature … Third, you might like, for a while, to take the clauses of the prayer one by one and make each in turn your 'prayer for the day' (*The Lord and His Prayer* [Grand Rapids: Eerdmans, 1996], pp. xiv-xv).

[7] Thomas Merton, *Praying the Psalms* (Collegeville, MN: Liturgical Press, 1956), p. 8. The Psalms are, he insists, 'the very expression of [the church's] inner life', and therefore a kind of sacrament of our 'union with the Incarnate Word' and 'contemplation of God in the Mystery of Christ' (*Praying the Psalms*, pp. 8-9).

[8] No doubt at some point in the move toward visible unity, the church will have to engage disagreements about the canon. Until then, we have to trust that the canon we have – and the translations we have – are adequate for the Spirit's work of making us the kind of people who can engage in those discussions savingly.

[9] Land, *Pentecostal Spirituality*, p. 100.

[10] *LRE* (Nov 1912), p. 23.

[11] Radner, *Hope Among the Fragments*, p. 92.

[12] See Robert W. Jenson, *Canon and Creed* (Interpretation; Louisville: WJKP, 2010), pp. 13-16.

to one story, witnessing in many voices to the one Word.[13] The Fathers were right about this, I believe: Scripture is 'undecipherable in its fullness and in the multiplicity of its meanings … an infinite forest of meanings' so that 'the more involved one gets in it, the more one discovers that it is impossible to explore it right to the end'.[14] Scripture is a 'true labyrinth'[15] – insuperably mysterious, endlessly complex, and inexhaustibly meaningful. Because they are divinely inspired, the canonical texts make a 'quarrelsome cohesiveness'[16] that incorporates us into one body as we learn to quarrel with it and with one another faithfully.

As we read, we should acknowledge and respect genre differences – as a rule, a proverb cannot be read like a Psalm, and a story needs to be read differently from both. But who knows how the Spirit might make use of these texts at any given time for this person or that community? Perhaps the Spirit can even make use of *misinterpretations*, if we distinguish between that and outright misuse or misappropriation of Scripture. The first, it seems to me, has to do with transgressing the literal sense of a text, its 'letter', while the latter has to do with violating its 'spirit'. Only the latter grieves the Spirit of the Word present in the act of reading.

Be that as it may, we must never mindlessly 'leap over' those texts that trouble us or seem to make no sense. Some passages will no doubt remain undecipherable for us. But we cannot say they make no sense, only that they make no sense to us.[17] We can be sure the Spirit has used them for the good of other believers in other times and places. Besides, that opacity can work for our good, much as speaking in tongues or contemplative prayer do – edging into our awareness a sense of the infinite excess of meaning in God's Word,

---

[13] As I mentioned at the beginning of the book, Chris Thomas recommends the metaphor of the black gospel choir, with the great variety of biblical texts as the individual voices that people the choir. The first goal of biblical exegesis is to let the voices be heard in all of their individuality and *only then* to move on to a hearing of the whole choir. The beauty of the singing is a beauty only enriched and textured by the 'dissonance'.

[14] de Lubac, *Medieval Exegesis Vol. 1*, p. 75

[15] de Lubac, *Medieval Exegesis Vol. 1*, p. 75.

[16] Borrowing the term one scholar uses to describe early Christianity. See Richard Norris, 'Articulating Identity', in Frances Young, Lewis Ayers, and Andrew Louth (eds.), (Cambridge: Cambridge University Press, 2004), pp. 71-90 (71).

[17] Robert W. Jenson, *Song of Songs* (Interpretation; Louisville: WJKP, 2005), p. 69.

an excess that often overwhelms us into awed and adoring silence before God.

(Re)Reading in the Spirit

It is good to be reminded that when we come to the Scriptures we are coming late to a conversation that has been going on for a very long time without us. This conversation gave shape to the Scriptures themselves, as well as to the numerous traditions that have emerged in the history of interpretation, including, of course, whatever traditions are shaping our readings now.[18] The Scriptures as we know them have come to us via 'innumerable discernments, assessments, discriminations, selections, writings and rewritings, editings, translations, disputes, critiques, power struggles, communal decisions, and responses to new events and situations'.[19] And if this long, difficult history teaches us anything, it teaches us that our engagements with the biblical texts are going to be long and difficult, too. Striving together to hear what the Spirit is saying to us, we will be caught up in interminable reading and rereading in changing circumstances and situations, preferably without the power struggles and communal dissension. Here is some good news: because God saves us not from but by interpretation and for it, these difficulties are a sign that the Spirit is truly at work among us, drawing us along, however agonizingly, toward perfection in Christ, the wisdom of God and our sanctification.[20]

One way that rereading teaches us wisdom is by requiring us to acknowledge that any reading we make is already drawing deeply from the well of other readings. In other words, we are inescapably indebted to those who have come to the text before us – a debt of love that exceeds all calculation. This is why Williams says,

> If I have read St Paul in 1 Corinthians carefully I should at least be thinking of my identity as a believer in terms of a whole immeasurable exchange of gifts, known and unknown ... an exchange no less vital and important for being frequently an

---

[18] Ford, *Christian Wisdom*, p. 66.
[19] Ford, *Christian Wisdom*, p. 67.
[20] Ford, *Christian Wisdom*, p. 66.

exchange between living and dead. There are no hermetic seals between who I am as a Christian and the life of a believer in, say, twelfth-century Iraq – any more than between myself and a believer in twenty-first century Congo, Arkansas, or Vanuatu. I do not know, theologically speaking, where my *debts* begin and end. [21]

Rereading also makes us wise by teaching us to own the fact that our readings invariably fall short, and not to be ashamed or frustrated by that. Ricoeur draws attention to the hard truth: 'It is *always* possible to argue for or against an interpretation, to confront interpretations ...' [22] Thus, no reading, except for God's reading at the Last Judgment, can be a final reading. This should not have caught us by surprise, because Scripture is *God's* Word, and we are finite and fallen readers, and we are not yet at the End of history. It only makes sense, then, that we are bound always to be reaching beyond our interpretive grasp when we handle the sacred texts. But precisely for that reason, the best readings are readings that gladly acknowledge their incompleteness and imperfection, so as to invite and make room for other readings – and even more the readings of others.

If it is true that we read Scripture not merely to gain knowledge, but to be moved by and toward wisdom that comes in truly loving God and neighbor, then the Spirit makes the most of Scripture for our and others' good when our attempts to make sense of the text remain open-ended. What George Steiner says about reading fiction and poetry applies equally well to interpreting Scripture:

A major act of interpretation gets nearer and nearer to the heart of the work, and it never comes too near. The exciting distance of a great interpretation is the failure, the distance, where it is helpless. But its helplessness is dynamic, is itself suggestive, eloquent and articulate. The best acts of reading are acts of incompletion, acts of fragmentary insight, of that which refuses paraphrase, metaphrase; which finally say, 'The most interesting in all this I haven't been able to touch on'. But which makes that inability not a humiliating defeat or a piece of mysticism but a kind of

---

21 Williams, *Why Study the Past*, p. 27.
22 Paul Ricoeur, *Interpretation Theory: Discourse and the Surplus of Meaning* (Fort Worth: Texas Christian University Press, 1976), p. 79.

joyous invitation to reread.[23]

Despite what some seem to think, reading in the Spirit does not mean we are free to make the text mean whatever we want it to mean. On the contrary, because we trust that the Scriptures are peculiarly useful for God's work in us, we can risk letting the texts speak for themselves, on their own terms. Of course, given the intractable difficulties of interpretation, we can never be sure that we have been entirely successful. But in faith we trust that God can enliven our readings of the text in such a way that we can hear what we need to hear, without forcing our own agenda on the text.[24] Reading Scripture faithfully means quieting our own voice so we can hear the Word that whispers to us with, in, and from the texts.

Many – or, more likely, all – of us have been trained to go to Scripture and to draw out of it a meaning that serves a purpose or meets an immediate felt need. Worst of all, we have been conditioned to use it to make and win arguments. But that kind of reading has little, if any, long-term sanctifying effect. In fact, if we continue to do it, it will only make it increasingly harder for us to tell the difference between what is true and what we want to be true. So, we need, instead, to settle down into the work of reading, allowing the texts to weigh on us. And that kind of reading takes time and so demands both patience and courage. Against our own instincts and the pressures of what we sometimes call 'real life', we have to learn how to dwell in the interpretive moment, pushing past the readings that come easiest to us, straining to hear the harmonies that lie just outside our normal range of hearing.

We need to avoid using the Scripture-interprets-Scripture principle to play one text off against another in some kind of rivalry of truthfulness or authoritativeness.[25] Instead, we should explore the meanings of the biblical texts in their own integrity and their own right.[26] Then – and only then – 'can we do justice to the convergence

---

[23] George Steiner, 'The Art of Criticism 2', *The Paris Review* 137 (Winter 1995); available online: http://www.theparisreview.org/interviews/1506/the-art-of-criticism-no-2-george-steiner; accessed: 1 September 2014.

[24] My Doktorvater, Chris Thomas, provides an excellent model for this kind of disciplined reading in his recent commentary on Revelation: *The Apocalypse: A Literary and Theological Commentary* (Cleveland, TN: CPT Press, 2012).

[25] Williams, 'Historical Criticism and Sacred Text', p. 223.

[26] Williams, 'Historical Criticism and Sacred Text', p. 223.

of scriptural meanings …'[27] For this reason, it is crucial as we are reading the Scriptures to pay attention to the use one scriptural passage makes of another, to listen for intertextual echoes and resonances, and to follow the lines of the emerging theological trajectories. Consider, for example, how Paul uses Ps. 44.22 at the end of Romans 8: 'Because of you we are being killed all day long, and accounted as sheep for the slaughter' (Rom. 8.36). In the Psalm, this is a line of protest, even accusation. But Paul reads it as a line of praise. His reasoning seems to work like this: because we are being slaughtered for God's sake, we are identified with Christ, the one who by God's will was slaughtered like a sacrificial lamb for us. Indeed, we are so identified with him that God's love for him falls on us as well, and for that reason nothing can separate us from God's love any more than it could separate the Father from the Son.

Or, for yet another example, consider the fact that the necromancer cares for the disgraced King Saul when everyone else – including God – has forsaken him (1 Sam. 28.20-25). Seeing that he is helpless and tormented, she kills the fatted calf for him, as the prodigal's father does for his helpless and tormented son. And like the priests of Israel, she bakes unleavened cakes for him. In this way, this witch, against all of our expectations, reveals that God prepares a table for us in the presence of our enemies so that we can see that our enemies are not his.

If our interpretation of Scripture is to work our sanctification, then we have to resist the temptation to explain away difficulties and ambiguities and contradictions by facile harmonizations. And we will be able to resist that temptation only if we have a deep confidence in the Spirit as our teacher, a readiness to trust ourselves and others, and the patience to wrestle with the text together in ways that move us toward God. In other words, we will have to learn to read with and for the community.

(Re)Reading with Community

Because of what we have been told to believe about the Scriptures, and because of the ways we have learned to read them – most of which we do not even realize we did learn, because we assume it is

---

[27] Williams, 'Historical Criticism and Sacred Text', p. 223.

merely natural – we come to the canonical texts with deeply held pre-commitments that more or less predetermine what they can say to us. If, then, we hope to read these texts in ways that work our sanctification,[28] we are bound to devote ourselves to the alter-native life of the church, to the sanctified and sanctifying community whose life bodies forth 'the mind of Christ' (1 Cor. 2.16).[29] As Hauerwas puts it, 'the right reading of the gospel requires an ecclesial location'.[30] Tragically, many in our tradition have come to believe that the Spirit's work is in the life of the individual over against and apart from the life of the community. And so, they have come to hold that there is no need to be trained to read the Bible. In fact, many seem to believe that the Scriptures are rightly read only by those who have not been prepared for the work. As if all that is needed is for us to follow our own instincts unquestionably. As if the authority of an interpretation comes from the reader's lack of theological preunderstanding, and the indifference he shows to traditional beliefs and practices.

But this runs hard against the grain of Scripture's own wisdom. Take, for example, Paul's words to Timothy, his son in the faith. Before he says anything about the Scriptures themselves, Paul instructs Timothy to remember that he was taught the truth and who taught it to him. This is true, first, of Timothy's church family: 'continue in what you have learned and firmly believed, knowing from whom you learned it' (2 Tim. 3.14). But it is also true of Timothy's father in the faith: 'Now you have observed my teaching, my conduct, my aim in life, my faith, my patience, my love, my steadfastness, my persecutions …' (2 Tim. 3.10-11). Clearly, then, Paul does not want Timothy coming to the Scriptures without an awareness of those who have trained him for the life of faith. In other words, Paul's instructions show that he believed Timothy could read the Scriptures rightly of if he was following the apostolic example, and living in communion with the people who had shaped his faith. Needless to say, the same goes for us, too.

---

[28] See Green, *Seized by Truth*, pp. 1-6.

[29] This is a key feature of the emerging Pentecostal hermeneutics. See Green, *Foretasting the Kingdom*, pp. 190-94.

[30] Stanley Hauerwas, 'Why "The Way the Words Run" Matters: Reflections on Becoming a "Major Biblical Scholar"', in J. Ross Wagner, A. Katherine Grieb, and C. Kavin Rowe (eds.), *The Word Leaps the Gap: Essays on Scripture and Theology in Honor of Richard B. Hays* (Grand Rapids: Eerdmans, 2008), pp. 1-19 [11].

The Scriptures belong to the God, not to the church or to one or another of its members. But they are entrusted by God again and again to the church – and only so also to you and to me, as individual believers. Faithful readings, then, are in that sense always 'traditional'. Even if they are innovative, or in some sense new, they always arise from and within a shared conversation that includes the whole people of God. And they are offered always only for the good of that community, and the fulfilment of its responsibility to bear witness to the goodness and faithfulness of God. Therefore, undisciplined, self-directed readings of Scripture are both a faithless denial of our indebtedness to the mothers and fathers and sisters and brothers who have taught us the faith, and a self-willed assertation that the Spirit rests on us individually, independent of the other members of Christ's body.

This is why Christian engagement with Scripture happens, paradigmatically, in the church's worship.[31] Pentecostalism is a mystical tradition, but it is a shared mysticism, communal and intercessory. So, the definitive 'place' for biblical interpretation is not the 'prayer closet' or 'the public square', vital as those places are; instead, the definitive place is the worship gathering, the set-aside time and space of the liturgy. For Pentecostals, in other words, the Scriptures are authoritatively read in the shared space of the mutual experience of God and one another in prayer, testimony, singing, and preaching.[32] Readings that arises in other places prove their worth, their trustworthiness, in this setting.

This all comes into focus through the 'anointed sermon',[33] in which a biblical text or, more often, a set of texts, 'comes alive' in both preacher and audience alike.[34] As the preacher attends both to the texts and to the ways they move her, she gathers up past, present,

---

[31] Ford, *Christian Wisdom*, p. 78.

[32] For an exploration of how form affects and effects content, see Arthur C. Danto, 'Philosophy and/as/of Literature', in Garry L. Hagberg and Walter Jost (eds.), *A Companion to the Philosophy of Literature* (Malden, MA: Blackwell Publishing, 2010), especially pp. 54-56. Thinking specifically about the 'canonical literary format' of the 'professional philosophy paper', Danto wonders if in the process of moving away from the dialogue (e.g. Plato's) and meditation (e.g. Descartes'), professional philosophers and their work have not 'lost something central'.

[33] Cheryl Bridges Johns, 'What Makes a Good Sermon: A Pentecostal Perspective', *Journal of Preachers* 26.4 (Pentecost 2003), pp. 49-50.

[34] Johns, 'What Makes a Good Sermon', pp. 46-48. See also James McClendon, *Systematic Theology Vol. 1: Ethics* (Nashville: Abingdon Press, 1986), p. 31.

and future all at once, binding them together by means of a 'this is that' vision. Her vision directs the hearers' attention toward God and what God wants to do in the world, and in this way frees herself and her hearers to believe that God is truly at work in all things – and moves them to find ways to participate in that work as it is already happening in and around them.[35]

But we cannot participate rightly in what God is doing or answer fully the call to read with and within community, if we limit ourselves to communion with those who already share our theological pre-commitments and interpretative practices. As I have said, we have to read with and for all God's people, living and dead and not yet born, within and without our own tradition. We cannot truly open our-selves to the whole counsel of God if we do not read with and for the whole people of God. 'No scripture is of any private interpreta-tion, and it is with all saints that we are to comprehend what is the height and depth and length and breadth, and know that love which passeth knowledge.'[36]

This is easier said than done, of course, but we have to seek out ways to hear interpretations of Scripture that differ from our own. This can be done through reading, of course, but also in conversa-tion. However we do it, we must trust the process, allowing the Spirit to teach us as we learn from them.[37] Only intentionally rereading in 'company different from usual' opens us to new horizons of mean-ing.[38]

Attending to the whole counsel of God in conversation with the whole people of God means nothing if we forget that we are called to serve the world. To put it bluntly, we are reading only for ourselves and our 'faithful remnant' unless we take up the Scriptures always also in the hearing of the 'cries, calls, appeals, and shouts' of those for whom he gave and gives his life.[39] If we want to read for Christ, and not for ourselves, then we have to attend to their needs, their voices. As David Ford reminds us,

> the discernment of cries is … a fundamental responsibility of communities and their members, and the reading of scripture is a

---

[35] Johns, 'What Makes a Good Sermon', p. 52.
[36] *WE* 127 (February 19, 1916), p. 9.
[37] Ford, *Christian Wisdom*, p. 69.
[38] Ford, *Christian Wisdom*, p. 68.
[39] Ford, *Christian Wisdom*, p. 65.

schooling in this discernment as an accompaniment to the cries of praise, joy, thanks, interrogation, repentance, petition, intercession, lament, hope, proclamation, blessing and love in which readers are summoned to join.[40]

I have been rewriting this chapter during a global pandemic, which seems to have triggered a world-wide economic crisis. I have heard cries of desperation from cities in Mexico, filled with gang violence, Putin's Russia, horrible outbreaks of the virus in prisons and on Native American reservations in the US. Just a few days ago, I watched the video of Ahmaud Arbery's murder, and I have seen some of the ugly justifications of what was done to him, and many stubborn refusals to face the sickness of white supremacy that diseases everything in our lives. But I have also seen and heard so much that is beautiful and joyful. Conversations with friends. Movies with my wife. Games with my children. I know all of these experiences are impacting me, at least superficially. But I hope the Spirit is seeding them all deeply in my spirit, in my subconscious. If I can be touched there by the experiences of others, if I can truly be moved by compassion, weeping with those who weep and rejoicing with those who rejoice, then my readings of Scripture will have to change as I am changed.

Faithful engagement with God and neighbor in worship sanctifies us for the reading of Scripture because in that engagement we begin to develop a 'feel' for the ways of God – this, we might say, is our share in the 'sense of the faithful' – that guides our interpretations.[41] Reading like this does not come to us naturally – or supernaturally. We must learn to do it together in community over time by doing it and seeing others do it. In other words, we need to be 'apprenticed to past and present wise readers of scripture who have lived their lives in response to its message'.[42] In these ways, we may learn to 'read the Spirit', attending to what God the Spirit is doing in our lives, as well as the lives of our neighbors and our enemies. We cannot read

---

[40] Ford, *Christian Wisdom*, pp. 68-69.

[41] David Kelsey, *Proving Doctrine: The Uses of Scripture in Modern Theology* (Harrisburg, PA: Trinity Press International, 1999), p. 167. See also Daniel J. Trier, *Virtue and the Voice of God: Toward Theology as Wisdom* (Grand Rapids: Eerdmans, 2006), pp. 198-99.

[42] Ford, *Christian Wisdom*, p. 86.

the Scriptures without at the same time trying to read the activity of the Spirit of the Scriptures in our lives.[43]

(Re)Reading for Christ

At its heart, the practice of reading in the Spirit and with the community is reading for Christ. This is true in two interrelated and mutually-determining senses: first, we should always be asking how a particular passage bears witness to the character or effect of Christ's life and work; and we should be always be open to allow that reading to press us toward living like Christ, submitting to his teaching, leaning on his wisdom. Abraham's offering of Isaac, for example, prefigures obliquely the Father's 'giving over' of the Son. But we need to allow the spirit of that story to stir up our affections so that we feel ourselves moved by it, edged toward ways of living that are good for us and others. We should read until we feel ourselves wanting to be made like Christ – even if that means all of our desires, including the desire to be with God and like God, must be, in a sense, sacrificed.

When we come to the Scriptures, then, although we are paying attention to the literary shape and movement of the texts, to the 'way the words run', we are not trying simply to rediscover 'original intent', or to uncover what the words actually 'meant' in the ancient world so we can work out how they might be made to 'mean' something for us today. Instead, as I have just said, we are trying to find the point of convergence of the literary, theological, and spiritual truth. Nothing more or less than that. Hence, as we 'read the way the words run', we do so in confidence that the Spirit 'shapes our imaginations in a manner that forces us to read the world scripturally rather than vice versa'.[44] In fact, that is, in the final analysis, the one rule of interpretation: any reading that moves us along toward oneness in Christ(likeness) and our shared participation in his intercessory

---

[43] As Stephen Fowl contends, 'if Christians are to read with the Spirit (as they agree they must) then they must also become adept at reading the Spirit's activity in their midst' (*Engaging Scripture: A Model for Theological Interpretation* [Eugene, OR: Wipf & Stock, 1998], p. 127).

[44] Stanley Hauerwas, *Working with Words: On Learning to Speak Christian* (Eugene, OR: Wipf & Stock, 2011), p. 108. Hauerwas' use of the language of 'force' is strange, if not problematic. See Keen, *The Transgression of the Integrity of God*, pp. 150-52. See also Hauerwas' response in the Forward to that same book (p. xxviii).

mission is a good reading; any reading that does not lead to that end is a bad reading.[45] And perhaps more than anything, we should remember that we should be humbled by Scripture, not exalted in our abilities to read it.[46]

To that end, we have to give up the idea of reading 'literally', because, as I have said already, that way of reading is false both to the letter and to the spirit of the biblical texts. We need to read literarily, theologically, and spiritually instead, paying attention to what the texts seem to want to do on their own terms, to the ways that the texts give witness to Christ in his relation to the Father, and to the ways that our hearts are stirred as we read. We will find all of that, I believe, if we commit ourselves to looking for the 'christological plain sense', because in the truth about him the art of the biblical narrative, the movements of the Spirit, and the will of the Father are perfectly aligned.[47] 'For indeed Christ – as the creed tells us – is God's agenda in Scripture, and it is God whom we should always try to discern, as what the text before us "really" imports.'[48]

Rereading for Christ assumes that the Scriptures are uniquely bound to him and his work. As Rowan Williams puts it, 'At the heart of scripture the prophetic word becomes the Incarnate Word. At the heart of scriptures is the fire of God's presence, of God's gift perfectly given and perfectly received in Jesus Christ'.[49] The Spirit leads us into the fullness of God in Christ by directing us into the fullness of the Scriptures' witness to Christ.

This is why we believe that Jesus is to be found in the OT with the 'same particularity as in the Gospels'.[50] In his commentary on Isaiah, Goldingay contends that the doctrine of the Trinity 'seriously skews our theological reading of Scripture', because it 'excludes most of the insight expressed in the biblical narrative's portrayal of the

---

[45] See Augustine, *De doctrina christiana* 1.35.39.

[46] As Williams reminds us, 'the difficulty of the sacred text [does not offer] a kind of elevated recreation for advanced souls' ('Language, Reality and Desire', p. 143).

[47] Jason Byassee, *Praise Seeking Understanding: Reading the Psalms with Augustine* (Grand Rapids: Eerdmans, 2007), pp. 247-54.

[48] Jenson, *Canon and Creed*, p. 82.

[49] Rowan Williams, *Open to Judgment: Sermons and Addresses* (London: Darton, Longman and Todd, 2014), p. 160.

[50] Radner, *Hope Among the Fragments*, p. 92.

person and its working out of the plot'.[51] In his view, listening for Jesus in the OT is to ignore what the OT actually says. And he argues, for example, that Isaiah's vision of God is not a vision of the Trinity, and that the angelic 'holy, holy, holy' witnesses not to God's tri-personal oneness, but to the 'distinctively supernatural, dangerous, almost frightening, divine nature, which should make people bow their head simply because they are creatures – let alone because they are people polluted by their wrongdoing'.[52] But this is to misunderstand entirely who Jesus is and how Scriptures speak of him. There can be no vision of the divine nature that is not a vision of Jesus, the person of God in whom God's fulness is presented to us. Hence, the Gospel of John understands Isaiah's vision to be exactly what Goldingay says it cannot be (Jn 12.37-41):

> [37]Although he had performed so many signs in their presence, they did not believe in him. [38]This was to fulfill the word spoken by the prophet Isaiah: 'Lord, who has believed our message, and to whom has the arm of the Lord been revealed?' [39]And so they could not believe, because Isaiah also said, [40]'He has blinded their eyes and hardened their heart, so that they might not look with their eyes, and understand with their heart and turn – and I would heal them'. [41]Isaiah said this because he saw his glory and spoke about him.

The Gospel insists that it is just because Isaiah has in some sense seen Jesus that the prophet knows the fate of those to whom the God's glory is revealed. Isaiah sees in the glory of the exalted Christ the character of God and understands the effects it must have on those who love darkness rather than light.

In spite of what Goldingay believes, then, literary, theological, and spiritual readings of the OT emerge from the dual recognition of the fact that the God to whom Jesus prays is none other than the God of Abraham and that the God to whom Abraham prayed was none other than Jesus Christ. For Christians, Israel's Scripture are true to

---

[51] John Goldingay, 'Biblical Narrative and Systematic Theology', in Joel B. Green and Max Turner, *Between Two Horizons: Spanning New Testament Studies and Systematic Theology* (Grand Rapids: Eerdmans, 2000), p. 133.

[52] John Goldingay, *The Theology of the Book of Isaiah* (Downers Grove, IL: Inter-Varsity Press, 2014), pp. 11, 24.

themselves just in their witness to Jesus as the revelation of the God Abraham and Sarah, the God of Moses and Miriam and Aaron.[53]

Of course, those stories are almost always stories of failure and loss. They are always, without exception, stories of suffering. So, to read the OT for figures of Christ is to look for the ways in which those failures and that suffering make possible new ways to pray, new ways to speak to the past and to the future, new ways to hold sorrow in hope, new ways to recognize the worth of others. If we read them well, we will come away with an awareness that everyone we meet – including everyone we meet in Scripture – bears a likeness to Christ, and is claimed by him as beloved. And if it is true of them, then it is also true of us. Knowing this, we can read with confidence that God's sanctifying work in our lives is bound up with our readings of the biblical texts – but not in such a way that we are saved by our good readings.

> We need to read the Bible … around Christ, and read it, therefore, in the confidence that our own mishearing and misapprehending, our own confusions and uncertainties … are going to be part of God's triumphant work in us … As the text of encounter and contest is fulfilled in our own struggles, so we pray that the culmination of that text, the Word Incarnate, may triumph in each of us, in our reading, in our praying and in our living.[54]

Rereading for Christ brings us again and again to moments of repentance, times in which a truth in the Scriptures stands over against us as that word of reproof or correction (2 Tim. 3.16). In fact, I would argue we cannot be faithful readers of Holy Scripture unless we accept that Scripture shares in God's authority, so that it has a priority over our readings of it. The Bible is effective in that the authoritative God acts in my reading of it, and my submission to the process of interpretation created for me, for us.[55] Bound by this conviction, we are sure to find that much of the time the sacred texts at least seem to be saying something very different from what we want them to say, suggesting meanings very much at odds with what we expected to find. Many times, if not always, we will find ourselves 'torn

---

[53] Steinmetz, 'The Superiority of Pre-Critical Exegesis', p. 37.

[54] Williams, *Open to Judgment*, p. 160.

[55] Thomas R. Yoder Neufeld, *Killing Enmity: Violence and the New Testament* (Grand Rapids: Baker, 2011), p. 13.

between wishing the text did not say "that" and knowing [we] need in some sense to submit to its authority'.[56] So much depends on our not overreacting in those moments, our willingness to wait, to give the Spirit time to teach us what we need to learn – even if it requires a lifetime.

We can, perhaps, get a better sense of what is required of us in rereading for Christ if we think of it as like Samuel's search for the chosen one (1 Samuel 16). Like the prophet, we come to the biblical texts looking for someone. And we also fail to recognize him. As we dwell in the interpretive moment, meditating and reflecting on what it is that we are to hear, waiting for that moment of recognition, we have to allow reading after reading after reading to pass by, knowing 'the Lord has not chosen any of these' (1 Sam. 16.10). In fact, it is perhaps not too much to say that we have not truly 'heard' a text (or set of texts) until we find ourselves at our wit's end, baffled and disoriented by the failure of our expectations. But once we find ourselves asking, in some desperation, 'Are there any possible readings left?', we are perhaps just then primed for revelation.

Reading for Christ so often leads to disappointment. But it is not surprising, really. We are tempted to make interpretations of Scripture that fit our expectations and do the work we think needs doing; so, it is for our good that he frustrates us. Besides, the Christ we are searching for in these texts, the Christ we are trying to persuade to 'speak up' and to 'show himself' is in the God who is 'meek and lowly of heart' (Mt. 11.29). Perhaps that is the primary reason he makes us search for him? How else would we learn just how humble and unassuming he is?

(Re)Reading from the Heart

Rabbi Jonathan Sacks, in *The Dignity of Difference*, comments on what he takes to be the most astonishing aspect of the Genesis stories, in particular:

> Perhaps the most remarkable thing in the narrative of the covenant is the way in which, stylistically and substantively, the Book of Genesis signals G-d's love and concern for those of Abraham's family who are *not* chosen: Ishmael and Esau. Two scenes – the

---

[56] Neufeld, *Killing Enmity*, p. 13.

one in which Hagar and Ishmael are sent away into the desert and Hagar turns away from seeing her son about to die of thirst, the other in which Esau comes in to his blind father and both realise the deception Jacob has practised against them – are among the most emotionally intense in the whole Torah. Our sympathies are drawn to Ishmael and Esau ...[57]

Think about that last line for a moment: 'Our sympathies are drawn to Ishmael and Esau ...' He is right. But why? These are stories about election – in particular about God electing the younger instead of their elders. But, as Sacks observes, our sympathies are with those who are rejected; we stand with them – against God! And yet, if Sacks is right, that is precisely what the story and God want from us. Written by the elect community, they are intended to call into question whatever we think we know about election and the electing God. They do this almost exactly as Nathan does, confronting David: by telling us stories that move us to care about those whom we and God seem to have forgotten or passed over. And exactly in this way, they show us that we are in the wrong, and have wronged others, because we have completely misunderstood what election means and what the God of election wants.

This way of reading may strike us as strange, at first, because most of us have been trained to expect the text – and preachers and teachers of the text – to provide us with easy, straightforward knowledge about God, ourselves, and the way the world works. But what if God gives us these stories to test our hearts, to see where our sympathies lie, to cast doubt on our perspectives? What if the wisdom of God is formed in us only as our affections are worked against the grain of our knowledge and judgments?

As I suggested in the previous chapters, some of us come to the Scriptures, and especially the OT, embarrassed, if not outraged by what we are sure it says. We find so much of it mistaken, inappropriate, misguided, disgusting – even wicked; so, we are left to question if texts this difficult and troubling could possibly be the work of the God of Jesus Christ. It is true, of course, that we do not know these texts half as well as we think we do. And it is also true that some of our embarrassment and outrage is the result of our own moral

---

[57] Jonathan Sacks, *The Dignity of Difference: How to Avoid the Clash of Civilizations* (London: Bloomsbury Academic, 2003), p. 14.

confusion and bad faith. All that notwithstanding, I agree that the Scriptures are filled with offenses. But perhaps that is by design? Perhaps our embarrassment and confusion and outrage are what the text and the God of the text want from us? Perhaps the text and the God of the text know what they are doing, and are purposefully provoking us?

Without advising despair, I want to argue that we have been much more poorly instructed for the work of making good – that is gospel – sense of the biblical texts than we imagine. In fact, I believe it would be difficult to exaggerate just how unprepared we are for reading the Scriptures the ways they are meant to be read. This is because we have come to insist that the Scriptures make sense on our own terms and in our own time. As a result, we open the Scriptures looking for easy, final answers, answers that we can immediately put to effective use accomplishing ends of our own making. Or, to put it a bit less polemically, much too much of our interpretation focuses on the 'indicative and imperative moods', which stress 'cognitive clarity, sharp divisions and rejections, decisiveness, and focussed concentration'.[58] Whatever good reading in these 'moods' might do for us, if those are the only ways of reading that we know and enact, we are setting ourselves and others up for disaster. We become wise only as we read also in and for other 'moods', such as 'the interrogative mood of Job in the midst of suffering and bewilderment'; 'the subjunctive mood of exploration and openness to surprise'; and, perhaps above all, 'the optative mood of longing, hoping and imaginative anticipation of God's future'.[59]

On this score, Lee Roy Martin is exactly right: 'every [biblical text] includes an affective dimension'.[60] Our responsibility is to attend painstakingly to those dimensions, and we do that just by tracing the lineaments of our *responses* to the text. As we read, together or alone, we have to reflect theologically on what the reading is doing to us, how it is making us feel, why certain responses are being provoked in us (and not others), what connections are being sparked for us.

---

[58] Ford, *Christian Wisdom*, p. 78.

[59] Ford, *Christian Wisdom*, p. 78.

[60] Lee Roy Martin, '"Oh give thanks to the Lord for he is good": Affective Hermeneutics, Psalm 107, and Pentecostal Spirituality', *Pneuma* 36.3 (2014), pp. 1-24 (9). See also Lee Roy Martin, 'Longing for God: Psalm 63 and Pentecostal Spirituality', *JPT* 22.1 (2013), pp. 54-76, and Lee Roy Martin, 'Delighting in the Torah: The Affective Dimension of Psalm 1', *Old Testament Essays* 23.3 (2010), pp. 708-27.

Continuing to reflect, we need to offer those responses and provocations up in prayer and in conversation with others for discernment.

Some of the various wisdoms of the Enlightenment advise us to work out our troubles by theorizing about hermeneutics. Aquinas, however, directs us to prayer. For many of us, starting with me, the temptation to choose theorizing over prayer has to be faced again and again. Of course, Aquinas also insists that 'the interpreter who prays well' is sure to find that 'prayer improves the interpretation', mostly by altering the character of the interpreter herself.[61]

Once, in a Seminary chapel sermon, Chris Thomas took Ps. 137.9 as his text: 'Happy are those who seize your infants and dash their heads against the rocks'. Having acknowledged that we are rightly horrified by such a claim, Thomas asked us to consider how God's people could come to desire such a terrible retribution against their enemies. He encouraged us to hear in this cry for vengeance the inconsolable sorrow of Israelites in exile, a people alienated from everything they had known as right and good, held captive in the godforsakeness of a strange land. He then turned to the prophet of exile, Ezekiel, and traced the stories of Ezekiel's visions, beginning with his vision of God in Ezekiel 1 and ending with the vision of the restored Temple and renewed land in Ezekiel 47. In closing, he drew our attention to what is said there, in that last vision, about the children of Israel's enemies:

> [21]So you shall divide this land among you according to the tribes of Israel. [22]You shall allot it as an inheritance for yourselves and for the aliens who reside among you and have begotten children among you. They shall be to you as citizens of Israel; with you they shall be allotted an inheritance among the tribes of Israel. [23]In whatever tribe aliens reside, there you shall assign them their inheritance, says the Lord God.

The story began in exile, in the cries of the exiles for vengeance. But it ends in restoration and in assurances of mercy and care for the very children they had formerly cursed. And Thomas's sermon, precisely because it is so careful to listen to the text on its own terms, attends to this arc, this progression, so that we can see in it the arc of the gospel story, which leads us from the night of weeping into the day

---

[61] Roger, 'How the Virtues of an Interpreter Presuppose and Perfect Hermeneutics', p. 81.

of rejoicing. This, I would argue, is a model of what it means to read in the Spirit with the community from and for the heart of Christ, moving through the various 'moods' to arrive, broken open and emptied out, at the optative: longing for the God who makes all wrongs right and draws everything and everyone into full flourishing.

(Re)Reading toward Faithful Performance

It should go without saying: we are called to read and reread the Scriptures in service of the Spirit's work in making us like Christ for the sake of the world. That is, we are called to be 'hearers' of the Word in ways that make us 'doers' of it – co-embodiments with Christ of the divine nature (Jas 1.22). But, as Nicholas Lash reminds us, what matters is not simply interpreting the ancient texts that we call the Scriptures so that they have meaning for us here-and-now. No, what matters is that in and from our readings of the Scriptures we as the people of God come to body-forth and act-out the same life and mission 'achieved, intended, and "shown"' in Jesus, the sanctifying revelation of God.[62] So, Balthasar is right:

> We can say, 'Lord, Lord!' in the depths of spirituality and mysticism, we can 'eat and drink with him' sacramentally, but it is all in vain if we do not carry out the will of our heavenly Father … Neither faith, contemplation nor kerygma can dispense us from *action*. And the libretto of God's saving drama which we call Holy Scripture is worthless unless, in the Holy Spirit, it is constantly mediating between the drama beyond and the drama here.[63]

In the words of an early Pentecostal, no hermeneutical sophistication can cover for an untrue heart. We have to 'keep the heart, the inward man, in line with the truth already revealed'.[64]

This is a terrifying truth, and one that we ignore not only to our own hurt, but to the hurt of everyone we care for: Christians from the beginning have read the Bible in ways that justified bigotry and abuse, oppression and mistreatment. Look, for example, at the way

---

[62] Nicholas Lash, 'What Might Martyrdom Mean?' *Ex Auditu* 1 (1985), pp. 14-24 (23).

[63] Hans Urs von Balthasar, *Theo-Drama: Theological Dramatic Theory Vol. 1* (San Francisco: Ignatius Press, 1988), p. 22.

[64] *PHA* 4.10 (July 8, 1920), p. 9.

so many of the Fathers spoke of the Jews and of women. Look at what they said – and, even more, what they have failed to say – about slavery.

In June 1999, Al Mohler, then, as now, a leading public figure in American Evangelicalism, appeared on Larry King's show to discuss a 'submission statement' made by the Southern Baptist Convention. The statement drew heavily on Ephesians 5, and during the show, Patricia Ireland, the president of the National Organization of Women, asked how Mohler's 'literal' reading of Ephesians 5 did not entail an endorsement of slavery. Of course, as she knew, and as Mohler knew, the overwhelming majority of Christian theologians had read that passage in just that way. He tried to argue that because nothing in Paul's words suggests slavery should exist perpetually, and that now it in fact is no longer practiced, the call to submit to slave-masters is irrelevant. But King and others were unsatisfied, and asked if Mohler condemned the runaway slaves, like Harriet Tubman, who gained their freedom. Mohler responded, 'I want to look at this text seriously and it says submit to the master, and I really don't see any loophole there, as much as our popular culture would want to see one'.[65]

In July 1968, an AG minister, Calvin Bacon, who lived in Atlanta, felt compelled to attend Martin Luther King Jr.'s funeral at the Ebenezer Baptist Church. Bacon stood outside, along with thousands of others, listening to the songs and the sermon. And he asked himself why he had come: 'I had told my wife I was going to write an article about it. But I had never done anything like that before; I am a pastor, not a reporter. So was this really the reason?' Bacon admits that 'the American Negroes had not been treated right', but he did not appreciate King's approach: 'I can't say I fully agreed with his "nonviolent civil disobedience." Nonviolence, yes. But I wasn't sure our definitions were the same. Civil disobedience, no: I knew the Scriptures state that we were to submit to our rulers.'

After the service, Bacon looked at the wreath on the door of the church and asked himself, 'Why all the trouble? How long will such violence last? Who is responsible? What is the solution?' With these questions heavy on his mind, he returned to his car and during the

---

[65] 'The Long Shadow of the Civil War: Moral Meanings for Our Time', *Proceedings of Maryville Symposium Vol. 6* (Maryville, TN: Maryville College, 2013), pp. 23-24.

drive home, a passage from 1 Timothy came to mind: 'Let as many servants as are under the yoke count their own masters worthy of all honour, that the name of God and his doctrine be not blasphemed'. Reflecting on this passage, Bacon came to a conclusion:

> I had wondered why I went. I now had a clearer understanding – and a new appreciation for God's Word and its ability to show us the root and the solution to our problems. Civil rights legislation and government spending cannot, I believe, meet the basic needs of the ghettos, but the gospel can. Perhaps the day is past when whites can minister directly to blacks. They tend to distrust the whites because of the way they have been exploited by them, But if we whites cannot minister directly to the American negroes, surely we can support qualified Negro ministers who will provide some of the spiritual leadership they so desperately need in this crisis hour.[66]

Bacon is troubled that 'their ministers are now preaching social revolution instead of the gospel of Christ's saving power', and he is left hoping that 'all who love God and who love all the people of the world may find some way to help our black neighbors spiritually – through gospel preaching and Bible teaching'. He insists that violence and 'racial unrest' are deplorable, and that 'revolution and lawlessness' are the consequence of God's judgment. The time, then, has come for repentance, for the sake of America. And he concludes: 'But what we do must be done quickly'.

I am not singling Mohler and Bacon out for censure. As we all know, their way of reading is shared by many, many others, including perhaps a majority of white Evangelicals and Pentecostals in the US. But their willingness to say loudly and clearly what is more often mumbled in private should make it unmistakable to us that this 'literalist' way of reading (although, in fact, it almost always violates the literary sense), and the doctrine of Scripture that upholds it, betrays the gospel. The way Bacon and Mohler read these texts, and others like them, absolve us of responsibility for others and attributes the subjugation of women and the horrors of slavery to God's providence.

---

[66] *PE* (July 14, 1968), p. 21.

Those who read these texts like Mohler and Bacon do, take them as divine guarantors of the social norms they cherish and want to conserve because they have come to imagine that they are divinely given. Tellingly, these readings keep them in their social and political place – and, by default, keep blacks and other minorities in theirs, as well. Can anyone really doubt that the reason 1 Tim. 6.1 comes to mind for Bacon has to do with the ways his socialization as a white man in the American South runs deeper than his spiritual and theological formation?

If we take them at their words, Mohler and Bacon believe that if only black folk knew their place and kept it, as Scripture commands, then violence and lawlessness would not happen. And it suggests, too, not so subtly, that if Tubman and King and other blacks disobey the authorities, it is the Christian's responsibility to force them back in line. So, in saying that King is wrong to protest and Tubman wrong to escape, they are saying that the slavers were not only right to own slaves, but also right to punish them for their refusal to comply with it. And they are saying that the police and the FBI were right to do what they could to stymie the civil rights movement. It is difficult not to think that this is why Bacon says not one word about the violence or lawlessness of chattel slavery and the Atlantic slave trade. Not one word about the violence or lawlessness of the Jim Crow era. Not one word about unjust laws or abuse of police powers or corrupt court authorities. He does not even lament the fact that King is murdered.

In the end, then, it is hard to deny that those who read these passages in these ways are driven by a nostalgia for a segregated America, one in which blacks serve blacks with a gospel approved by whites. This is especially strange for Bacon, because his Pentecostal tradition is rooted in black spirituality and theology, which is why so much of the early movement was marked by civil disobedience, including above all the transgression of racial laws. And his views are made all the stranger because the modern Pentecostal movement arose from the experience of the first church, which was persecuted by the authorities for preaching the message of Jesus. But in truth, it is strange for any Christian to doubt the need for civil disobedience, given that Israel's deliverance began in the disobedience of the midwives, and led to Moses defying Pharaoh's orders. How is it possible for people to deny the need for civil disobedience when they acclaim Jesus, whose ministry was marked by these transgressions and was killed, at last, as a criminal among criminals?

In a word, then, I believe Mohler's and Bacon's way of reading these texts is terribly wrong. Even more than that: it is a betrayal of the gospel. And so, I am haunted by the fact that the last words in Bacon's article echo the last words Jesus spoke to Judas: 'But what we do must be done quickly'. It is as if he realizes, in spite of himself, that in turning away from the black community, he is turning away from Jesus, as well.

Years previous to that, a contributor to the *Pentecostal Holiness Advocate* warned that refusals to see the truth, willful resistance to the Spirit, resulted in Scripture becoming untrue, so that the Scriptures 'grow dark'.[67] And that, I believe, is what has happened and is happening to us, as we persist in reading the Scriptures in ways that deaden us to the needs of others, so we are no longer moved, as Christ was, by compassion. To put it as bluntly as I can, any way of interpreting Scripture that necessarily requires us to condone slavery and the subjugation of women is necessarily an anti-Christian one, and one that we should reject absolutely and abandon immediately. If we hope to read the Scriptures faithfully, or to talk about them truthfully, then we need to learn from the very people we have abused and neglected, trusting that God has spoken to them what we were too rebellious to hear.

I know what I have said in the previous paragraphs is provocative for some, and perhaps disappointing for many. So, let me quickly add perhaps the most critical dimension of performing the Scriptures has to do with how we negotiate our deepest disagreements with one another, especially our disagreements about what the Spirit's Scriptures require of us. MacIntyre is correct, I think: a living tradition is 'an historically extended, socially embodied argument ... in part about the goods that constitute that tradition'.[68] A dead tradition, of course, is one in which such arguments are no longer lively, no longer loving, no longer hopeful, no longer ways of drawing close to one another. Thus, in this time before the End, wisdom demands that we submit our readings of Scripture humbly and with a sense of humor, inviting discernment, leaving room for other readings, and giving time for the

---

[67] *PHA* 4.10 (July 8, 1920), p. 9.
[68] Alasdair MacIntyre, *After Virtue: A Study in Moral Theory* (London: Duckworth Publishing, 1981), p. 222.

various readings and counter-readings to prove themselves.[69] Until the End – and even after the End, in a different way – we are bound to interpretation. And that is just as it should be. Because interpretation is just what God is saving us by and for.

The Divine Performance

With that in mind, let me offer one final example: a reading of Romans 9-11.[70] As a rule, this passage has been read as a single coherent theological argument, assuming that the apostle had a particular point to make, which he crafted with perfect success, and that a good reading of the passage discovers that point and makes it understandable so that it can be used to build or support a particular Christian teaching. Against that consensus, I want to suggest that Romans 9–11 can more fruitfully be read not as a tidy doctrinal treatise but as a torrid theological performance, a transfiguring work playing out across a series of rhetorical moves and countermoves that in the end leave us not with nothing but with more than we could have imagined possible.

I have hanging in my kitchen at home a large, untitled, abstract painting. I was there the night it was created. The artist began with a line-drawing of a samurai fighting a dragon. Once this sketch was finished, he immediately began painting an image over it. In the original drawing, the warrior's right arm was thrown up, fingers splayed in spasm, as the dragon fell on him. To create the second image, the artist used the lines of that arm to paint a large, deeply rooted and widely branching tree under the moon in a perfectly green meadow. But as soon as the second image was finished, he began to paint a third image over it, reworking the trunk of the tree into the mast of a boat and the meadow into a sea in storm. Once that image was finished, he threw down his brushes, and grabbed handfuls of paint, which he smeared wildly. At the end of everything, then, the canvas was a sea of colors with two swirling vortices in the center: one in blues and whites, the other in yellows, reds, and greens. Keeping that image in mind, I want to argue that we can read Romans 9-11 as a

---

[69] See Luke Timothy Johnson, *Scripture and Discernment: Decision Making in the Church* (Nashville: Abingdon Press, 1983).

[70] See Chris E.W. Green 'Provoked to Saving Jealousy: Readings Romans 9-11 as Theological Performance' *Pneuma* 38.1 (2016), pp. 1-13.

similar performance, one that happens in waves and ends by flooding us with something more than a 'message'.

Right at the beginning, Paul admits that he is deeply troubled, much like Christ in Gethsemane. That fact alone should arrest our attention: his realization of the all-conquering love of God at the end of Romans 8 has led him to this troubledness, this sorrow. Precisely because he knows in Christ we are 'more than conquerors' (8.37), precisely because he knows 'nothing can separate us' (8.39), he is pressed into the heart of intercession: 'I have great sorrow and unceasing anguish in my heart' (9.2). His sense of the infinite depths of God's love and God's loveliness, as well as his sense of his own belovedness, stirs up his desire for others to know this love, too. In fact, his desire presses him to want to make of his life a sacrifice like Christ's: 'I could wish that I myself were accursed and cut off from Christ for the sake of my own people, my kindred according to the flesh' (9.3).

But he is also troubled by the fact that such a sacrifice is required in the first place. If, in fact, it is true that 'neither death, nor life, nor angels, nor rulers, nor things present, nor things to come, nor powers, nor height, nor depth, nor anything else in all creation, will be able to separate us from the love of God in Christ Jesus our Lord' (8.38-39), then how can it be that Israel, God's covenanted people, have been separated from Christ? He knows that Israel holds a privileged place in God's purposes – 'to them belong the adoption, the glory, the covenants, the giving of the law ...' (9.4-5). And yet they somehow have not received what is rightfully theirs and so have been 'cut off from Christ'. What has happened? Has God failed to keep covenant? Paul insists that this is not true (9.6-8): 'It is not as though the word of God had failed. For not all Israelites truly belong to Israel, and not all of Abraham's children are his true descendants: "It is through Isaac that descendants shall be named for you"'. This means that it is not the children of the flesh, but the children of the promise, who are counted as Abraham's descendants.

Paul is quick to insist that God did not fail Israel, in part because 'not all Israelites truly belong to Israel, and not all of Abraham's children are his true descendants' (9.6-7). Instead, God has given Abraham children through Isaac, who was born through faith. So, those who believe in God are Abraham's children as surely as Isaac was. In fact, they are the truest of his descendants, the spirit-children of the promise. On the basis of this reading, Paul then takes up the story of Rebecca's sons, Jacob and Esau, although it is not at all clear how one leads to the other. A few selected quotations from the OT narrative secures his point: before the boys had been born, 'before they had done anything good or bad', Rebecca was told that the older would serve the younger because God hated Esau but loved Jacob. And so, Paul concludes that is just God's way: he elects not only Israel from among the nations, but also a remnant from within Israel, and his reasons for his elections remain inaccessible to us. We cannot call God unjust because God is beyond our reckoning of good and evil. And we, only creatures, have no right to speak against the creator in any case (Rom 9.9–21):

> [19]You will say to me then, 'Why then does he still find fault? For who can resist his will?' [20]But who indeed are you, a human being, to argue with God? Will what is molded say to the one who molds it, "Why have you made me like this?" [21]Has the potter no right over the clay, to make out of the same lump one object for special use and another for ordinary use?

Notice, Paul has led us far from where we began. And just at this point, Paul changes course yet again. No sooner has he refused our right to question God's designs, than he offers a justification for God's actions, showing that he does believe, against what he has just said, that there are reasons for them and reasons we can know. God has saved the true, spiritual Israel and rejected 'Israel according to the flesh' – because God wants in that way to 'show his wrath and to make known his power' (9.22).

He cites three passages of Scripture to seal the claim (9.25-29), one from Hosea and a pair from Isaiah:

> [25]As indeed he says in Hosea, 'Those who were not my people I will call "my people", and her who was not beloved I will call "beloved". [26]And in the very place where it was said to them, "You are not my people", there they shall be called children of the living God'. [27]And Isaiah cries out concerning Israel, 'Though the number of the children of Israel were like the sand of the sea, only a remnant of them will be saved; [28]for the Lord will execute his sentence on the earth quickly and decisively'. [29]And as Isaiah predicted, 'If the Lord of hosts had not left survivors to us, we would have fared like Sodom and been made like Gomorrah'.

The logic of Paul's interpretation is shocking, or it would be if we had not been over-familiarized with watered-down versions of it. In Christ, God has saved those who were not his people and damned all but a remnant of his own people to share the same fate suffered by Sodom and Gomorrah. Along the way, as he has worked out his strange purposes in history in his own way, purposes which run across each other like contradictions. God has used the 'vessels of wrath' – Esau, Pharaoh, and the majority of Israelites – for the freeing of 'vessels of mercy' – Jacob, Israel, and the remnant, made up of Jews and Gentiles who have Abraham's faith. He has done all of this, Paul argues, to reveal the divine power and to lavish 'the riches of his glory' on those predestined and called (9.22-24). In this vision, the non-elect, it would seem, exist just for the sake of the elect.

But as soon as he has shown us this vision, he begins to paint another. Israel's unenlightened zeal (10.2) has driven them into faithlessness. Stumbling in the dark of their self-righteousness, they have failed to see Christ, God's righteousness, who in his life, death, and resurrection accomplishes the realization of all God's promises as the telos of the covenant (10.4). Therefore, as Paul puts it, 'Gentiles, who did not strive for righteousness, have attained ... righteousness through faith; but Israel, who did strive for the righteousness that is based on the law, did not succeed in fulfilling that law'. Why did Israel fail where the Gentiles succeeded? Because they 'did not strive for it on the basis of faith, but as if it were based on works' (9.30–32).

But Paul still will not let the troubledness resolve, asking why Israel did not have faith. It is not, he says, due to any failure on God's part. God gave them every chance. There is 'no distinction between Jew and Greek' because 'the same Lord is Lord of all and is generous to all who call on him' (10.12). Because of God's love for all and generosity to all, God sends messengers to bring the 'good news' to Israel and to the nations, so that 'no one who believes in [Christ] shall be put to shame' and 'everyone who calls on the name of the Lord shall be saved (10.11-13). And where the divine witness to Christ comes, faith awakens – or so it should. 'So faith comes from what is heard, and what is heard through the word of Christ' (10.17). The trouble is, Israel has heard the divine witness and yet does not believe. The nations, against all odds, have inadvertently stumbled into the revelation of God in Christ, and Israel, in spite of God's constant nurturing and wooing, has given God only disobedience and disregard (10.18-21):

> [18]But I ask, have they not heard? Indeed they have, for 'Their voice has gone out to all the earth, and their words to the ends of the world'. [19]Again I ask, did Israel not understand? First Moses says, 'I will make you jealous of those who are not a nation; with a foolish nation I will make you angry'. [20]Then Isaiah is so bold as to say, "I have been found by those who did not seek me; I have shown myself to those who did not ask for me." [21]But of Israel he says, 'All day long I have held out my hands to a disobedient and contrary people'.

Previously, Paul had argued that everything depended on God's ineffable decisions. Now, he argues that God is utterly at the mercy of human decision. In the first image, God has the power to do whatever he elects to do. But in this later image, he seems powerless to nurture a faithful response in his people.

At this moment in his performance, Paul has presented his readers with several contrasting images. At times, he has shown one that says we simply cannot know why Israel has turned from God, because God's ways are inscrutable. At other times, he has shown its opposite, which says that we can in fact know why Israel has been condemned, and that it has everything to do with their own choices, not God's. One image says everything that happens to the vessels of mercy and vessels of wrath happens through divine initiative alone. Another image says that God is merciful to all, and that those who reject it bring the consequences of their faithlessness on themselves. Is God the potter who makes some vessels simply to break? Or is God the jilted lover, begging his unfaithful wife to return to him?

Paul, a true artist, forces us to face these alternatives, and then invites us to reject them both. They both fail to do justice to the majesty and ingenuity of God. So, in his performance's next act, Paul strives to show that God has always been doing more than meets the eye. He begins by refuting what it seems he has assumed from the first: God has not rejected his people, in spite of their apostasy. 'Has God rejected his people? By no means!' (11.1). All of Israel will be saved, and not only 'Israel' – the remnant of true believers in Abraham's God.

Creating this third image, Paul returns, briefly, to what he said in the beginning: God has saved a remnant out of Israel. But this time he also claims that God not only has saved a few from Israel but has also 'hardened' the rest. God has now done to Israel what God once did to Pharaoh, and Israel, which Paul first introduced as 'vessels of mercy', is seen to be at the same time 'vessels of wrath'. And this, Paul begins to reveal, is the surprising form of the good news: if once God hardened Pharaoh to save Israel, now God is hardening Israel only to save 'Pharaoh' (11.7-10):

> [7]What then? Israel failed to obtain what it was seeking. The elect obtained it, but the rest were hardened, [8]as it is written, 'God gave them a sluggish spirit, eyes that would not see and ears that would not hear, down to this very day'.[9]And David says, 'Let their table become a snare and a trap, a stumbling block and a retribution for them; [10]let their eyes be darkened so that they cannot see, and keep their backs forever bent'.

As Paul paints, a new image is emerging, although it is more abstract: Israel is being hardened so that the Gentiles might be saved. But the Gentiles are being saved only so that Israel might be saved. This is the great 'mystery' he proclaims: 'a hardening has come upon part of Israel, until the full number of the Gentiles has come in. And so all Israel will be saved' (11.25-26).

How does the salvation of the Gentiles work the salvation of Israel? Because the Gentiles' share in God's blessings provokes Israel to jealousy, and just so moves them to repentance. In the mysteries of providence, God is using the Gentiles, who are 'not a people', to provoke Israel, the people of God, to saving jealousy (11.11-16).

> [11]So I ask, have they stumbled so as to fall? By no means! through their stumbling salvation has come to the Gentiles, so as to make Israel jealous. [12]Now if their stumbling means riches for the world, and if their defeat means riches for Gentiles, how much more will their full inclusion mean! [13]Now I am speaking to you Gentiles. Inasmuch then as I am an apostle to the Gentiles, I glorify my ministry [14]in order to make my own people jealous, and thus save some of them. [15]For if their rejection is the reconciliation of the world, what will their acceptance be but life from the dead! [16]If the part of the dough offered as first fruits is holy, then the whole

batch is holy; and if the root is holy, then the branches also are holy.

These dramatic reversals, subversions, and overlays were already pre-figured for us earlier in the performance, in an appeal Paul makes to a line from the prophet Hosea: 'As indeed he says in Hosea, "Those who were not my people I will call 'my people,' and her who was not beloved I will call 'beloved'. And in the very place where it was said to them, 'You are not my people,' there they shall be called children of the living God'" (9.25-26). Masterfully, Paul is bending the Greek text of Hosea to make a startling and ironic point: In the prophet's original words, those who are 'not my people' are in fact Israel, whom God has rejected for their unfaithfulness. But in Paul's reworking, God rejects those he elects, and elects those who reject him, claiming both those who are faithful as his people and those who are not as 'my people'. In this image, it becomes impossible to tell where Israel begins and ends. Jacob, the beloved has become like Esau. And Esau has become like Jacob. Now, Israel, by and large, is at enmity with God. But they remain beloved for the sake of the fathers – who, of course, were themselves men of the nations who were made 'Jews' by God's creative word.

At first glance, Paul's reading of Hosea seems untenable. But a closer look shows us that Paul has read it well. The opening of the prophet's story tells us that the Lord directed Hosea to take 'a wife of whoredom and children of whoredom ...' (Hos 1:2). So, as the story goes, Hosea 'takes' Gomer and she bears him three children: Jezreel, Lo-ruhamah, whose name means 'not pitied', and Lo-ammi, whose name means 'not my people'. Each time a child is born and named, God declares the dissolution of the covenant. And when the last son is born, God severs the final thread holding him to Israel: 'And God said "Call his name Not My People, for you are not my people and I am not your God"' (Hos. 1.9).

Suddenly, however, everything is reversed and overturned: 'And it shall be, in the very place where it was said to them, "you are not my people", they too shall be called "sons of a living god"' (Hos. 1.10). Somehow, Paul recognizes in this astonishing reversal the sig-nature 'move' of the God revealed in Jesus Christ, the same 'crossing of the hands' that had surprised and troubled Joseph (Gen. 48.17-19). He sees what Jonah long before him had angrily discerned: God's mercy runs deeper than his wrath, and his threats are always in service of his promises. He sees that election is for the sake of the non-elect. He sees that mercy triumphs over judgment (Jas 2.13). Yes, God 'hands over' the wicked to their wickedness (Rom 1.26) – this is the divine wrath. But God also 'hands over' his own Son for us and for our salvation (Rom. 8.32) – this is his mercy. And that mercy 'in Christ' is the 'deeper magic' that overcomes and undoes the judgment that falls on us. Therefore, the divine wrath on the 'vessels of wrath' – the Pharaohs and the Esaus – somehow works God's mercy both for them and for the elect – Israel and the nations. And God's mercy on the 'vessels of wrath' also works good for all involved, provoking the rebellious elect to jealously, provoking them to return to their estranged lover. Paul is arguing that God hardens Pharaoh for Israel's sake and saves Israel for Pharaoh's sake. And then hardens Israel for Pharaoh's sake and saves Pharaoh for Israel's sake. Of course, he does not mean that God is forcing people to disobey and then punishing them for their disobedience. No, somehow, God is working with human freedom, creatively engaging what they do and fail to do in order to make something truly good of it all for all. We may be tempted to ask what this could possibly mean. But Paul has no more words for it and can only conclude: 'God has imprisoned all in disobedience so that he may be merciful to all' (11.32). Then he throws down his brushes and floods the canvas in praise (11.33-36)

> [33]O the depth of the riches and wisdom and knowledge of God! How unsearchable are his judgments and how inscrutable his ways! [34]"For who has known the mind of the Lord? Or who has been his counselor?' [35]'Or who has given a gift to him, to receive a gift in return?' [36]For from him and through him and to him are all things. To him be the glory forever. Amen.

I do not mean to suggest that this passage has no bearing on our doctrines. Not at all. What I do mean is that if we are not moved by the 'spirit' of this performance, if we are not enthused by its energy, then our readings are sure to be misguided. The last thing we should do is 'proof text' lines from this passage to win an argument or to validate a doctrine. We need, instead, to read and reread until we are taken up into the joy that comes in knowing that God is better than good, and that whatever we expect of him is nothing compared to what he is accomplishing for us. No eye has seen, no ear has heard what God has prepared for those who live him – not even those eyes that have read these texts, not even the ears that have heard these words.

AFTERWORD

I want to end by sharing a testimony. But first, I need to re-view the ground we have covered and offer some final reflections.

I tried in the three immediately preceding chapters to make a case for thinking differently about how and why we read Scripture, focusing on the ways the Holy Spirit uses our readings to work sanctification in and through us. But, as I said in the Introduction, thinking along these lines about Scripture and the God who makes use of Scripture requires a radical reframing of the conversation. Protestants, as a rule, talk about Scripture from above, so to speak, focusing on the nature of Scripture, attempting to explain how this collection of texts can serve as a fit vessel for divine revelation. Usually, this is done by attributing to Scripture the attributes of God, and then calling us, as believers, to trust the Scriptures just as we would trust God. Against those assumptions, I have tried to argue from below, attending to the ways the Spirit works with our readings of Scripture, exploring how the work of interpretation is fitted to teach us how to fulfill our calling as Christ's fellow intercessors. And on that basis, I argued that Scripture is designed to make us work, to challenge and provoke and offend and confuse us. The work of interpretation is difficult, not because we are doing it wrongly but precisely because the Spirit is training us for lives of priestly ministry.

With that in mind, I laid out in Part 1 an account of Christian vocation, in hopes of showing that we are called to participate in Jesus' ongoing work, joining him in bringing God's holiness to bear on all things in the world in ways that awaken hope in God and what he has promised to do. But if we have a warped sense of what God's holiness is and what it means for us, obviously it would do no one any good to talk about mediating it to others. So, bearing that concern in mind, I tried in Part 2 to argue for stranger, richer ways of imagining and describing holiness and the sanctified life. Along the way, if I did anything at all close to what I wanted to do, my engagements with the Scriptures provided a kind of model for how I think God means the Scriptures to work for us. Assuming that I did, I believe those are the most important parts of this work.

Now, the testimony I promised to share. I grew up in independent Holiness-Pentecostal churches that held the Scriptures – the King James Version only – in very high regard. At least, that is how it seemed to me at the time. We certainly took great pride in our commitment to the Bible as the only 'rule of faith and practice'. But now I can see that our interpretations of Scripture were often if not always irreconcilably at odds with the gospel, and what I then believed to be pure devotion to Holy Scripture I recognize now as in fact mixed with a love for my reading of certain passages and for the authority I believed I had at my disposal because those readings were drawn from God's Word. Our canon-within-the-canon included and emphasized texts like Deut. 22.5, 1 Cor. 11.2-16, Heb. 12.14, and 1 Pet. 3.3-4. Most of our sermons, as I recall, were crafted around typological readings of OT narratives, or the stories in the Gospels or Acts, and most of the time the thrust of the sermon had to do with one or more of the following themes: God's hatred for 'lukewarm' Christianity, the dangers of backsliding into worldliness, and/or how to 'get right with God' in order to avoid God's wrath, in this life and the next. Now, I sometimes suspect that we held so tenaciously to a high view of Scripture because that was the best way to secure an even higher view of our interpretations. Be that as it may, I am convinced that because we did not hold to the gospel, our readings inevitably veered into disaster – sometimes comically, sometimes tragically.

As I reflect on those experiences, what troubles me is not that we misinterpreted the Scriptures. Given our limitations as readers and the difficulties of these texts, certain kinds of misreading are inevitable. What troubles me is that I so often, and sometimes so easily misappropriated the Scriptures. In other words, I was taught to misread them in ways that grossly distorted the image of God for us and for others. We made uses of the biblical texts that wreaked havoc on us and on our neighbors. The more we used the Scriptures, therefore, the harder our hearts became and the duller our imaginations, so that we became less and less capable of fulfilling our call to mediate God's holiness to the world.

Thanks to the grace of a few teachers and friends, by the time I had graduated from Bible school I knew that learning to speak 'straight'[1] to God and of God required a dramatic re-learning of what

---

[1] Moore, 'Raw Prayer and Refined Theology', pp. 35-48.

it means to engage the Scriptures. Obviously, that re-learning continues and will continue. Along the way, I am accumulating other,
deeper debts to my friends and teachers – many of whom are my
students, as well. One story captures the essence of that re-learning
process for me, and I have kept it until last because I think it bears
witness to what I believe it means to sanctify interpretation and how
I think sanctified interpretation sanctifies us.

My earliest memory of Scripture is having heard the story of
Achan in Joshua 7, which ends, or so I thought at the time, with him
and his entire family, including his children as well as all of his animals, being stoned to death, burned to ash, and then covered with
rocks. I remember pacing back and forth in the living room of our
home in Oklahoma, weeping, fists balled up, asking my Dad why
God would allow such a thing, much less require it. I do not remember what he said to me, although I remember it did little to calm me
down and nothing to answer my questions.

I still live with that question. And a lot of other questions have
formed around it. (Why did Achan's confession not move Joshua to
mercy? Why does God not intervene?) Now, however, I do not read
that story as a report on something horrific God required Israel once
to do. I read it as a test of what God wants from and for me for
others. I believe the text is meant to function exactly as it has func-
tioned in Pentecostal preaching from the beginning: as a parabolic
provocation, a severely disturbing warning about the effects the sins
we hide have on us, our children, our communities, as well as animals
and the earth itself.

It turns out, though, that the text is much more ambiguous than I
realized at that first hearing. It is not clear, for example, if Achan
alone was killed, along with his animals, or if his children were stoned
to death, too. Regardless, what impresses me is that the story was
able to affect me like it did. And I think the response it provoked in
me is exactly the response it was designed to provoke.

A few years ago, I was giving a sermon in which I tried to explore
in some detail the intricacies of Gregory of Nyssa's reading of the
story of the rich man and Lazarus (Lk. 16.14-31), which I believe
shows us so much about the character of God's just mercy. As I recall, I was trying in the sermon to argue that Jesus is not concerned
to tell us the architecture of the afterlife – whatever that might be –
but to call us to freedom from our sins through the love of our

neighbor. Afterwards, one of my closest friends, Ken Teal, forced on me a question I had not thought to ask: 'What if Jesus tells us this story just to see how we respond to the rich man's cries for water?' I knew immediately that *that* question would never leave me alone. From then until now, whenever I come to the Scriptures, I find myself being drawn into the depths by the possibilities hidden in that 'What if …?'

Here is the wonder: those depths of possibility hidden in the Scriptures open out on the depths of the human spirit. To search those depths is to share in the Spirit's searching of the deep things of God where Christ, our sanctification, is found. Therefore, as we are searching, we are participating in the divine life, fighting – or playing – with God in conversation.

Here is the wonder: the depths of possibility hidden in the Scriptures open out on the depths of our spirit and our experiences of the world. And to search those depths is to share in the Spirit's searching of the deep things of God where Christ, our sanctification, is found. That is at least near the heart of what it means to say that Scripture is inspired – breathed by God. The Spirit provokes us, first, to ask God and those whom God has given us, 'Why?' And then to ask, 'What if?' In the process, as we are searching, we can be sure we are participating in the divine life, fighting – or playing – with God in the very conversation that is his life.

At times, of course, we will fall silent in the conversation. This is only right. We may fall silent because we realize we do not know what to say or because what we think we need to say seems wrong. Or we may fall silent because we are not sure if we even mean what we have said. Best of all, we may fall silent to listen, although even then we are sure that we will not hear everything that is said to or about us. Regardless, we need never fall silent from desperation or resignation. Even if we lack understanding, even if we are horrified by what we think we do understand, we can lean into God and into one another in simple trust: God has all the time we need, so we can wait for the right words to come. And if they do not come, that is alright, too.

BIBLIOGRAPHY

Early Pentecostal Periodicals
The Apostolic Faith (Azusa Street Mission, Los Angeles, CA)
The Church of God Evangel (Church of God, Cleveland, TN)
The Pentecostal Holiness Advocate (The Pentecostal Holiness Church, Falcon, NC; Franklin Springs, GA)
Pentecostal Testimony (William H. Durham, Chicago, IL; Los Angeles, CA)
The Latter Rain Evangel (Stone Church, Chicago, IL)
The Bridegroom's Messenger (The Pentecostal Mission, Atlanta, GA)
The Pentecost (J. Roswell Flower, Indianapolis, IN)
Weekly Evangel (Assemblies of God; St Louis, MO; Springfield, MO)
Confidence (A.A. Boddy, Sunderland, England, UK)

Other Works Cited
Abraham, William J., *The Bible: Beyond the Impasse* (Dallas, TX: Highland Loch Press, 2012).
Adewuya, J. Ayodeji, *Holiness and Community in 2 Cor. 6.17-7.1: Paul's View of Communal Holiness in the Corinthian Correspondence* (New York, NY: Peter Lang, 2001).
Albrecht, Daniel E., *Rites in the Spirit: A Ritual Approach to Pentecostal/Charismatic Spirituality* (JPTSup 17; Sheffield: Sheffield Academic Press, 1999).
Alter, Robert W., *The Art of Biblical Narrative* (New York, NY: Basic Books, 2011).
Althouse, Peter, 'Ascension-Pentecost-Eschaton: A Theological Framework for Pentecostal Ecclesiology', in John Christopher Thomas (ed.), *Toward a Pentecostal Ecclesiology: The Church and the Fivefold Gospel* (Cleveland, TN: CPT Press, 2010), pp. 225-47.
Archer, Kenneth J., *A Pentecostal Hermeneutic: Spirit, Scripture, and Community* (Cleveland, TN: CPT Press, 2009).
Augustine, Daniela, *Pentecost, Hospitality, and Transfiguration: Toward a Spirit-Inspired Vision of Social Transformation* (Cleveland, TN: CPT Press, 2012).
Augustine of Hippo, *The Trinity* (Washington, DC: Catholic University of America Press, 2010).
Ayres, Lewis, '"There's Fire in That Rain": On Reading the Letter and Reading Allegorically', in Hans Boersma and Matthew Levering (eds.), *Heaven On Earth: Theological Interpretation in Ecumenical Dialogue* (Malden, MA: Wiley-Blackwell Publishers, 2013), pp. 33-51.
—'The Soul and the Reading of Scripture: A Note On Henri de Lubac', *Scottish Journal of Theology* 61.2 (2008), pp. 173-90.
Baker, Anthony D., *Diagonal Advance: Perfection in Christian Theology* (Eugene, OR: Cascade Books, 2011).
—'Things Usually So Strange: Nature and Grace Reconsidered', *Syndicate* (August 2014); accessed 4 August 2014; http://syndicatetheology.com/anthony-d-baker/.
Balthasar, Hans Urs von, 'Vocation', *Communio* 37.1 (Spring 2010), pp. 111-27.
—*The Glory of the Lord: A Theological Aesthetics Vol. 1-Seeing the Form* (San Francisco, CA: Ignatius Press, 1982).
—*Theo-drama: Theological Dramatic Theory Vol. 1* (San Francisco, CA: Ignatius Press,

1988).

Barton, Stephen C., *Holiness: Past and Present* (London: T&T Clark, 2003).

Beacham, Paul F., *Advanced Catechism for the Home, Sunday School, and Bible Classes* (Franklin Springs, GA: PH Church Publishing House, 1971).

Begbie, Jeremy, 'Language: Can We Speak About God Without Words?' Third Lecture in the 2010 New College Lectures, Sydney, Australia, 2010; accessed 1 June 2014; http://youtu.be/4fyNg8cupls.

Behr, John, *Formation of Christian Theology Vol. 1: The Way to Nicaea* (Crestwood, NY: SVPS, 2001).

Betz, Hans Dieter, '2 Cor. 6.14-7.1: An Anti-Pauline Fragment?', *JBL* 92.1 (March 1973), pp. 88-108.

Betz, John R., *After Enlightenment: The Post-Secular Vision of J.G. Hamann* (Malden, MA: Wiley-Blackwell Publishers, 2009).

Billings, J. Todd, *The Word of God for the People of God: An Entryway to the Theological Interpretation of Scripture* (Grand Rapids, MI: Eerdmans, 2010).

Bloesch, Donald G., *The Church: Sacraments, Worship, Ministry, Mission* (Downers Grove, IL: IVP, 2002).

Boersma, Hans, *Embodiment and Virtue in Gregory of Nyssa: An Anagogical Approach* (New York, NY: Oxford University Press, 2013).

Bonhoeffer, Dietrich, *Berlin: 1932–1933* (Dietrich Bonhoeffer Works 12; Minneapolis: Fortress, 2009).

—*Ethics* (Dietrich Bonhoeffer Works Vol. 6; Minneapolis, MN: Augsburg Fortress Press, 2005).

—*Sanctorum Communio: A Theological Study of the Sociology of the Church* (Dietrich Bonhoeffer Works Vol. 1; Minneapolis, MN: Fortress Press, 1998).

—*Life Together* (Minneapolis, MN: Fortress Press, 1996).

—*Meditating On the Word* (Nashville, TN: Cowley Publications, 1986).

Bretherton, Luke, *Holiness as Hospitality: Christian Witness Amid Moral Diversity* (Burlington, VT: Ashgate, 2010).

Brueggemann, Walter, *A Pathway of Interpretation: The Old Testament for Pastors and Students* (Eugene, OR: Cascade Books, 2008).

—'Counterscript', *Christian Century* (Nov 29, 2005), pp. 22-28 (23).

—*Deep Memory, Exuberant Hope: Contested Truth in a Post-Christian World* (Minneapolis, MN: Augsburg Fortress Press, 2000).

—'Divine Council', in *Reverberations of Faith: A Theological Handbook of Old Testament Themes* (Louisville, KY: Westminster John Knox Press, 2002), pp. 55-56.

—*Inscribing the Text: Sermons and Prayers of Walter Brueggemann* (Minneapolis, MN: Augsburg Fortress Press, 2004).

—*Theology of the Old Testament: Testimony, Dispute, Advocacy* (Minneapolis: Fortress Press, 1997).

Buber, Martin, *Meetings: Autobiographical Fragments* (New York: Routledge, 2002).

—*The Letters of Martin Buber: A Life in Dialog* (New York: Knopf Doubleday, 1991).

Byassee, Jason, *Praise Seeking Understanding: Reading the Psalms with Augustine* (Grand Rapids, MI: Eerdmans, 2007).

Byrne, Brendan, *The Hospitality of God: A Reading of Luke's Gospel* (Collegeville, MN: St Benedict, 2000).

Cartledge, Mark J., *Speaking in Tongues: Multi-Disciplinary Perspectives* (Milton Keynes:

Paternoster, 2006).

Castelo, Daniel, 'A Holy Reception Can Lead to a Holy Future', in Lee Roy Martin (ed.), *A Future for Holiness: Pentecostal Explorations* (Cleveland, TN: CPT Press, 2013), pp. 225-34.

—*Revisioning Pentecostal Ethics: The Epicletic Community* (Cleveland, TN: CPT Press, 2012).

—'Tarrying On the Lord: Affections and Virtues in Pentecostal Perspective', *JPT* 13.1 (2004), pp. 31-56.

Chan, Simon, 'Jesus as Spirit Baptizer: Its Significance for Pentecostal Ecclesiology', in John Christopher Thomas (ed.), *Toward a Pentecostal Ecclesiology: The Church and the Fivefold Gospel* (Cleveland, TN: CPT Press, 2010), pp. 139-56.

—'The Language Game of Glossolalia, or Making Sense of the "Initial Evidence"', in Wonsuk Ma and Robert Menzies (eds.), *Pentecostalism in Context: Essays in Honor of William W. Menzies* (JPTSup 11; Sheffield, UK: Sheffield Academic Press, 1997), pp. 231-53.

—*Liturgical Theology: The Church as Worshipping Community* (Downers Grove, IL: IVP, 2006).

Charette, Blaine, 'Reflective Speech: Glossolalia and the Image of God', *Pneuma* 28.2 (Fall 2006), pp. 189-201.

Chryssavgis, John, *In the Heart of the Desert: The Spirituality of the Desert Fathers and Mothers* (Bloomington, IN: World Wisdom Publishing, 2008).

Clendenin, Daniel B., *Eastern Orthodox Christianity: A Western Perspective* (2nd edn; Grand Rapids, MI: Baker Academic, 2003).

Coakley, Sarah, *God, Sexuality, and the Self: An Essay On the Trinity* (Cambridge: Cambridge University Press, 2013).

Cole, Casey S., 'Taking Hermeneutics to Heart: Proposing an Orthopathic Reading for Texts of Terror via the Rape of Tamar Narrative', *Pneuma* 39.3 (2017), pp. 264-74.

Cooper, Jordan, *Christification: A Lutheran Approach to Theosis* (Eugene, OR: Wipf & Stock, 2014).

Daniels, Bruce C., *New England Nation: The Country the Puritans Built* (New York, NY: Palgrave Macmillan, 2012).

Danto, Arthur C., 'Philosophy and/as/of Literature', in Garry L. Hagberg and Walter Jost (eds.), *A Companion to the Philosophy of Literature* (Malden, MA: Blackwell-Publishing, 2010), pp. 135-62.

Davies, Andrew, 'Reading in the Spirit: Some Brief Observations on Pentecostal Interpretation and the Ethical Difficulties of the Old Testament', *Journal of Beliefs and Values* 30.3 (December 2009), pp. 303-11.

Davies, Oliver, *Theology of Transformation: Faith, Freedom, and the Christian Act* (Oxford: OUP, 2013).

Dawn, Marva, *A Royal Waste of Time: The Splendor of Worshiping God and Being Church for the World* (Grand Rapids, MI: Eerdmans, 1999).

Dayton, Donald W., 'The Holiness Churches: A Significant Ethical Tradition', *The Christian Century* (26 February 1975), pp. 197-201.

—*The Theological Roots of Pentecostalism* (Grand Rapids: Baker Academic, 1987).

Dempster, Murray, 'The Church's Moral Witness: A Study of Glossolalia in Luke's Theology of Prayer', *Paraclete* 23.1 (1989), pp. 1-7.

Denaux, Adelbert, 'Stranger on Earth and Divine Guest: Human and Divine Hospitality in the Gospel of Luke and the Book of Acts', in E. Van der Borght and P. van Geest (eds.), *Strangers and Pilgrims On Earth* (Leiden: Brill, 2012), pp. 87-100.

Denaux, Adelbert, *Studies in the Gospel of Luke: Structure, Language and Theology* (Münster: LITVerlag, 2010).

Donaldson, Terence, 'The Vindicated Son: A Narrative Approach to Matthean Christology', in Richard N. Longenecker (ed.), *Contours of Christology in the New Testament* (Grand Rapids: Eerdmans, 2005), pp. 100-121.

Drury, John L., 'Hospitality and the Grammar of Holiness'; paper presented at 41st Annual Meeting of Wesleyan Theological Society (Kansas City, MO, March 2-4, 2006).

Duffey, Michael K., *Be Blessed in What You Do: The Unity of Christian Ethics and Spirituality* (New York, NY: Paulist Press, 1988).

East, Brad, *The Doctrine of Scripture* (A Cascade Companion; Eugene, OR: Cascade, forthcoming).

Ekblad, Bob, *A New Christian Manifesto* (Louisville: WJKP, 2008).

Ellul, Jacques, *The Humiliation of the Word* (Grand Rapids, MI: Eerdmans, 1985).

—*The Subversion of Christianity* (Grand Rapids, MI: Eerdmans, 1986).

Enns, Peter, *Ecclesiastes* (Two Horizons Old Testament Commentary; Grand Rapids, MI: Eerdmans, 2011).

Flood, Gavin, *The Importance of Religion: Meaning and Action in Our Strange World* (Malden, MA: Wiley-Blackwell Publishers, 2012).

Ford, David F., *Christian Wisdom: Desiring God and Learning in Love* (Cambridge: Cambridge University Press, 2007).

Fowl, Stephen E., *Engaging Scripture: A Model for Theological Interpretation* (Eugene, OR: Wipf & Stock, 1998).

—*Theological Interpretation of Scripture* (Eugene, OR: Cascade Book, 2009).

Goldingay, John, 'Biblical Narrative and Systematic Theology', in Joel B. Green and Max Turner (eds.), *Between Two Horizons: Spanning New Testament Studies and Systematic Theology* (Grand Rapids: Eerdmans, 2000).

—*The Theology of the Book of Isaiah* (Downers Grove, IL: InterVarsity Press, 2014).

Gorman, Michael J., *Inhabiting the Cruciform God: Kenosis, Justification and Theosis in Paul's Narrative Soteriology* (Grand Rapids, MI: Eerdmans, 2009).

Green, Chris E.W., *Foretasting the Kingdom: Toward a Pentecostal Theology of the Lord's Supper* (Cleveland, TN: CPT Press, 2012).

—'I Am Finished: Christological Reading(s) and Pentecostal Performance(s) of Psalm 88', *Pneuma* 40 (2018), pp. 150-66.

—'"Not I, but Christ": Holiness, Conscience, and the (Im)Possiblity of Community', in Lee Roy Martin (ed.), *A Future for Holiness: Pentecostal Explorations* (Cleveland, TN: CPT Press, 2013), pp. 127-44.

—'Provoked to Saving Jealousy: Readings Romans 9-11 as Theological Performance', *Pneuma* 38.1 (2016), pp. 1-13.

—'The Altar and the Table: A Proposal for Wesleyan and Pentecostal Eucharistic Theologies', *Wesleyan Theological Journal* 53.2 (2018), pp. 54-61.

Green, Joel, *Seized by Truth: Reading the Bible as Scripture* (Nashville, TN: Abingdon Press, 2007).

Gregory of Nazianzus, 'To Cledonius the Priest against Apollinarius', in Edward R. Hardy (ed.), *Christology of the Later Fathers* (Philadelphia, PA: Westminster, 1954), pp. 215-54.

Griffiths, Paul J., *Song of Songs* (BTC; Grand Rapids, MI: Brazos Press, 2011).

Guder, Darrell L., 'Mission', in Richard Burnett, *The Westminster Handbook to Karl Barth* (Louisville, KY: WJKP, 2013), pp. 150-51.

Harink, Douglas, *1 & 2 Peter* (BTC; Grand Rapids, MI: Brazos Press, 2009).

Harmless, William H., *Desert Christians: An Introduction to the Literature of Early Monasticism* (Oxford: OUP, 2004).

Harrison, Verna E.F., 'Allegory and Asceticism in Gregory of Nyssa', *Semeia* 57 (1992), pp. 113-30.

Hauerwas, Stanley, *Matthew* (BTC; Grand Rapids, MI: Brazos Press, 2007).

— 'Salvation and Health: Why Medicine Needs the Church', in Stephen E. Lammers and Allen Verhey (eds.), *On Moral Medicine: Theological Perspectives in Medical Ethics* (2nd edn; Grand Rapids, MI: Eerdmans, 1998), pp. 72-83.

—*Sanctify Them in the Truth: Holiness Exemplified* (Nashville, TN: Abingdon Press, 1998).

—*Unleashing the Scripture: Freeing the Bible from Captivity to America* (Nashville, TN: Abingdon Press, 1993).

—*War and the American Difference: Theological Reflections On Violence and National Identity* (Grand Rapids, MI: Baker Academic, 2011).

—'Why "The Way the Words Run" Matters: Reflections on Becoming a "Major Biblical Scholar"', in J. Ross Wagner, A. Katherine Grieb, and C. Kavin Rowe (eds.), *The Word Leaps the Gap: Essays On Scripture and Theology in Honor of Richard B. Hays* (Grand Rapids, MI: Eerdmans, 2008), pp. 1-19.

—*Working with Words: On Learning to Speak Christian* (Eugene, OR: Wipf & Stock, 2011).

Hays, Richard B., *Echoes of Scripture in the Letters of Paul* (Binghampton, NY: Vail Ballous Press, 1989).

—*First Corinthians* (Interpretation; Louisville, KY: WJKP, 2011).

Hollenweger, Walter, 'The Social and Ecumenical Significance of Pentecostal Liturgy', *Studia Liturgica* 8 (1971-1972), pp. 207-15.

Hovenden, Gerald, *Speaking in Tongues: The New Testament Evidence in Context* (JPTSup 22; Sheffield: Sheffield Academic Press, 2002).

Hunsinger, George, *How to Read Karl Barth: The Shape of His Theology* (New York, NY: OUP, 1991).

—*Eucharist and Ecumenism: Let Us Keep the Feast* (Cambridge: Cambridge University Press, 2008).

—'Sanctification', in Richard Burnett (ed.), *The Westminster Handbook to Karl Barth* (Louisville, KY: WKJP, 2013), pp. 192-98.

Jenson, Robert W. and Carl E. Braaten (eds.), *Christian Dogmatics Vol. 2* (Philadelphia, PA: Fortress Press, 1984).

Jenson, Robert W., 'Can We Have a Story?', *First Things* 101 (March 2000), pp. 16-17.

—*Canon and Creed* (Interpretation; Louisville: WJKP, 2010).

—*The Knowledge of Things Hoped For: The Sense of Theological Discourse* (New York, NY: OUP, 1969).

—'Liturgy of the Spirit', *The Lutheran Quarterly* 26.2 (May 1974), pp. 189-203.

—*On the Inspiration of Scripture* (Delhi, NY: American Lutheran Publicity Bureau, 2012).

—*A Religion Against Itself* (Richmond, VA: John Knox Press, 1966).

—'The Religious Power of Scripture', *Scottish Journal of Theology* 52.1 (1999), pp. 89-105.

—*Song of Songs* (Interpretation; Louisville: WJKP, 2005).

—*Systematic Theology Vol. 1: The Triune God* (New York, NY: OUP, 1997).

—*Systematic Theology Vol. 2: The Works of God* (New York, NY: OUP, 1999).

—'Theosis', *Dialog* 32.2 (1993), pp. 108-12.

—'What if It Were True?', *Center for Theological Inquiry Reflections* 4 (2002), pp. 2-20.

Jerome, *Commentary On Matthew* (Trans. Thomas P. Scheck; Washington, DC: The Catholic University of America Press, 2008).

Johns, Cheryl Bridges, 'Grieving, Brooding, and Transforming: The Spirit, the Bible, and Gender', *JPT* 23.2 (Fall 2014), pp. 141-53.

—*Pentecostal Formation: A Pedagogy Among the Oppressed* (JPTSup 2; Sheffield: Sheffield Academic Press, 1993).

—'What Makes a Good Sermon: A Pentecostal Perspective', *Journal for Preachers* 26.4 (Pentecost 2003), pp. 45-54.

—'Yielding to the Spirit: A Pentecostal Understanding of Penitence', in Mark J. Boda and Gordon T. Smith (eds.), *Repentance in Christian Theology* (Collegeville, MN: Liturgical Press, 2006), pp. 287-306.

Johns, Jackie D., 'Yielding to the Spirit: The Dynamics of a Pentecostal Model of Praxis', in Murray W. Dempster, Byron D. Klaus, and Douglas Peterson (eds.), *The Globalization of Pentecostalism: A Religion Made to Travel* (Carlisle, CA: Regnum, 1999), pp. 70-84.

Johnson, Luke Timothy, *The Acts of the Apostles* (Sacra Pagina; Collegeville, MN: Liturgical Press, 1992).

—*Scripture and Discernment: Decision Making in the Church* (Nashville, TN: Abingdon Press, 1983).

Jones, Gregory L., 'Formed and Transformed by Scripture: Character, Community, and Authority in Biblical Interpretation', in William P. Brown (ed.), *Character and Scripture: Moral Formation, Community, and Biblical Interpretation* (Grand Rapids, MI: Eerdmans, 2002), pp. 18-33.

Just, Arthur A., *The Ongoing Feast: Table Fellowship and Eschatology at Emmaus* (Collegeville, MN: Liturgical Press, 1993).

Kärkkäinen, Veli-Matti, *One with God: Salvation as Deification and Justification* (Collegeville, MN: Unitas, 2004).

Kearney, Richard, 'On the Hermeneutics of Evil', in David M. Kaplan (ed.), *Reading Ricoeur* (Albany, NY: State University of New York Press, 2008), pp. 241-55.

—*Poetics of Imagining: Modern to Post-Modern* (New York, NY: Fordham University Press, 1988).

Keen, Craig, *After Crucifixion: The Promise of Theology* (Eugene, OR: Cascade Books, 2013).

—'A Quick "Definition" of Holiness', in Kevin W. Mannoia and Don Thorsen (eds.), *The Holiness Manifesto* (Grand Rapids, MI: Eerdmans, 2008), pp. 237-38.

—*The Transgression of the Integrity of God: Essays and Addresses* (Eugene, OR: Cascade

Books, 2012).

Kelly, Joseph F., 'Niceta of Remesiana', in Robert Benedetto (ed.), *The New Westminster Dictionary of Church History Vol. 1* (Louisville, KY: WJKP, 2008), p. 463.

Kelsey, David, *Proving Doctrine: The Uses of Scripture in Modern Theology* (Harrisburg, PA: Trinity Press International, 1999).

Kennedy, Joel, *The Recapitulation of Israel: Use of Israel's History in Matthew 1.1-4.11* (Tübingen: Mohr Siebeck, 2008).

Kerr, Alan, *The Temple of Jesus' Body: The Temple Theme in the Gospel of John* (JSNTSup 220; London: Sheffield Academic Press, 2002).

Knight, Henry H., 'Worship and Sanctification', *Wesleyan Theological Journal* 32.2 (1997), pp. 5-14.

LaVerdiere, Eugene, *Dining in the Kingdom of God: The Origins of the Eucharist according to Luke* (Chicago, IL: Liturgy Training Publications, 1994).

Laird, Martin, 'Under Solomon's Tutelage: The Education of Desire in the Homilies on the Song of Songs', *Modern Theology* 18.4 (October 2002), pp. 507-27.

Land, Steve J., *Pentecostal Spirituality: A Passion for the Kingdom* (Cleveland, TN: CPT Press, 2010).

Lash, Nicholas, *Holiness, Speech, and Silence: Reflections On the Question of God* (Aldershot: Ashgate, 2004).

—'What Might Martyrdom Mean?', *Ex Auditu* 1 (1985), pp. 14-24.

Leithart, Peter, 'Salvation and Mission', *First Things* (blog); accessed 11 July, 2014; http://www.firstthings.com/blogs/leithart/2014/06/salvation-and-mission.

Levering, Matthew, *Participatory Biblical Exegesis: A Theology of Biblical Interpretation* (Notre Dame, IN: University of Notre Dame Press, 2008).

Lincoln, Andrew, *New Testament Theology: The Theology of the Later Pauline Letters* (Cambridge: Cambridge University Press, 2000).

Lossky, Vladimir, *The Mystical Theology of the Eastern Church* (Crestwood, NY: SVSP, 1976).

Louth, Andrew, 'The Place of Theosis in Orthodox Theology', in Michael J. Christensen and Jeffery A. Wittung (eds.), *Partakers of the Divine Nature: The History and Development of Deification in the Christian Traditions* (Grand Rapids, MI: Baker Academic, 2008), pp. 32-44.

de Lubac, Henri, *Medieval Exegesis Vol. 1: The Four Senses of Scripture* (Grand Rapids, MI: Eerdmans, 1998).

Ma, Julie C., and Wonsuk Ma (eds), *Mission in the Spirit: Towards a Pentecostal/Charismatic Theology* (Oxford, UK: Regnum Publishers, 2010).

MacDonald, George, *Phantastes* (Grand Rapids, MI: Eerdmans, 1981).

MacIntyre, Alasdair, *After Virtue: A Study in Moral Theory* (London: Duckworth Publishing, 1981).

Macchia, Frank, *Baptized in the Spirit: A Global Pentecostal Theology* (Grand Rapids, MI: Zondervan, 2006).

—'Sighs Too Deep for Words: Toward a Theology of Glossolalia', *JPT* 1 (1992), pp. 47-73.

Mann, Mark H., *Perfecting Grace: Holiness, Human Being, and the Sciences* (London: T&T Clark, 2006).

Marchadour, Alain, and David Neuhaus, *The Land, the Bible and History* (Bronx, NY: Fordham University Press, 2007).

Marion, Jean-Luc, 'The Invisibility of the Saint', *Critical Inquiry* 35.3 (Spring 2009), pp. 703-10.

Martin, Lee Roy (ed.), *A Future for Holiness: Pentecostal Explorations* (Cleveland, TN: CPT Press, 2013)

—*Pentecostal Hermeneutics: A Reader* (Leiden: Brill, 2013).

—'Delighting in the Torah: The Affective Dimension of Psalm 1', *Old Testament Essays* 23.3 (2010), pp. 708-27.

—'Longing for God: Psalm 63 and Pentecostal Spirituality', *JPT* 20.1 (2013), pp. 54-76.

—'Oh Give Thanks to the Lord for He Is Good', *Pneuma* 36.3 (2014), pp. 1-24.

McCabe, Herbert, 'Eucharistic Change', *Priests and People* 8.6 (June 1994), pp. 217-21.

—*God, Christ, and Us* (London: Continuum Books, 2003).

—*Law, Love and Language* (London: Continuum, 2003).

McClendon, James, *Systematic Theology Vol. 1: Ethics* (Nashville, TN: Abingdon Press, 1986).

Merleau-Ponty, Maurice, *Sense and Non-Sense* (Evanston, IL: Northwestern University Press, 1964).

Merton, Thomas, *Praying the Psalms* (Collegeville, MN: Liturgical Press, 1956).

—'War and the Crisis of Language', in Robert Ginsberg (ed.), *The Critique of War: Contemporary Philosophical Explorations* (Chicago, IL: Henry Regnery Company, 1969). accessed 1 June 2014; http://www.aloha.net/~stroble/merton2.html.

Migliore, Daniel, *Faith Seeking Understanding* (2nd edn; Grand Rapids, MI: Eerdmans, 2004).

Milbank, John, *The Word Made Strange: Theology, Language, Culture* (Malden, MA: Blackwell Publishing, 1997).

Mittledstadt, Martin William, *The Spirit and Suffering in Luke-Acts: Implications for Pentecostal Pneumatology* (JPTSup 26; London: T&T Clark, 2004).

Moltmann, Jürgen, *The Crucified God* (Minneapolis, MN: Fortress Press, 1993).

Moore, Rickie D, 'Canon and Charisma in the Book of Deuteronomy', *JPT* 1 (1992), pp. 75-92.

—'Raw Prayer and Refined Theology: You Have Not Spoken Straight to Me as My Servant Job Has', in Terry L. Cross and Emerson B. Powery (eds.), *The Spirit and the Mind: Essays in Informed Pentecostalism* (New York, NY: University Press of America, 2000), pp. 35-48.

Murdoch, Iris, *The Sovereignty of Good* (London: Routledge, 2001).

Myers, Ben, *Christ the Stranger: The Theology of Rowan Williams* (London: T&T Clark, 2012).

Neufeld, Thomas R. Yoder, *Killing Enmity: Violence and the New Testament* (Grand Rapids, MI: Baker, 2011).

Nicetas of Remesiana, 'The Power of the Holy Spirit', *The Fathers of the Church Vol. 7* (Washington DC: Catholic University of America Press, 1970), pp. 23-41.

Nichols, Aidan, *Wisdom from Above: A Primer in the Theology of Father Sergei Bulgakov* (Leominster, UK: Gracewing Publishing, 2005).

Nolland, John, *The Gospel of Matthew* (NIGTC; Grand Rapids, MI: Eerdmans, 2005).

Norris, Richard, 'Articulating Identity', in Frances Young, Lewis Ayers, and Andrew Louth (eds.), *Cambridge History of Early Christian Literature* (Cambridge:

Cambridge University Press, 2004), pp. 71-90.

O'Brien, Peter T., *The Letter to the Ephesians* (The Pillar New Testament Commentary; Grand Rapids, MI: Eerdmans, 1999).

O'Donovan, Oliver, *Desire of the Nations: Rediscovering the Roots of Political Theology* (Cambridge, UK: Cambridge University Press, 1996).

—*The Ways of Judgement* (Grand Rapids, MI: Eerdmans, 2005).

Oden, Thomas C., *John Wesley's Scriptural Christianity: A Plain Exposition of His Teaching on Christian Doctrine* (Grand Rapids, MI: Zondervan, 1994).

Oliverio, William, *Theological Hermeneutics in the Classical Pentecostal Tradition: A Typological Account* (Leiden: Brill, 2012).

Ortland, Dane C., *Zeal Without Knowledge: The Concept of Zeal in Romans 10, Galatians 1, and Philippians 3* (London: T&T Clark, 2012).

Peppiatt, Lucy, *Women and Worship at Corinth: Paul's Rhetorical Arguments in 1 Corinthians* (Eugene, OR: Cascade Books, 2015).

Peterson, Cheryl M., *The Holy Spirit and the Christian Life: Historical, Interdisciplinary, and Renewal Perspectives* (New York, NY: Palgrave Macmillan, 2014).

Peterson, Eugene, *Christ Plays in Ten Thousand Places: A Conversation in Spiritual Theology* (Grand Rapids, MI: Eerdmans, 2005).

—*The Contemplative Pastor: Returning to the Art of Spiritual Direction* (Grand Rapids, MI: Eerdmans, 1993.

—*Eat This Book: A Conversation in the Art of Spiritual Reading* (Grand Rapids, MI: Eerdmans, 2006).

Poloma, Margaret, *Main Street Mystics: The Toronto Blessing and Reviving Pentecostalism* (Walnut Creek, CA: AltaMira Press, 2003).

Radcliffe, Timothy, 'Christ in Hebrews: Cultic Irony', *New Blackfriars* 68 (1987), pp. 494-504.

—'Preaching: Conversation in Friendship', Lecture, To All the World: Preaching and the New Evangelization Conference (University of Notre Dame; 25 June 2014); accessed 4 August 2014; https://www.youtube.com/watch?v=3ePWG ez_xP0.

Radner, Ephraim, *A Brutal Unity: The Spiritual Politics of the Christian Church* (Waco, TX: Baylor University Press, 2012).

—*Hope Among the Fragments: The Broken Church and Its Engagement with Scripture* (Grand Rapids, MI: Brazos Press, 2004).

—'The Church's Witness of Reconciliation in the Twenty-First Century', Lecture, 2009 Palmer Lecture Chapel (Seattle Pacific University; 10 March 2009); accessed 2 July 2014; https://itunes.apple.com/itunes-u/palmer-lectures-in-wesleyan/id 389794952?mt=10.

Rahner, Karl, 'Holy Scripture as a Book', in *Theological Investigations* 22 (London: Darton, Longman and Todd, 1991).

—'Listening to Scripture', in *Theological Investigations* 16 (London: Darton, Longman and Todd, 1979).

—'Reflections on the Unity of the Love of Neighbour and the Love of God', in *Theological Investigations* 6 (London: Darton, Longman and Todd, 1969).

Ratzinger, Joseph, *The Spirit of the Liturgy* (San Francisco, CA: Ignatius Press, 2000).

Ricoeur, Paul J., *Interpretation Theory: Discourse and the Surplus of Meaning* (Fort Worth, TX: Texas Christian University Press, 1976).

Rogers, Eugene F., *After the Spirit* (Grand Rapids, MI: Eerdmans, 2005).

—'How the Virtues of an Interpreter Presuppose and Perfect Hermeneutics: The Case of Thomas Aquinas', *Journal of Religion* 76.1 (January 1996), pp. 64-81.

Root, Michael, 'The Achievement of Wolfhart Pannenberg', *First Things* 221 (March 2012), pp. 37-42.

Sacks, Jonathan, *The Dignity of Difference: How to Avoid the Clash of Civilizations* (London: Bloomsbury Academic, 2003).

Schell, William G., *The Ordinances of the New Testament* (Guthrie, OK: Faith Publishing House; n.d.)

Senn, Frank C., *New Creation: A Liturgical Worldview* (Minneapolis, MN: Augsburg Fortress Press, 2000).

Sider, J. Alexander, *To See History Doxologically: History and Holiness in John Howard Yoder's Ecclesiology* (Grand Rapids, MI: Eerdmans, 2011).

Siedell, Daniel A., 'You Will Make Bells and I Will Paint Icons', *Cultivare* (12 March 2012); accessed 26 September 2014; http://www.patheos.com/ blogs/cultivare/ 2013 /03/you-will-make-bells-i-will-paint-icons/.

Smith, James K.A., *Desiring the Kingdom: Worship, Worldview, and Cultural Formation* (Grand Rapids, MI: Baker Academic, 2009).

—'Lift up Your Hearts: John Calvin's Catholic Faith', Lecture, Meeter Center Lecture (Calvin College and Seminary; October 2012); accessed 24 August 2014; http://www.scribd.com/doc/109817080/Lift-Up-Your-Hearts-John-Calvin-s- Catholic-Faith.

—'The Closing of the Book: Pentecostals, Evangelicals, and the Sacred Writings', *JPT* 11 (1997), pp. 49-71.

—*The Fall of Interpretation* (2nd edn; Grand Rapids, MI: Baker Academic, 2012).

—*Thinking in Tongues: Pentecostal Contributions to Christian Philosophy* (Grand Rapids, MI: Baker Academic, 2010).

Staniloae, Dumitru, *The Experience of God Vol. 1: Revelation and Knowledge of the Triune God* (Brookline, MA: Holy Cross Orthodox Press, 1994).

Steiner, George, 'The Art of Criticism 2', *The Paris Review* 137 (Winter 1995), n.p.; accessed 1 September 2014; http://www.theparisreview.org/interviews /1506 /the-art-of- criticism-no-2-george-steiner.

Steinmetz, David C., 'The Superiority of Pre-Critical Exegesis', in Stephen E. Fowl (ed.), *The Theological Interpretation of Scripture: Classic and Contemporary Readings* (Malden, MA: Blackwell Publishing, 1997), pp. 26-38.

Stout, Jeffrey, *Ethics After Babel: The Languages of Morals and Their Discontents* (Boston, MA: Beacon Press, 1988).

Stithatos, Nikitas, 'On the Inner Nature of Things', *The Philokalia Vol. 4* (London: Faber and Faber, 1995), pp. 121-22.

Stubbs, David L., *Numbers* (BTC; Grand Rapids, MI: Brazos Press, 2009).

Swinton, John, *Dementia: Living in the Memories of God* (London: SCM Press, 2012).

Symeon the New Theologian, 'Discourse Ten', in *The Discourses*; translated by C.J. de Cantanzaro; (New York, NY: The Missionary Society of St Paul, 1980).

Synan, Vinson, *The Holiness-Pentecostal Tradition: Charismatic Movements in the Twentieth Century*. (2nd edn; Grand Rapids, MI: Eerdmans, 1997).

Taylor, Charles, *Sources of the Self* (Cambridge: Cambridge University Press, 1989).

Thiselton, Anthony, *The First Epistle to the Corinthians* (NIGTC; Grand Rapids, MI:

Eerdmans, 2000).

Thomas, John Christopher (ed.), *Toward a Pentecostal Ecclesiology: The Church and the Fivefold Gospel* (Cleveland, TN: CPT Press, 2010).

—'The Spirit, Healing and Mission: An Overview of the Biblical Canon', *International Review of Mission* 93.370-371 (July-October 2004), pp. 421-42.

—*The Apocalypse: A Literary and Theological Commentary* (Cleveland, TN: CPT Press, 2012).

—*The Spirit of the New Testament* (Blandford Forum: Deo Publishing, 2005).

Torrance, T.F., *Hermeneutics of John Calvin* (Edinburgh: Scottish Academic Press, 1988).

—*The Trinitarian Faith* (London: T&T Clark, 1997).

Trembath, Kern Robert, *Evangelical Theories of Biblical Inspiration: A Review and Proposal* (Oxford: Oxford University Press, 1987).

Trible, Phyllis, *Texts of Terror: Literary-Feminist Readings of Biblical Narratives* (London: SCM Press, 2002).

Trier, Daniel J., *Virtue and the Voice of God: Toward Theology as Wisdom* (Grand Rapids, MI: Eerdmans, 2006).

Tupper, E. Frank, *A Scandalous Providence: The Jesus Story of the Compassion of God* (Macon, GA: Mercer University Press, 1995).

Turner, Denys, *Thomas Aquinas: A Portrait* (New Haven, CT: Yale University Press, 2013).

Turner, Max, *Power from On High: The Spirit in Israel's Restoration and Witness in Luke-Acts* (JPTSup 9; Sheffield: Sheffield Academic Press, 2000).

Van de Walle, Bernie, '"How High of a Christian Life?": A.B. Simpson and the Classic Doctrine of Theosis', *Wesleyan Theological Journal* 43.2 (Fall 2008), pp. 136-53.

Vanhoozer, Kevin J., *Biblical Narrative in the Philosophy of Paul Ricoeur: A Study in Hermeneutics and Theology* (Cambridge: Cambridge University Press, 1990).

Verhey, Allen, and Joseph S. Harvard, *Ephesians* (Louisville, KY: WJKP, 2011).

Vondey, Wolfgang, *Beyond Pentecostalism: The Crisis of Global Christianity and the Renewal of the Theological Agenda* (Grand Rapids, MI: Eerdmans, 2010).

Ward, Graham, *Christ and Culture* (Challenges in Contemporary Theology; Malden, MA: Blackwell, 2005).

Watson, Francis, *Paul and the Hermeneutics of Faith* (London: T&T Clark, 2004).

Webb, William, *Returning Home: New Covenant and Second Exodus as the Context for 2 Corinthians 6.14-7.1* (JSNTSup 85; Sheffield: JSOT Press, 1993).

Webster, John, *Holiness* (London: SCM Press, 2003).

—*Holy Scripture: A Dogmatic Sketch* (New York, NY: Cambridge University Press, 2003).

—'Reading Scripture Eschatologically', in David M. Ford and Graham Stanton (eds.), *Reading Texts, Seeking Wisdom* (London: SCM Press, 2003), pp. 245-56.

—*The Grace of Truth* (Farmington Hills, MI: Oil Lamp Books, 2011).

—'T.F. Torrance on Scripture'; Paper presented at 2009 Annual Meeting of the T.F. Torrance Theological Fellowship (Montreal; 6 November 2009); accessed 3 June 2014; http://www.tftorrance.org/meetings/tftonscript ure.pdf.

—*Word and Church: Essays in Christian Dogmatics* (Edinburgh: T&T Clark, 2001).

Wesley, John and Charles, *Hymns on the Lord's Supper with a Preface Concerning the*

Christian Sacrament and Sacrifice Extracted from Dr. Brevint (5ᵗʰ edn; Bristol: William Pine, 1762).

Williams, Rowan, *Being Christian: Baptism, Bible, Eucharist, Prayer* (Grand Rapids, MI: Eerdmans, 2014).

—'Historical Criticism and Sacred Text', in David F. Ford and Graham Stanton (eds.) *Reading Texts, Seeking Wisdom: Scripture and Theology* (Grand Rapids, MI: Eerdmans, 2003), pp. 217-28.

—'Language, Reality and Desire in Augustine's *de Doctrina*', *Journal of Literature and Theology* 3.2 (July 1989), pp. 138-150.

—*On Christian Theology* (Malden, MA: Blackwell Publishers, 2000).

—*Open to Judgement: Sermons and Addresses* (London: Darton, Longman and Todd, 2014).

— 'Religious Language under Pressure'; Edward Schillebeeckx Lecture (Radboud University; Nijmegen, Netherlands; 13 December 2013); accessed 24 August 2014; http://jasongoroncy.com/2014/04/10/religious-language-under-press ure-rowan -williams-edward-schillebeeckx-lecture/.

—'Sacramental Living: Living Baptismally', *Australian Journal of Liturgy* 9.1 (2003), pp. 3-18.

—*Silence and Honey Cakes: The Wisdom of the Desert* (Oxford: Lion Publishing, 2003).

—*Teresa of Avila* (London: Continuum Books, 2003).

—'The Deflections of Desire: Negative Theology in Trinitarian Discourse', in Oliver Davies and Denys Turner (eds.), *Silence and the Word: Negative Theology and Incarnation* (Cambridge: Cambridge University Press, 2002), pp. 115-35.

—*The Edge of Words: God and the Habits of Language* (London: Bloomsbury, 2014).

—'The Theological World of the Philokalia', in Brock Bingman and Bradley Nassif (eds.), *The Philokalia: A Classic Text of Orthodox Spirituality* (Oxford: OUP, 2012), pp. 102-21.

—*Where God Happens: Discovering Christ in One Another* (Boston, MA: New Seeds Books, 2005).

—*Why Study the Past: The Quest for the Historical Church* (Grand Rapids, MI: Eerdmans, 2005).

Wiman, Christian, *My Bright Abyss: Meditation of a Modern Believer* (New York, NY: Farrar, Straus and Giroux, 2013).

Wolterstorff, Nicholas, *Until Justice and Peace Embrace* (Grand Rapids, MI: Eerdmans, 1983).

Work, Telford, *Living and Active: Scripture in the Economy of Salvation* (Sacra Doctrina; Grand Rapids, MI: Eerdmans, 2002).

—'Pentecostal and Charismatic Worship', in Geoffrey Wainwright and Karen B. Westerfield Tucker (eds.), *The Oxford History of Christian Worship* (Oxford: OUP, 2006), pp. 574-85.

Wright, Christopher J.H., *Knowing God the Father through the Old Testament* (Downers Grove, IL: IVP, 2007).

Wright, N.T., *The Lord and His Prayer* (Grand Rapids, MI: Eerdmans, 1996).

—*Matthew for Everyone Pt. 1* (Louisville, KY: WJKP, 2004).

—*Paul and the Faithfulness of God* (Minneapolis, MN: Fortress Press, 2013).

—*Paul for Everyone: 2 Corinthians* (Louisville, KY: WJKP, 2004).

Wright, Steven J., *Dogmatic Aesthetics: A Theology of Beauty in Dialogue with Robert W.*

Jenson (Minneapolis, MN: Fortress Press, 2014).

Yong, Amos, *The Spirit Poured Out On All Flesh: Pentecostalism and the Possibility of Global Theology* (Grand Rapids, MI: Baker Academic, 2005).

INDEX OF BIBLICAL REFERENCES

Old Testament

Genesis
4.9   85
6.6   147
7   141
7.23   147
8.21   147
9.20   147
9.21-25   147
12.1   36
12.3   14
18.21   148
18.22-33   161
19   141
19.24, 26   148
19.31-32   148
48.17-19   212
49.22-24   132

Exodus
15.11   83
13.18   164
17.14-16   149
17.16   133
20.21   82
32.32   161
34.14   106

Leviticus
12   136

Numbers
6.24-26   76
16   120
16.3   120
16.41   121
16.44   121
16.46   121
16.48   121
25.6-13   158

Deuteronomy
12.2-8   62
22.5   216

Joshua
7   217
7.24-26   146

Judges
19.29   148

Ruth
2.11   36

1 Samuel
13.13-14   148
15   xi
15.1-3   144
15.3   141
15.7-10   144
15.22   42
15.22-23   144
15.26   145
15.28-29   145
15.33   145
15.35   145, 147
16   197
16.10   197
16.14   149
18.10   149
19.9   149
19.24   149
25.1   150
28.19   150
28.20-25   188
28.21   149

1 Kings
17   70
22.22   141

1 Chronicles
16.29   97

Job
42.3   141

Psalms
1   70, 199
8   11-12, 91
23   132
29.2   97
31.5, 15   108
34.8   70
36.9   82
44.22   188
63   xi, 199
82.1   92
88   138
88.4, 5   138
88.14, 15   138
106.28-31   158
107   199
129.3   179
137.9   200
139.12   82
145.16   98

Song of Songs
3.3-4   98
5.16   98

Isaiah
1.15   70
6   194-95
29.11   xiii
53.2   97
53.12   81
55.8   116

Jeremiah
15.16   70
20.7   141

23.29	177		13.3-9	176		5.39-40	157
31.12	132		13.11-17	178		6.56	70
42.9-10	148		13.36	178		7.19	157
			13.43	178		7.24	93
Ezekiel			15.21-28	178		8.17	157
1	200		16.16	89		9.4	14
36.26-27	179		16.17	88		10.34	157
47	200		16.21	178		10.38	13
			19.16-22	161		12.37-41	195
Hosea			20.20-23	178		14.3	106
1.2	212		21.28-32	178		14.15	41
1.9	212		22.36-40	40		15.9-10	41
1.10	212		25.31-46	105		15.25	157
11.1	14		25.40	41		16.13	72
			26.6-13	178		16.25-27	104
Joel			26.26	70		18.31	157
2	133					19.7	157
			Mark			19.30	21
Jonah			8.34-35	91			
4.2	161					**Acts**	
			Luke			2.5	50
Zechariah			1.38	65		2.17	35, 89
12	133		1.79	150		10	35
			3.23-28	50		10.34-45	89
Haggai			8.10	162		17.11	67
2.7	98		9.23	114		17.28	41
			10	127			
			10.25-37	81		**Romans**	
New Testament			10.26	127		1.4	39
			10.3-4	48		1.26	213
Matthew			16.14-31	217		2.19	82
2.15	14		19.1-10	102		4.1-3	158
3.13-17	39		19.42	150		5.3-5	165
3.17	14		22.32	109		5.5	85
5.3-10	38		22.38	48		6.2	91
5.14	25		22.51	48		6.3-5	16
5.16	34		24.13-32	102		6.10	21
5.24	41		24.27, 44	131, 160		8	166
5.38	115					8.2	157, 207
6.1-6	34		**John**			8.20-21	165
9	127		1.1	106		8.24	91
9.13	41, 127		1.4	76		8.32	213
10.24	18		1.9	137		8.36	188
11.19	27		1.10	98		8.36-37	100
11.29	197		1.18	106		8.37, 39	207
12.1-8	127		3.16	118		9-11	xi, 206-214
			5.36-47	160		9.3	207

9.4-5	207
9.6-8	207
9.9-21	208
9.22	208
9.22-24	209
9.25-26	212
9.25-29	208
9.30-32	209
10	158
10.2	209
10.4	209
10.11-13	209
10.17	209
10.18-21	210
11.1	210
11.7-10	211
11.11-16	211
11.25-26	211
11.33-36	213
12.1-2	40
12.5	91
12.21	40
13.9	40
13.12	82
14-15	93
15.4	160, 165

1 Corinthians

1.17	111
1.18-25	156
1.27-28	156
1.23	88
1.24	34
2.7	35
2.16	189
4.3-5	93
4.9	34
5.9-13	92
6.2	91
9.19	114
9.21	113
9.22	107
10.11	133
10.15	93
11.2-16	xi, 170-76
11.3	170

11.5-6	170
11.7-12	170
11.13	93
11.14	170
11.16	171
11.31-32	93
12.13	16
13.1-7	41
14	66
15.24-25	12
15.27	12
15.28	12, 173
15.30	12

2 Corinthians

2.15	42
3.18	31
4.6	76, 82
5.14	24
5.16-17	175
5.19	38
5.20	29
6.14-7.1	76, 79-82
7.2	80

Galatians

1	158
2.11-14	89
3	159
3.26	175
5.14	40
6.2	40, 114

Ephesians

1.6	16
1.18	137
1.23	24
2.1-3	30
2.3	121
2.13-14	32
2.15	31, 175
2.19	31
2.21-22	31-32
3.1	32
3.6	32
3.17	37

3.18-20	32
3.20	116
4.1	70
4.4-5	16
4.12	16
5	202
5.1	32
5.8	82
5.26	16

Philippians

1.10	78
1.18	48
1.23	118
2	106
2.12-13	19
3	158
3.6	77
3.6-8	158
3.8-11	77
3.10-11	118
3.12	49
4.7	49
4.18	42

Colossians

1.13	169
1.15, 19	31
1.24	21
2.7	179
2.10-12	77
2.12	16
2.17, 20	25
2.20-23	115
3.4	41
3.5, 8	77

1 Timothy

4.13	67, 182
4.14	21
5.22	78
6.1	204
6.16	82

2 Timothy

3.10-11	189

3.14	189	10.5	37	**1 John**	
3.15	156	10.5-7	34	1.5-7	14
3.16	126, 129, 156,	10.10	35	2.15	78
	196	10.12	111	3.2	87
3.17	166	10.26	77	3.3	78
		12.2	35	3.9	77
Philemon		12.14	81, 216	3.11	40
1	120	12.15	82	3.14	41
		13.11-12	110	3.17	71
Hebrews		13.13	26, 111	3.18-19	41
1.3	24			3.19-21	119
2.5-7	11	**James**		4.17	104
2.8	11, 12	1.23-24	155	4.18	119
2.9	24	1.27	78	5.16	119
2.9-10	11				
2.11	12	**1 Peter**		**Jude**	
4	130	1.1	78	1.21-23	81
4.12	147, 154, 177	1.16	78		
5.8-9	18	3.3-4	216	**Revelation**	
7.3	29	3.18	21	3.21	106
7.25	29			10.8-9	70
7.26	81	**2 Peter**		19.10	159
9.28	21	3.11, 14	78	19.11	85

INDEX OF AUTHORS

Aquinas, Thomas 4, 13, 175, 200
Abraham, William J. 2, 5, 128
Adewuya, J. Ayodeji 76, 80
Archer, Kenneth J. 130
Augustine, Daniela 30
Augustine of Hippo 18, 98, 166-67, 182, 194,
Baker, Anthony D. 18-19, 49, 55, 76, 85, 91
Balthasar, Hans Urs von 13, 21, 201
Beacham, Paul 4-5, 70
Behr, John 44, 135
Betz, Hans Dieter 79-80
Billings, J. Todd 126, 169
Boersma, Hans 153, 168
Bonhoeffer, Dietrich 5, 29, 63, 71, 82, 90-91, 101, 114-15, 128, 138, 163
Brueggemann, Walter 17, 43, 46, 89-90, 92, 138, 152, 155
Buber, Martin 27-28, 30, 112-13, 145, 147
Castelo, Daniel 69, 76, 97, 107, 167-68
Chan, Simon 16, 29
Coakley, Sarah 164
Cole, Casey S. 160
Coulter, Dale 75
Drury, John L. 98-100
East, Brad xii
Ellul, Jacques 55
Ford, David F. 191-92
Fowl, Stephen E. xii, 193
Goldingay, John 194-95
Gorman, Michael J. 83
Green, Joel 65, 189
Gregory of Nazianzus 27
Hauerwas, Stanley 38-39, 51-52, 56, 107, 120, 189, 193
Hunsinger, George 24, 174
Jenson, Robert W. 2-3, 13, 31, 44, 47, 57-58, 70, 86, 98, 104-108, 153, 181-84, 194
Johns, Cheryl Bridges 60, 108, 129-30, 150-52, 190-91
Johnson, Luke Timothy 50, 206

Keen, Craig 83-86, 99, 119-20, 193
King, J.H. 117
Land, Steve J. 17-18
Lash, Nicholas 52, 201
Leithart, Peter xiii, 17, 143
Levering, Matthew 166
Lossky, Vladimir 87
de Lubac, Henri xiii, 126, 131, 184
Luce, Alice 132
Macchia, Frank 12, 17, 75, 103
Marion, Jean-Luc 82-83, 101
Martin, Lee Roy 5, 176, 199
McCabe, Herbert 20, 44-51, 65, 97
Mason, C.H. 69
Merton, Thomas 183
Milbank, John 88
Mittledstadt, Martin William 104
Moltmann, Jürgen 111
Moore, Rickie D 55, 135, 152, 161, 216
Myers, Ben 112, 118
Myland, D. Wesley 134
O'Donovan, Oliver 92, 114
Oliverio, William 2
Origen xiii-xv, 142
Peppiatt, Lucy 171-73
Radcliffe, Timothy 7, 30, 110-12
Radner, Ephraim 37-40, 90-91, 135-36, 183, 194,
Rahner, Karl 41, 56, 66
Ratzinger, Joseph 64
Ricoeur, Paul J. 108-109, 186
Rogers, Eugene F. 16, 39, 168
Smith, James K.A. 45, 53, 61, 134
Staniloae, Dumitru 83
Steiner, George 186-87
Steinmetz, David C. xiii, 142, 196
Symeon the New Theologian 87
Taylor, G.F. 64, 131
Thomas, John Christopher 4, 184, 187, 200
Torrance, T.F. 25, 164
Trible, Phyllis 159
Vanhoozer, Kevin J. 108-109

Watson, Francis   171
Webb, William   80
Webster, John   18-19, 22, 83, 85, 105, 125, 150, 162-63, 168-69
Wesley, John   22-23
Williams, Rowan   20, 25-26, 30, 32, 47, 49, 60, 64-65, 68, 71, 107, 116-18, 154, 160, 163-68, 185-88, 194, 196

Wiman, Christian   87, 154
Wolterstorff, Nicholas   71
Work, Telford   47, 58, 150
Wright, Christopher J.H.   15
Wright, N.T.   15, 80, 158, 183,
Wright, Steven J.   98
Yong, Amos   17

Made in the USA
Monee, IL
03 August 2023

40395506R00144